DATE DUE

~~JUL 2 '03~~			
~~DE 0 '04~~			

DEMCO 38-296

HUMAN RIGHTS AND CHOICE IN POVERTY

HUMAN RIGHTS AND CHOICE IN POVERTY

Food Insecurity, Dependency, and
Human Rights-Based Development Aid
for the Third World Rural Poor

Alan G. Smith

Westport, Connecticut
London

Library of Congress Cataloging-in-Publication Data

Smith, Alan G.
    Human rights and choice in poverty : food insecurity, dependency,
and human rights-based development aid for the Third World rural
poor / Alan G. Smith.
        p.   cm.
    Includes bibliographical references and index.
    ISBN 0–275–95826–4 (alk. paper)
    1. Rural development—Developing countries.   2. Rural development
projects—Developing countries.   3. Agricultural assistance—
Developing countries.   4. Human rights—Developing countries.
5. Dependency.   I. Title.
HN981.C6S63   1997
307.1′412′091722—dc21   96–47616

British Library Cataloguing in Publication Data is available.

Library of Congress Catalog Card Number: 96–47616
ISBN: 0–275–95826–4

First published in 1997

Praeger Publishers, 88 Post Road West, Westport, CT 06881
An imprint of Greenwood Publishing Group, Inc.

Printed in the United States of America

The paper used in this book complies with the
Permanent Paper Standard issued by the National
Information Standards Organization (Z39.48–1984).

10 9 8 7 6 5 4 3 2 1

Contents

Preface

Any interdisciplinary approach to a multifaceted real world involves trying to build bridges between different modes of analysis. In addressing third world poverty, the chasm between the philosophers and the social scientists has been a wide one. Yet, to be practically meaningful with regard to our duties under the moral rubric of human rights, philosophy must be coupled with an awareness of the actual grass-roots situations facing the poor and a sense of the practical difficulties involved in addressing them. Certainly, any particular model of human rights based duty will remain unpersuasive in the absence of such awareness.

A second gap to be bridged in an interdisciplinary effort is that between two sectors of human rights thinking, the freedom sector and the economic-social sector, as they pertain to the predicament of third world rural poverty. Economic-social rights (to food, health, employment, etc.) have been considered by some to be relevant, while civil-political rights assessment in the third world has been mainly limited to critically appraising national political systems and their use of violence and detention against their citizens. The loss of choice suffered by the rural poor at the village level, in which uncertainty of attaining even minimal food and health is intertwined with the deprivation of significant choice, has not been the subject of an integrated human rights assessment. While "dependency" on government relief is roundly decried by some Western commentators on poverty, little thought is given to the implications of the dependency on a wide variety of patron-like neighbors, relatives, and others in the social environment that rural food insecurity imposes on its victims.

With a background in both the philosophical and social science approaches, I felt compelled, some years ago, to try to bridge these gaps. This work presents a human rights related model of the "clientelistic dependency" of food-insecure individuals and households that are materially better off. It then proceeds to illustrate the concepts with a look at the rural poor in three countries: Bangladesh, Botswana, and Tanzania. It aims to present, and illustrate empirically, a strategy for fulfilling the international duties of the world's advantaged inhabitants under the moral rubric of human rights.

I owe a special debt of thanks for the support given me in this project by people at the Christian Michelsen Institute (CMI) in Bergen, Norway, in its Program of Human Rights Studies, and its Department of Social Science and Development. Dating back to the beginning of this work during a five-month visit to the CMI over a decade ago, their hospitality, encouragement, and material aid with the expenses of my visits to Scandinavian libraries and to the countries treated in the study were indispensable. My several opportunities to conduct human rights country assessments for the Nordic human rights yearbook project, *Human Rights in Developing Countries*, on behalf of the CMI, the Norwegian Human Rights Institute, and the Danish Institute of Human Rights, were also of great help. I received invaluable consultation in the preparation of the manuscript from an old friend, Patrick O'Connor. Finally, making it down a long road such as this would not have been possible without the emotional support of my dear wife and my two wonderful young sons.

Chapter 1

The Predicament and Its Background

A Bangladeshi family that owns only .6 acre of paddy land must periodically turn to a better-off uncle to make up a food deficit, borrowing against the future sale to the latter of a small portion of the paddy land. Another Bangladeshi household is able to sharecrop a precious half-acre of high land from a better-off neighbor to grow high-yielding variety (HYV) irrigated rice in the winter, but only with the obligation to buy the necessary water from the neighbor's tubewell and/or become one of the neighbor's supporters in village politics. In Tanzania, a peasant household with four children farms two acres of land from which the family is fed maize at malnutrition or near-malnutrition levels. The family depends on a shopowner for seed for the next crop as well as for credit for food in the lean seasons. Another large Tanzanian family depends primarily on a precious job held by one of its members in a nearby town amid widespread underemployment. A woman in rural Botswana is able to feed her five children provided that, at plowing time, she can continue to borrow a team of oxen from a relative, and also receive a small remittance from her husband, who works on a construction project in the capital city. In each of these cases, minimal nutrition—and, hence, protection from infections and other diseases that prey on people with the low resistance associated with malnutrition—is conditional on maintaining some sort of relationship with a better-off household or households. Such relationships, which constitute what I here call "clientelistic dependency," must be maintained in order to ward off weeks or months of much-heightened risk to the health and survival of one or more household members. They also render the dependent peasants vulnerable to constraint in their civil-political behavior, as they are likely to consider what they think to be the preferences of their "patron" by "anticipating" the latter's "reaction" (as it is termed by political scientists).[1] Each such case, I will argue, poses a human rights predicament, not only in the economic-social sector of human rights, but also in the civil-political sector. That predicament, I will suggest, can only be remedied over the long run by a certain sort of development aid involving simple and cheap appropriate technology, which must be offered as an option to a clearly defined category of poor households.

The debate about freedom in poverty is, by now, an old one. To what extent might conditions of poverty serve to constrain choice in ways that threaten the freedoms enshrined in human rights? On the one hand, recently, the tradition of "positive liberty" has emphasized that a minimal level of economic and social well being provides a necessary physical platform for the possibility of the kind of free and full social and political participation associated with democratic rights. In its dimensions affecting the individual, this position has been developed further in the late twentieth century (as we shall see in Chapter 2) in Henry Shue's *Basic Rights* (1980). On the other hand, the "negative freedom" argument—represented significantly in the mid-century analysis of Frederick Hayek in his *Constitution of Liberty* (1960)—suggests that preserving rights to freedom involves no more than removing institutional barriers to free choice. In this volume I propose to reconstruct elements of each of these views in a theoretical model combined with a concrete analysis focusing on the predicament of poverty and the clientelistic dependency it promotes. This predicament affects a large proportion of the world's population, undercutting the momentum for democracy building in the third world.

In the third world, the great majority of the population still lives in rural areas. There, typically, as many as the poorer 30 to 50 percent may lack even the minimal dietary volume (not to mention nutritional balance) needed to provide resistance to common illnesses. Food insufficiency malnutrition—primarily in the form of general protein/energy deficiency, but also of specific nutrient deficiencies (especially of iron, folic acid, and vitamin A)—has the effect of profoundly suppressing immune response to infectious disease, including respiratory and diarrheal infections, malaria, tuberculosis, measles, and intestinal parasites, in a variety of ways.[2] The obvious fact for third world rural dwellers is that those suffering from a food shortage get sicker and fall ill more often than those with sufficient food, thereby suffering effects ranging from an incapacity to work effectively to death (Spurr 1990). Children are notably affected (Chen et al. 1980).

The dependency on a relative, a neighbor, a local government bureaucrat, or even an aid official with a nongovernmental organization (NGO)—amounts to a requirement for whatever temporary degree of access they currently have to the minimal level of food intake that is necessary to ward off malnutrition-related health threats. Their plight can result in constraint of significant economic choice by the poorer-stratum peasants, that tends to be linked to constraint of civil-political choice as well. Their vulnerability to the loss of current or possible future opportunities makes them vulnerable to constraint on their politically relevant expression and association, which is limited to the range likely to be acceptable to their current or potential patron. Being nearly or already at risk of malnutrition-related health problems, they cannot afford to lose any opportunity they now have, or might get, to maintain or augment the family survival package, since no component can be lost without significantly increasing the risk of malnutrition and the resultant health threat. Such peasants may still have many choices in minor areas of life, and those on whom they depend for temporary minimal survival may choose to leave them free of any sociopolitical expectations regarding expression, association, and political participation. However, their clientelistic dependency nonetheless leaves them *vulnerable* to the constraint of significant choice in these areas. Significant alternatives to their current strategy involving clientelistic dependency tend to be barred to all but the most risk-tolerant individuals.

While the broad scope of this threat is well known to students of peasant poverty, it has tended to be papered over in recent assessments asserting that a rural economic revival of small-scale income-earning activities is taking place due to the effect of "structural adjustment" in opening up rural economies. Research reports on third world villages generally fail to focus on degrees of poverty as they are related to consequent differences in the character of clientelistic relationships deriving from poverty. Economically, important alternative strategies that are significant in the sense of having real potential to reverse the insecurity of access to food and health are often open to middle-stratum households. These range from gaining access to credit opportunities for agricultural inputs to improve food-crop output to going into a gainful sideline activity or educating both sons and daughters in hopes of their landing a good urban job. However, such options tend to be either out of the reach of poorer-stratum peasants or available only if they increase their clientelistic dependency on a more affluent individual or household. Relatively autonomous petty-trading, service, or small-industry activities tend to be cost-beneficial (in terms of improvement in food access versus labor cost) only for middle-stratum or better-off households, as opposed to the extremely low return on labor that resource-poor individuals tend to face in trying such options.

Many observers of poverty sense that along with their low level of resources for providing their families with nutrition, health, and education, the poor have a strikingly meager range of choice in their lives. Much depends, however, on how the reduction in choice is conceptualized. Earlier in this century, liberal critics who looked at poverty in light of the value of freedom tended to view it in terms of the lack of ability to actually do many of the things that formal freedoms permit one to do. For example, in 1927 John Dewey, in his *Liberalism and Social Action* (1963), called for a social guarantee of a minimum income, not only to enable doing certain things directly, but also to alleviate the insecurity and the all-consuming character of economic struggle among the poor, that tend to get in the way of exercising freedoms. More recently, Shue (1980) usefully extended this view to the third world by emphasizing the physiological and health deficiencies that can hinder the poor from taking the physical actions involved in the full exercise of rights to freedom. He called for guaranteeing subsistence needs as well as physical security against assault, to enable the normal exercise of freedom.

However, even Shue's "basic rights" approach stood analytically in isolation from the developing tradition of *human* rights, which, in practice, tended to assume that even those who are in poor health due to injury from assault or a nutritional deficiency can exercise civil-political rights in limited ways (to vote, speak, associate, etc.)—at least as long as they live. In part because of this fact—that while they live, the rural poor seem to remain at least minimally able physically to exercise their rights—it has been easy for many who concede respect for human rights to remain unpersuaded by Shue's overall argument. Moreover, the object of Shue's analysis of duty was a one-step guarantee of adequate food, clothing, shelter, preventive medical care, and environmental protection for all of the poor, to be provided directly, by conventional aid methods. While I sympathize with this as a long-term goal, as an immediate obligation it seems a tall order involving methods that in practice are difficult and problem ridden. In addition, alongside these subsistence rights, Shue's one-step approach required a thoroughgoing protection from assault (security rights), as a parallel prerequisite to the enjoyment and exercise of civil-political rights. Again, we have a laudable goal but one which is extremely unlikely and unrealistic as a prerequisite requirement for the third world, and apt to discourage anyone looking for a truly feasible immediate obligation under the human rights moral rubric.

However, alongside Shue's overall traditional analytical rubric of choice constrained by the inability to take action to exercise rights, he included a particularly interesting sort of "standard threat." Shue made the point that one's freedom may be removed by fear of economic retribution as well as of retribution by violence (1980, 26). Unfortunately, he failed to explore further this avenue of causation. Arguably, nonetheless, the most prevalent problem of choice among the third world poor is not that they normally cannot physically take any sort of action in the exercise of rights, but rather that they are vulnerable to the withdrawal of survival-providing economic opportunity if they stray beyond the limits set by what they believe to be their patrons' preferences; hence they perceive at least a potential risk in acting with full independence. This situation does not require that an overt exercise of "power" be made by the patron in an actual conversation, but only that there be an underlying *vulnerability* of the poor partner in the relationship, which can quite effectively constrain civil-political behavior (resulting either in silence and inactivity or in activity and expression that are thought by the client to be acceptable to the patron), *without* overt behaviors by either patron or client to make explicit the pattern of causation.

This situation can be shown to be explorable in ways conceptually independent of Shue's overall emphasis on the physical inability to act due to poverty. It is my purpose to develop an analysis, in terms of the existing rubric of human rights (that is, without trying to invent new sorts of rights), that can explain the predicament of choice constraint via clientelistic dependency, and that, in human rights terms, supports an immediate obligation to offer a certain type and level of subsistence-supporting development aid to the third world rural poor. What I call the "choice structure" facing poor peasants typically involves the absence of what I call "significant alternatives" to the pattern of clientelistic dependency facing the poor peasant. The rural poor depend on clientelistic relationships to get access to such things as credit or food to cover periods of food shortages, plots to sharecrop, wage labor in the slack season, an animal draft team to borrow for plowing, water for irrigation, and similar necessities which must be combined to provide the minimal survival package for the poor peasant. Available clientelistic options in a particular setting typically offer more or less the same combination of a temporary probability of survival with an absence of long-term assurance, given the ever-present risk of weeks or months of malnutrition each year and the resultant lowering of resistance to potentially fatal illness. The necessity of having (or obtaining) a clientelistic relationship with which to try to contend with survival threats tends to bar the pursuit of *significant alternatives* in expression and association as well as food and health. It thus rules out assurance of the options of minimal significant choice and of minimal well-being, which must be the first and most urgent immediate objective of human rights efforts.

I argue for introducing, via a particular type of development aid, a new and quite significant alternative, which provides the peasants with *comparatively autonomous control* over their most minimal survival requirements while avoiding the creation of a new line of clientelistic dependency. I have in mind the provision, for target-category peasants, of the option of acquiring certain simple types of agricultural equipment (e.g., animal draft teams, small plows, animal-drawn carts, and manual water pumps) that can save labor and enhance productivity sufficiently to assure, under the peasant's own control and with no clientelistic obligations, a crop that is minimally sufficient for the survival of all family members. In contrast, the best current approach, "integrated rural development," typically relies on local officials, providing a recurring supply of credit for recurring agricultural needs (like fertilizers, food, or water from someone else's facility). While this approach has the potential for targeting real poverty, in today's context it can often play the role of a new component of clientelistic dependency rather than a significant alternative to that system. However, when the targeted peasants have an available option of *comparatively autonomous self-provision*, then even those who do not take up the option (wishing instead to depend entirely on existing clientelistic alternatives), at least are no longer constrained into those relationships; they may become (or remain) clients without being clientelistically *dependent*. With the bargaining power that only an option of exit can supply, they may gain leverage toward achieving a minimal choice of expression and association as well as minimal access to food and health. Similarly, those who accept the new equipment may continue to benefit from integrated rural development programs and other clientelistic relationships while being less bound to them. Hence, conventional development aid approaches would lose their capacity of contributing to the dependency aspect of the problem, and instead take their intended place among human rights-sensitive solutions for rural poverty.

HUMAN RIGHTS BACKGROUND

With the fall of the Communist regimes of Eastern Europe and the former Soviet Union and the consequent demise of the cold war, a new identity crisis began in the field of human rights. For a long time, the alternative orientations toward human rights problems appeared to be the conventional Western emphasis on civil-political rights, on the one hand, and on the other, the economic and social rights emphasis of the socialist countries and many nations in northern Europe and the third world. On the civil-political side, the momentum of democratization in Eastern Europe, Russia, and parts of the third world may well give rise to a complacent sense that the human rights victory has already been won. The International Monetary Fund (IMF), the World Bank, and some donor governments have, under certain circumstances, made continued aid conditional on the acceptance of a package of market-oriented and democracy-promoting changes by the government, and these have contributed to civil-political change in national institutions in major urban areas, in the direction of democracy.

Civil-political democratization, however, presents itself primarily in a formal-legal sense and at the national centers only (e.g., with formal multi-party elections). At the village level, that at which politics is meaningful to most rural dwellers, contending national political parties are often little more than changing labels used by the same factional patron-client networks in village politics. Huge numbers of people in the lower strata in rural areas remain, in their civil-political behavior, silent or cooperative with their economic patrons. Third world governments often rely heavily, for support and stability, on the support of intermediate and local patron-client networks. Even in countries where the national government is well intended regarding human rights, the local conditions underlying the problems emphasized here tend to be well beyond the conventional formal-legal reach of central government policies. Nonetheless, what we in the West most often read about in our press are the gains made by "democracy" in the third world.

On the economic-social side of human rights, the momentum seems to be toward winding down government spending programs directed at economic needs generally. This is occurring under the relentless pressure of the International Monetary Fund (and donors) for monetarist reform to deal with deficits in government budgets in countries in both the world's North and South, and to free markets from government price controls and other restrictions. This gradual weakening of conventional governmental programs (though many smaller NGO efforts continue vigorously) may give rise to overall pessimism and to a focus solely on necessary relief for victims of the dislocations of war. However, for those most in need in third world rural areas, there may be less actual change than at first seems apparent. Regrettably, many of the previous economic aid programs failed to substantially reach the rural poor. In some countries experiencing market liberalization, higher market-based producer prices have replaced the old, artificially low procurement prices that used to be set by government officials in order to promote low urban food prices; this liberalization has helped farmers who produce substantial surplus for the market. However, for vast numbers of the rural poor, who produce little or no surplus for sale, the new era often means that either one sort of "trickle down" is replaced by another or that the flow stops altogether.

For human rights orientations overall, there is a real risk that this combination of civil-political complacency and economic-social pessimism will overwhelm the human rights movement, at a time when human rights standards should emerge into the forefront, out of the shadows of the old ideological conceptualizations stemming from the cold war. I shall argue here that both the complacency and the pessimism are misplaced, and that there is the possibility of a new understanding internationally of feasible human rights-related obligations in our era. I do not recommend the replacement of any ongoing, well-intended, and effective conventional aid efforts. In my view, however, these issues, conceptions, and practical efforts need to be *supplemented* with a qualitatively different, bottom-up component that is firmly rooted in the human rights rubric of analysis, moral evaluation, and obligation.

The predicament I try to address has to do with the vast numbers of third world rural dwellers who experience poverty-based protein/energy malnutrition and who must survive, at least in part, by means of economic opportunities offered by connections (often kinship based), with one or more better-off villagers. I call these relationships clientelistic dependencies to distinguish them from conventional patron-client relationships on the one hand, and classic economic dependency relationships on the other (e.g., of a child or an incapacitated relative). Like economic dependents, clientelistic dependents generally experience insecurity in obtaining minimal food and health access, and therefore cannot normally afford to risk losing the relationship. Under these circumstances, typically, the loss of even a small component of a household's economic package of opportunities can produce weeks or months of added malnutrition and harm to the family members' health. In this they differ from clients of patrons in the classical anthropological or political sense, who are seen as involved in a more voluntary and multidimensional relationship with their patron, having much of value to offer the latter. However, like classic clients and unlike economic dependents, clientelistic dependents are economically functioning, and indeed often must be hyperfunctional to scratch every grain of economic return out of the meager resources. In fact, in the foreseeable future there is no sense in condemning or trying to do away with clientelistic economic relationships involving the poor or anyone else; they are the lifeline of literally billions of the world's people and a key informal coordinating mechanism of political, economic, and social life. In any case, human rights provisions, as well as practical problems of feasibility and effectiveness, tend to rule out attempts at direct governmental intervention in such relationships. Indeed, relationships of clientelistic dependency among the rural poor cannot be affected substantially by traditional, top-down regulatory mechanisms.

As for currently functioning conventional methods of development aid, it is, on human rights grounds, unjustifiable to remove them simply because they may involve clientelistic dependency. The most effectively poverty-targeted of conventional aid interventions must be continued in order to address immediate economic-social and civil-political human rights problems; actual or potential victims of violence must be saved, and people who are threatened with malnutrition must be fed in whatever ways can help. Important work has been done in this regard on the right to food in international law.[3] At the same time, however, we must recognize that conventional methods alone are not likely to be effective in addressing the underlying context of poverty-based clientelistic dependency. In practice they tend, at most, to redirect or modify the channels of clientelistic dependency; they fail to alter either its attendant constraint on civil-political choice or its contribution to a persisting insecurity caused by inadequate food and access to health. The current aid approaches could be made far more effective if the missing bottom-up component could be provided, which they currently do not do.

If the effects of clientelistic dependency are to be addressed under the rubric of human rights-based obligation, some sort of practical, realistic, and politically feasible steps—both based on human rights and otherwise consistent with human rights—must be proposed to those who are most advantaged (mainly in the world's Northern Hemisphere). If possible, the new steps must be gauged at least to complement existing well-targeted aid, and perhaps even to neutralize any negative aspects for choice that the more conventional aid may create. A promising strategy of feasible and practical intermediate steps may have to be indirect rather than direct in terms of channels of impact on the problem. Moreover, it must be sufficiently affordable and realistically promising in their effectiveness that citizens and governments of advantaged societies accept them as essential for third world victims of health-threatening and choice-eliminating poverty.

With regard to the economic-social rights sector alone, in one initiative (to which I was privileged to contribute), the idea was proposed to focus human rights-based development aid on building a "minimal threshold" of food, health, employment, and education in the third world, as a preliminary foundation for further progress in realizing the whole range of socioeconomic rights (Andreasson, Smith, and Stokke 1992).[4] The following discussion also pursues a minimalist human rights foundation with respect to improving development aid. It extends beyond the economic-social rights sector, however, into the realm of civil-political rights to depict a prerequisite ground-level nexus of fundamental civil-political and economic-social rights.

To some extent standing in the way of such an approach are certain conventional ideas, mostly stemming from a traditional legal outlook on human rights. One such barrier takes the approach that human rights responsibility is confined, in one way or another, to the borders of each nation, thus calling into question the universality of both the rights and any potential correlative duties. However, the universal applicability of these rights seems evident from the human rights documents and the international arrangements drawn up to implement them (Donnelly 1989, 205–228). Claims to particular exemptions or idiosyncratic interpretations on the grounds of particular cultural or other local differences have been powerfully refuted in the work of Donnelly (1989) and others. On the side of related duty, the view that the human rights rubric implies international duty is again evident, both in the international instruments, which have been widely signed or otherwise supported around the world, and in an increasing volume of commentary. For many, the issue of international responsibility of all humans for fostering respect for human rights everywhere is that of ensuring consistency with human rights provisions for national self-determination—finding routes for international intervention in which the third world nation-states can, comparatively easily, cooperate.

A related barrier to viewing this predicament as a human rights problem and taking feasible action on it (to be explored in more detail in Chapter 2) has to do with traditional legal conceptions of the means by which international obligation is to be acted upon. In the traditional legal view on human rights, obligations fall only on government (principally, the national "sovereign" government of the territory in which the problem exists), which must respond to valid claims, by ceasing to violate human rights and by punishing individual government officials who have violated them. It is even controversial to some to consider governments as falling under a specific human rights obligation to apply laws and programs to private citizens, in order to punish perpetrators of deeds that would clearly be human rights violations if they were done by government officials.

In the face of this barrier, I focus on the reality of human rights problems in the third world and of our ordinary language of human rights. We quite normally extend talk of human rights beyond matters of violations by governmental officials to those by other groups in society, not least because of the ease with which governmental actors can do their violating via private allies or informal activities without being held accountable in the courts. Major thinkers contend that the moral rubric of human rights obligates all humans, as such, to at least refrain from violations of life and liberty. As Braybrooke (1970, 1972) and Singer (1970, 1972) contend against Lyons (1970), private threats or acts of violence against those assembling to hear a speaker are taken to be violations of rights of assembly as well as of physical security. By the same token, exercising a right is not limited to making a claim before a court or court-like tribunal; more commonly, it involves engaging in the protected activity.

Another barrier to discovering new sorts of approaches to ground-level human rights problems is the tendency of some commentators with a legalist bent of mind to focus the human rights obligation on protecting the "exercise" of rights, viewed only in terms of *making claims* before governmental tribunals. Certainly it is necessary that a route of claim making and recognition be *available* when an attempt to shut down the protected activity is made (which may conceivably be found in the realm of customary sanction as well as formal modern law and courts, as per Shue 1980, 16–17), but this requirement does not mean that exercising a right is synonymous only with asserting a claim. This seems to be suggested by Donnelly (1989, 10–11), if I am not misinterpreting his otherwise useful distinction between a right's "assertive exercise," its "direct enjoyment," and its "objective enjoyment" (1989, 11). In ordinary language, I maintain (whether or not in technical legal language), the option of the exercise of rights that we

aim to protect under the human rights moral rubric—the goal—refers especially
to the ordinary doing of the activity or possession of the value that is protected
by the right, such that the exercise is not challenged, in certain circumstances:
(a) wherever the activity or value would be threatened in the absence of the pattern, in local social practice, of respect for the right, and (b) whenever there are
available procedures for making a valid claim if the exercise is challenged or
threatened. Particularly in the third world context, we want to work toward protecting—if necessary through efforts *quite independent of* traditional formal-legal mechanisms—the exercise of rights of ordinary people who know
nothing of the nature of a right.

If we wish to avoid arguments that view the human rights obligation in too
weak and restrictive a form, we must also avoid those that unrealistically and
infeasibly assume too large a scope of immediate duty under the human rights
rubric. To be sure, there is some truth to the contention that if it seems physically
possible to address a human rights problem, then a persuasive moral obligation
to act on it now exists. An economic-social sector example is the contention that
the world's food production capacity is sufficient to feed the world's malnutrition sufferers and that only "political decisions about its distribution" stand in
the way (Donnelly 1989, 33; see also p. 93). To leave the matter at that, however, is to go only part way toward showing the feasibility of the discharge of a
duty to protect rights. Political barriers and barriers of widespread perception
regarding difficulties in the mechanism of resource extraction and delivery—
whether they be found at the source of aid supply, at the target level of the third
world village, or somewhere in between—are, regrettably, real barriers. Given
the nature of human beings and their currently workable patterns of political and
economic organization and coordination at all levels (international, national,
regional, and local), difficult political, social, financial, and other problems do
exist at many levels. What a particular lawyer, for example, thinks possible and
workable may be actually impossible, unworkable, or subject to unacceptable
costs in other values in the light of what an eminent economist or another variety
of social scientist may have observed at another level of the process of possible
remedy. The perceived existence of a moral obligation requires that it be feasible
to perform, regardless of the reasons for any actual infeasiblity.

THE STRATEGY AND MODEL OF THE STUDY

Social scientists have known for a long time about the aspects of dependency
at work in the conventional, widely recognized relationships of tenant farmers to
landlords and landless laborers to employers. Little, however, has been done to
conceptualize, under the human rights rubric, the whole range of poverty-related
economic dependencies, including a wide variety of types of dependencies of
smallholder clients who live as close to the margin of survival as do pure tenants
or landless laborers. The client household receives (for one or more of its members) one or more of a variety of values, such as a job, a sharecropping plot, access to oxen for plowing, and political protection. In return, the patron gets po-

litical support or other cooperation, such as aid in emergencies or guaranteed labor supply in peak periods. The varying particular kinds of dependency situations have in common a key risk for the client—that if the poor individual or household displeases the patron in some sort of civil-political related behavior, there may be a withdrawal or foreclosure of present or possible future patron-offered access to a resource or opportunity that is critical for survival. The dependents' vulnerability undercuts the development of a reliable, ground-level social practice of respect for human rights generally.

To understand the civil-political dimensions inherent in such economic relationships, we should take our cue from what political scientists call power by "anticipated reaction."[5] Even where no clear evidence exists of attempts by the patron to limit the behavior of the clientelistic dependent, the latter may feel a need to conform due to an "anticipation" of the patron's possible negative reaction, should the client depart from the perceived constraints. In this context, I suggest, a food-insecure, dependent peasant household is vulnerable to losing minimal significant choice in civil-political behavior and economic strategy for food access, due to the patron's *capacity* to impose sociopolitical preferences on the dependent household as a condition (perhaps unstated) of the continuation of the relationship and the survival-critical economic opportunities it provides to the poor household.

In place of Shue's emphasis on the actual exercise of a right, I focus on a third conceptual element lying in the gap between the merely formal-legal right, on one hand, and its particular exercise on the other. This element is the right's "observance" (in the language of the human rights Covenants), referring to the behavioral practice of respect of the right in ordinary social life, as a matter of the social situation and the social practice in the actual lives of average people. This practice will be referred to as an "operational right." Such a right (which must be clearly defined) will be considered as distinct from the actual doing of the thing for which the right provides scope (a distinctness not consistently maintained in Shue's formulation of enjoyment of a right), so as to direct attention to the sorts of factors that in the real world may have to go into deciding whether to exercise an actually available right. Such an operational right will be viewed as the assurance, in daily life, of the ready availability of an option, whether of significant choice among two or more significant alternatives or of access to a critical resource via a path of endeavor to gain the thing. To achieve civil-political freedom in practice, at least as ordinarily experienced in life in the Western democracies (e.g., freedom of expression and association), we demand significant alternatives for readily available choice; as noted in a founding work in the modern discipline of political science, a freedom composed of numerous trivial alternatives for choice is not a practically meaningful freedom.[6] To work with such a conception, however, we need to identify the nature of a significant alternative in realistic terms that are applicable in practice to various fields for choice and to particular predicaments of constraint and poverty facing the vast majority of third world people who live in rural areas. For an alternative to be called significant, there are four requirements: (a) being known, (b) being significantly different from other alternatives, (c) potential effectiveness for the intended goal, and (d) feasibility to try.

Thus the central components of the model presented here, then, will be access to minimal food and health in the economic-social sector of human rights and minimal significant choice of expression and association in the civil-political sector, which are linked to minimal choice of economic endeavor for food access as a catalyst of the other four. These factors will be viewed as interdependent. When assured as a minimalist package, I argue, they form a single, prerequisite springboard for autonomous, bottom-up movement toward the realization of the other human rights and of higher levels (beyond minimalist versions) of all these rights. Minimalist levels of the four key rights will thus be presented as fundamental causal stepping-stones to the fulfillment of the body of modern human rights as a whole, which must be the immediate focus of human rights-based correlative duty in the rural third world. As in the areas of food and health, we need to provide definitions of minimal-prerequisite degrees of access to food and health and of expression and association, and we must explain their interdependency relationships alongside a fifth factor in the minimalist complex: minimal choice of endeavor for food access.

This conceptualization of prerequisite conditions will form the basis of a recommendation of a certain sort of development aid strategy aimed at the third world rural poor. The practical focus of the recommendation will be on making available to the vulnerable third world rural poor, under the constraints of limited northern resources and the necessity of good cost-effectiveness in applying them, (a) certain simple and locale-suited items for food access, located at the low end of the appropriate technology scale, which can be used directly and independently in ways that are under the household's own control, and (b) in seasons and periods of maximum hunger, limited supplementary "food for work" opportunities in order to build necessary local infrastructure for the poor and to relieve survival anxieties that might accompany either trying the new, more independent route to minimal food access or sticking with the old sorts of clientelistic relationships.

The proposed approach will be aimed to supplement from below the more traditional approaches, by adding to the choice structure a new significant alternative which, for those willing to put in the necessary hard work, will be a comparatively autonomous one. Perhaps only a minority of the target group will take up this labor-intensive new option, but by offering a different, feasible, and promising alternative, and thus increasing (to two) the number of significant alternatives, it would render the existing options significantly more *voluntary* than before. Thereby, the proposed approach may reduce the tendencies of many of the traditional top-down aid approaches to leave unchanged the problem of vulnerability to coercion or even, as a kind of byproduct, contribute to it. At the same time, conventional approaches often prove costly, vulnerable to corruption and diversion, and unreliable in assuring food access to the target group by themselves. As a result of the widened availability of an option of significant choice for the rural poor, the prospects might thereby be raised of a turn for the better in local social practices, improving respect for human rights at the grass roots.

As will be made clear, however, analytical clarification is not enough in the sensitive and difficult area of persuading people of a moral duty that they do not currently recognize. The predicament's dimensions, terms, and solution must be applied to real-world problems and carefully illustrated in particular cases. Necessarily, there must also be the depiction of a feasible path of practical action to build respect for human rights on a sound foundation, incorporating it in the activities and local social practices at the village level. Subsequent chapters apply the model to an especially pressing area of human rights problems in the middle and late twentieth century, that of the third world rural poor, using the examples of Bangladesh, Botswana, and Tanzania.

THE THIRD WORLD RURAL PREDICAMENT

The absence of assurance of the option of significant choice may take various forms. For one, local social practices may actually authorize patron sanctions against noncompliance. This situation may, fairly openly, offer the poor peasant only one alternative for choice in political and economic association and endeavor. Here the poor may at times be mobilized in clientelistic support of the key resource owner's faction in local politics. In rural Bangladesh, there often occurs an enforced incorporation into active clientelistic compliance.

Alternatively, the ability to constrain may result simply in the success by local private or governmental elites in achieving non-involvement and *silence* by the poor on issues of real significance, as may be the case in much of rural Botswana and Tanzania. In such a case, local factional politics will remain an elite matter, with little or no participation in factional village politics by poorer strata among the political followings of higher-level leaders of patron-client networks. Social and economic dependencies, and the attendant vulnerability to coercion, may remain focused on traditional kinship and lineage-based patterns, or there may be many dependency linkages not based on kinship. Dependencies are typically on better off private patrons, but may also be on state officials (be the system socialist, capitalist, or mixed).

We may be tempted to sum up the relationship as uni-directional, with food insecurity causing choice constraint. It is also the case, however, that the choice constraint is, in turn, a causal contributor to continued food insecurity. The presence of significantly different alternatives of expression or association could serve to open up new and more secure forms of access to food, as in organization of cooperatives or political associations to support cooperatives or achieve land reform. The most essential of the minimal prerequisite rights from the two sectors of freedom and well-being prove to be interdependent.

This basic predicament will be illustrated in the cases of Bangladesh, Tanzania, and Botswana to illustrate how the categories in the theoretical framework may be applied to real-world situations. These chapters pull together, under the integrative model presented here, results of research that has been undertaken by social scientists from a variety of different disciplines. Such research results often remain buried on the consultancy shelves of bureaucrats or in specialized journals to which policy makers and concerned citizens seldom have recourse.

While we find many useful bodies of research on the village context of these clientelistic relationships, however, we do not possess systematic empirical studies of the exercise of political control in clientelistic relationships involving the poorer strata. Social science has not shown specific frequencies of the exercise of power by the well-off over poor individuals who, in one way or another, are dependent on them for the resources crucial for food capacity. Several reasons can be suggested for this lacuna in our empirical understanding of the situation for poor third world peasants: (a) as is evident from the discussion of power by anticipated reaction, constraint may arise even without *overt* power exercise, or even the intent thereof by the patron; (b) few other kinds of information are as sensitive and as secretively held as this, and honest and revealing responses from villagers on this subject are likely to be difficult to elicit without achieving virtually perfect conditions of participant observation, having gained the full confidence of the villagers; (c) even if candid responses can be had, they may not yield a conclusive explanation of the motives behind relevant behavior; and finally (d) it is difficult in practice to get permission to do research on such a sensitive question, which governments and local influentials are not apt to welcome with open arms. Accordingly, in trying to understand the rural sectors of Bangladesh, Botswana, and Tanzania, we cannot fall back on studies exploring the actual political behavior of clients of each identified stratum in relation to their patrons in village politics. Of course, this is not to suggest that such research is impossible; indeed, one of the aims of this book is to stimulate research in these and other particular country cases, carrying further the conceptual model elaborated here.

Our purposes here, however, do not require identifying the specific exercise of power among particular individuals, but only the context of the *capacity* for such exercise. This was also the case with the original civil-political natural rights claims against absolute monarchy, which attempted to achieve limited government, and were the earliest recognized precursors to human rights. It was not demonstrated empirically that all kings or their agents abused the wide prerogative given them under absolute monarchy, or that abuse occurred with any particular frequency. The key argument for natural rights to limit monarchic government was only that overly wide discretion placed kings *in a position* to abuse governmental power. What is necessary here is to reveal the common situations regarding these clientelistic dependency relationships among a defined category of poor individuals, and show that in the local, customary milieu, patrons have the capacity to exercise such control if they wish. Whether a patron does condition a poor person's access to survival on the constraint of behavior within patron-preferred limits is, of course, up to the patron, who may choose not to do so. However, a patron's tolerance may change, or a particularly helpful aid agent who had offered an alternative might leave for another post. The actual exercise of power need occur only often enough in the village context to influence the *perception* among poor clientelistic dependents that they might lessen their risk of malnutrition by anticipating patron reactions in their social and political behavior.

A further barrier to analysis oriented toward understanding these interrelationships has been the comparative isolation from one another of the different specialized approaches coming out of the different analytical disciplines involved in our understanding of the problem. To take a few examples, there has certainly been much debate and study of inequality and poverty as such by economists and sociologists, of patron-client relations in general by anthropologists and political scientists, of international dependency by all kinds of social scientists, of resource use and settlement patterns at the village level by geographers and environmental scientists, of development aid outcomes by development economists, of agricultural innovation attempts by agronomists and other farming systems researchers, and of well-being and needs as a human rights focus by philosophers. What has not emerged is the specific relevance, to human rights overall, of the intersection of these dimensions in the interpersonal environment of the third world poor. Given this lack of integrative focus, it is not so surprising that a clear sense of obligation to take practical action to address such problems is largely lacking from the discussion of human rights.

WHAT CAN BE DONE AND WHO IS TO DO IT?

Any such inquiry immediately raises the question of whether there is, indeed, a realistically practical way to go about solving the problem. Regarding any attempt to address economic-social minima, the traditional conception of providing for basic needs tends to involve conveying food directly, usually through centrally administered governmental channels, to those who need it. Increasingly, however, in today's international financial situation, and given today's awareness of the loss of aid to diversion and corruption in many third world contexts, to implement such an approach on a large and systematic scale is viewed as out of reach. International economic competition claims the lion's share of available discretionary capital, for investment to gain jobs or prevent job loss, leaving some advantaged countries hard pressed to maintain their own fraying national welfare programs. Each nation tends to view its own economic position as too precarious to risk recession by making major contributions to the economies of actual or potential third world competitors. While these considerations, I think, are much exaggerated as barriers to major contributions for international aid, the fact that they are so influential at the level of widespread *perception* is something we cannot ignore if we wish to have a real-world impact on research and action.

According to the widely influential view of Joel Feinberg (1973), there can be no current obligation to remedy the lack of a human right if we cannot identify duty holders due to insufficient means to remedy the problem. According to this view, economic-social rights, for example, become merely "manifesto rights," theoretical goals to be taken seriously only in a more plentiful hypothetical fu-

ture. The economic-social Covenant, on the other hand, more accurately identi-
fies an obligation to "take steps" to progressively realize economic-social human
rights. (International Commission 1977, 25). However, in the absence of knowledge or consensus on what sorts of steps are actually effective, almost anything
can be portrayed as such a step, thus substituting lip service for substance.

The civil-political sector of human rights seems to present a clearer picture.
Duty in this sector is recognized as immediate, and there is a conventional paradigm for analyzing impediments to human rights. It involves finding a guilty
"violator" or "perpetrator," and then effectively applying a legal rule and hierar-
chical governmental executive authority to his or her behavior so as to cause it to
cease. Indeed, however, in the civil-political sector, too, there is much disagree-
ment and ineffective efforts in fostering the impartial protection of personal security against assault, in the third world.

Certainly, from a point of view sensitive to both civil-political and economic-social human rights, we cannot deal with clientelistic dependency in this
way. At the outset, the behavior most approaching individual-perpetrator culpability would be the act of actual coercion; however, we rarely obtain clear information on such events. In any case, the cause of poor client constraint is not a
specific act by an individual perpetrator. Whatever we may think of the motives
of patrons or clients, it is, for practical purposes, the situation itself that imposes
clientelistic dependency, in combination with the susceptibility of the peasant to
perceptions that go with the relationship. The relationships themselves are
viewed by their participants as, at least in part, mutually beneficial. The poor
depend on having or obtaining them for whatever degree of survival assurance
(or risk reduction) can be achieved under the circumstances. The dependencies
are imbedded in local social practices and customs, and cannot unambiguously
be identified as the fault of specific individual perpetrators, as asserted by the
old human rights model.

Second, the individual perpetrator model does not yield a practical way of addressing the problem. Specific acts of coercion are likely to be authorized by
local custom, which cannot be readily altered by any center-imposed formal-legal approach. To attempt to do so by direct political or administrative
means, whether political, legal, or social-revolutionary, would in the first instance be likely to run counter to one or more other human rights. Moreover, the
track record of previous such top-down efforts suggests that they would be unlikely to accomplish more than modifying or rechanneling the culprit dependencies, sometimes resulting in more harm than good to economic-social, as well as
civil-political, rights. Actually, in any event, the most common initial approach
of international human rights efforts is not immediately and directly to pursue
individual perpetrators; that tends to be left to the affected country's legal appa-
ratus. Instead, the immediate goal of traditional international human rights effort
has been to bring the harmful practice to a halt, in ways consistent with human
rights generally.

The only practical focus must, rather, be on the degrees of poverty imposing
clientelistic dependency and just how they do so, so that means of remedy may

be crafted to simultaneously increase economic-social security and choice, each in the same step-by-step sequence. At minimal levels, choice and economic security tend to reinforce each other in an interdependent relationship. On one hand, a well-founded, autonomous economic base tends to increase choice, and on the other, such choice, particularly when involving the use of resources, tends to reinforce economic reliability. It is not useful for this predicament to imagine each right separately and try to finance its fulfillment only by the traditional means of top-down formal-legal programs. We need instead to focus more specifically on less expensive, concrete stimuli at the grass-roots level, in order to take advantage of the causal relationships among the appropriate sectors that can start a fruitful ground-up momentum in the right direction, and in so doing render more traditional development aid initiatives more harmless from a human rights point of view.

At least in agriculture, the poor tend to be really quite adept and skillful stewards of what they have, given their extremely adverse circumstances. As Holmboe-Ottesen puts it, "dietary adequacy is positively related to the proportion of homegrown food in the family diet, both in terms of nutrients and energy" (1992, 165). In contrast, income in cash comes in spurts and invites use for non-food items, so that food stocks run short later and food has to be purchased at high prices (Holmboe-Ottesen 1992, 164–166). Moreover, income in cash or donated food can invite clientelistic dependency on the person or persons who make up the immediate channel of the aid. With appropriate, food-productive tools (or other analogous resources) for autonomous agricultural self-provision, entrusting the poor with expanded choice can produce the steadiest and most resourceful guardianship over their own minimal well-being.

I will argue that initial cost-effective efforts to help under the human rights rubric must take the form of introducing, into the interdependent nexus of various fields of choice involved in the areas of minimal prerequisite rights, a new alternative of economic endeavor for food access. This must be a ready alternative, not posing additional risk in the already risk-heavy environment of the third world rural poor. A small productivity-enhancing implement, parcel of land, draft animal, or similar type of aid must be given to households or larger groupings, on condition that the transferred resource is not sold over, say, a two-year period. Second, food for work opportunities must be provided for the most desperate periods of the year, for both those who take up the new alternative and those who do not, in order to relieve the worst anxieties about survival and thus render substantially voluntary whatever choice is made between the two significant alternatives.

The target household may take up the new alternative (and all the hard work that may go with it) for the additional long-run security and independence it may provide, or it may look at its attendant responsibilities and prefer to continue in the current clientelistic dependency. The goal of human rights-sensitive research and action is not to coerce people into doing what the analysts consider to be in their interest. Rather, it is to introduce an alternative in the village that can combine with the existing relationships to provide the option of minimal significant choice and of minimal provision of food and health. Again, a peasant may (and perhaps most will) choose *not* to take up the new alternative, but he or she (and the patron) will nonetheless know it is available. The option of a more independent way out of the current clientelistic dependency (as opposed to that of merely changing patrons, which is often difficult or even impossible, and is seldom significantly different from the status quo in its consequences) may strengthen the bargaining power of those remaining in it. The goal is, then, the alteration of the local context for choice, in order to spearhead a turning of local social practices toward the habit of respect for human rights. When this bottom-up alteration of local social custom has been more or less completed, and a comparative assurance of minimal prerequisites of food, health, expression, and association thereby have been roughly built, the stage will be set for further steps, relying on bottom-up momentum, toward the completion of the human rights agenda and an improved effectiveness for existing, conventionally administered programs.

In conceptualizing the problem of founding local social practices of respect for civil-political and economic-social human rights in any given country or sector, I argue that it is necessary to accurately distinguish seven separate questions. The first two may be entertained generally, without thematic reference to illustrative particular cases. (1) Philosophically and empirically, what is a minimal prerequisite right for each of the two rights sectors of freedom and well-being, and what is its relationship to our ordinary language of rights in their actual operation? (2) What patterns of causal interaction and interdependency exist among such minimalist versions of the rights at the most basic foundations of the development of human rights progress? These questions will be explored in Chapter 3. Its jumping off point will be a sympathetic but critical exploration of the argument in Henry Shue's *Basic Rights* (1980), in contrast to the conservative approach of Frederick Hayek (1960), which culminates in a presentation of my own theoretical approach.

The theoretical side of this matter, however, is radically insufficient and unsatisfying by itself if the task is practical persuasion to an international duty that is not now seen. It must be operationalizable and adequate to a variety of cases and practical issues. The remaining questions will be taken up, therefore, in the context of comparative treatment of three country cases (Bangladesh, Botswana, and Tanzania), to illustrate how the concepts may be applied. (3) What are the most useful preliminary indicators showing just who are those who lack the most minimal foundations of choice and well-being? (4) What is the *choice structure* consequently facing the members of the vulnerable category—what are (and are not) their "significant alternatives" for economic and political choice? (5) What is the key resource or tool whose insufficiency may be said to be responsible for the subminimal capacities regarding choice and well-being in each specific context enforcing dependency on better-off individuals for economic opportunity? (6) For each given resource or tool, what is the qualitative and quantitative cutoff point for sufficient independent food capacity adequate for minimal choice and minimal well-being of the household, clearly indicating the vulnerable category? Finally, (7) What is the remedy; what are the form and amount of the key resource or resources that might feasibly be provided by development aid, as an attractive enough option for there to be enough takers to make it a viable alternative for the whole vulnerable category? It is these latter questions that must be taken up in the particular cases of Chapters 3, 4, and 5.

NOTES

1. For the political science concept of power by "anticipated reaction," see Dahl 1976, 30–31, and Jack Nagel, *The Descriptive Analysis of Power* (New Haven: Yale University Press, 1975). Additionally, Dahl refers the reader to Carl Friedrich, *Constitutional Government and Democracy* (New York: Harper and Bros., 1937), 16–18.

2. Ulijaszek includes, among other things, effects that are understandable only to individuals with the necessary technical knowledge, but that may nonetheless be mentioned: "hypoplasia of the lymphoid system and a reduction in circulating lymphocytes and phagocytic activity," harm to "the integrity of skin and mucuous membranes, which normally afford a high degree of protection against pathogens," harm to "the physiological response to pathogens in the intestinal mucosa, which may have profound effects on whether the pathogen is eliminated from the tissue, or stays," and reduction in all of the following: "cell-mediated immunity (CMI), bacteriocidal function of polymorphonuclear neutrophils, secretory IgA antibody response, activation of the C3 and factor B components of the complement system," and "responsiveness of lymphocytes to Interleukin 1" (1990, 137–140).

3. For example, see Philip Alston and Asbjorn Eide, "Advancing the Right to Food in International Law," in *Food as a Human Right*, edited by Asbjorn Eide, et al (Tokyo: United Nations University, 1984).

4. See also Andreasson, Skalnes, Smith, and Stokke, 1988, which was preceded by earlier work by the same group: "Rights and Needs in a Third World Context: a Model for Disaggregating Economic and Social Rights" (paper presented by author at the World Congress of the International Political Science Association, Paris, France, July 15–20, 1985).

5. See note 1 above.

6. Regarding the general concept of freedom on this point, see Robert Dahl and Charles Lindblom, *Politics, Economics, and Welfare* (New Haven: Yale University Press, 1953), 31.

Chapter 2

The Theoretical Model

Often, a useful way of presenting a conceptualization is to contrast it with alternatives, which may be discovered to have limitations, but also elements of value. The touchstones for the following argument will be approaches found in two theoretical discussions, which will be examined critically. Each, partly by similarity and partly by contrast, will contribute to the reader's understanding of the content and the significance of my own model, which will be elaborated and justified along the way. On the politically social-democratic (or "liberal," in the American sense) side of the issue, we shall look at Henry Shue's *Basic Rights* (1980), which is clearly the forerunner for the issues taken up by the inquiry at work here. On the conservative side, Friedrich Hayek's argument about freedom in relation to basic needs, in his *Constitution of Liberty* (1960), will be considered. These two works have had their most powerful influence, not in the most philosophically rigorous sector of human-rights-related thinking, but rather, in the realm of practical theory that is most important in the education of policymakers.

Shue's central concern, which I share, is that many countries have on the books formal civil-political rights that are not actually available in practice to many ordinary citizens, being denied in ways traceable to some sort of physical privation or the threat thereof. These latter conditions, he rightly argues, must be addressed if we wish to actually establish freedom rights in practice. Shue attempts to show that there are certain rights-related values that must be provided first—principally "security" and "subsistence"—as necessary to the actual exercise or enjoyment of "all other" (principally, the civil-political) rights. Shue's basic rights are called "basic" by him in that, in his view, their guaranteed enjoyment is necessary for the actual enjoyment of the full range of civil liberties and political rights, such as freedom of expression and association, the right to vote, and so forth. Shue refrains from explicit discussion of the human rights framework of thought and its traditional division of rights into freedoms and personal security against assault, on the one hand, and well being and basic material and cultural needs on the other. However, we may observe that among his basic rights, from the "freedom" side he takes only a single basic right of physical security against assault, while from the economic-social side, his general basic right to "subsistence" includes several categories of well-being: "unpolluted air, unpolluted water, adequate food, adequate clothing, adequate shelter, and minimal preventive public health care" (Shue 1980, 23).

According to Shue's view our duties toward the observance of "all other rights" require that worldwide, "social arrangements" be provided to guarantee the enjoyment of the basic rights by all. Such social arrangements must guarantee basic rights by (a) avoiding depriving anyone of any of them, (b) protecting potential victims from deprivation of any of them by others, and (c) aiding those who are already being deprived of their rights to security against assault and to subsistence (Shue 1980). The following discussion will find fault not with this overall direction of thought, which I hope to bolster. Rather, my contentions with Shue concern his methods, which I believe to be conceptually and practically flawed in grappling with (a) the practical meaning of respect for human rights at the grass roots and with (b) the task of clarifying a realistic obligation of the world's advantaged to address the minimal freedom and well-being of the third world rural poor.

I will examine these problems more closely, with an eye to redirecting and recasting the impulse to avoid conceptual confusions and practical difficulties, against the backdrop of that philosophical tradition that is so strikingly (and painfully) missing from Shue's discussion—the tradition of human rights philosophy. I will suggest that only the causally interdependent, minimal prerequisite protections conceptualized here can persuasively clarify the feasible immediate obligations of advantaged peoples toward those in the third world who lack assurance of civil-political and economic-social rights.

CAUSATION AMONG RIGHTS

There are two key requirements of any theory of obligation to fulfill the requirements that are prerequisite to the normal respect of rights. The justification for the obligation must be understandable in the light of ordinary language about rights, and the duties that are justified must be seen as workably and effectively *performable*. The following discussion is primarily concerned with the former. However, a word about the latter is necessary at the outset, because doubts about performability have, regrettably, played a significant role in Shue's failure to persuade many beyond those who were already converted to the 1970s orthodoxy of "basic needs."

In the human rights debate, a major barrier to a widespread sense of duty toward economic-social human rights is the perception that guaranteeing the values described in the Covenants at the indicated levels seems unrealistically expensive. One could point to the northern context of astronomical debt, capital shortage, government deficits, recession risks, and rising population and other pressures on the national resources of the developed countries, which are locked in competition with one another to gain and keep businesses and jobs. Part of the problem of expense is that of the often inefficient and corruption-ridden conventional delivery mechanisms (with the exception of ordinary disaster relief) for aid, particularly those channeled through the third world governmental levels themselves. Many conclude that the northern economies are too fragile and inadequate for what they see as a massive redistributive task. Most commonly considered to be in this category are the economic-social human rights, ranging from those to adequate food and health, to rights to employment and vacations with pay. In the view of Joel Feinberg, if a right cannot feasibly be guaranteed, no duty holders can be found for it; at best, it will be regarded only a "manifesto right," awaiting some future state of affairs in which resources are available to provide for it (Feinberg 1973). This prevalent outlook makes it easy to dismiss Shue's recommendations.

On the other hand, defenders of the basic needs orthodoxy would reply that this situation is one merely of self-serving illusion, covering a lack of will to simply decide to governmentally extract and distribute the necessary resources. In any case, persuasion of the citizenries and governments of their obligation to fully satisfy the Covenants' economic-social standards for the third world seems a long-term endeavor; in the meantime, we face an ethical demand to try to do something in the face of the political realities. However distasteful it may be to consider the level of material or other costs with regard to such compelling moral imperatives as human rights, it remains true in the real world that people will not readily believe in duties that they think their economies cannot actually handle.

Unfortunately, the aspect of Shue's argument that is most easily used to reject it out of hand by those less tutored in philosophy is the high perceived cost of the apparently massive redistribution and reshaping of the environment of the third world poor that would be required to satisfy the basic rights. The right to subsistence, for Shue, "includes the provision of subsistence at least to those who cannot provide for themselves" (1980, 24). Shue did not develop detailed standards for each of his "subsistence" categories of "unpolluted air, unpolluted water, adequate food, adequate clothing, adequate shelter, and minimal preventive public health care" (1980, 23). The only practical reference point we find in trying to specify these basic rights standards is to compare them to the implementation of human rights standards found in, say, northern Europe. The people Shue would see as proper recipients of the aid would surely number in the billions, and the cost would doubtless be quite high.

The proper conclusion to draw from this fact should not, however, be blanket pessimism. We still face the ethical question of what to do in the meantime, and whether to support intermediate steps which stand a better chance of persuading northern governments and voters. It should spur us to focus our attention more closely on the nature of the problem and its solutions, both philosophically and empirically. We must integrate in our thinking the full complexity of the task to see if a more realistic sequence of developments can in fact be stimulated at a politically feasible cost.

If we wish to turn from the broad quantitative aspects of aid to the qualitative aspects of aid strategy and sequencing, Shue's (1980) framework of analysis again gives us little clue as to which way to turn. Whether comparing the security and subsistence rights sectors, or examining the subsistence sector taken alone, Shue leaves the reader with an impression that the basic rights are more or less equivalent in their "basic" character. There are no priority relationships set out to indicate the causal importance or general significance of some over others in the overall buildup of respect for the basic rights as a whole or for the civil-political rights that require the basic rights' fulfillment. A person who is faced with insufficient available resources for a concerted attack on the whole list of basic rights of security and subsistence will discover no principle for ranking more and less essential elements from the subsistence list (of preventive health care, adequate food, clothing, shelter, clean air, and clean water) when trying to establish a strategic place to start.

Beyond the question of establishing the priorities among the values of the basic rights, there may be important strategic relationships between a lower degree of right satisfaction and the development over time of a higher degree, which we might call full satisfaction. There is no guide to be found in Shue's argument concerning what suboptimal levels of provision of each right might be much better than none, given conditions of perceived resource scarcity and major difficulties of implementation, in contributing to progress over time toward full observance. Shue's argument actually implies that since all the basic rights are basic, they must be fully enjoyed if the non-basic rights are to be exercised. Accordingly, if any one component of the basic rights is not provided fully, then all other rights are not truly available. The critic's conclusion would be, then, that we cannot provide all rights, how can anyone be held responsible for doing anything? It might be possible that aid directed toward a partial provision of one or two rights might facilitate a causal sequence toward subsequent gains in those and other rights as well, in part by rendering the recipient's *own efforts of self-provision* in those rights areas more effective. This, however, has to do with the question of empirical causal sequences *within* Shue's basic sector of rights, which Shue does not take up.

Again, this question has been taken up in a promising initiative (to which I contributed) arising in the context of Scandinavian outlooks on human rights thinking (Andreasson, Smith, and Stokke 1992). While that work was concerned with the implementation of economic-social human rights alone, it presented the need for what it called a "minimal threshold" approach for the third world, focusing on minimalist guarantees, and commencing in core areas of economic-social rights such as food, health, employment, and education, to trigger bottom-up momentum toward the later full provision of socioeconomic rights.[1]

ACTUAL OPTION VERSUS EXERCISE

More central, however, than the question of availability of adequate resources or other mechanisms to support Shue's duty to aid, is the conceptual dimension, involving the difficulties in Shue's justification itself and the relevant consequences for the persuasiveness of his conclusions (1980). First, we shall explore Shue's orientation toward the issue of what is necessary for the actual exercise of a right (what he calls "enjoyment") and contrast it with my own orientation toward an "operational right," which is an actual (rather than merely formal) option, the exercise of which one may accept or reject. Then, some of the implications of this distinction will be taken up with a focus on the two tiers of Shue's justification. The first tier seemed to take center stage in Shue's argument, while the second was mentioned briefly without analytical and empirical exploration. According to Shue: (a) basic right values such as adequate food and health are physically necessary for the sorts of actions involved in exercising such rights as free expression and association, and (b) the threat of a deficiency in the basic right can serve to coerce or intimidate action. The second of these tiers is a valuable starting point (once recast in form and deepened in content), but the first has weak spots that rule out its widespread persuasiveness.

Shue's underlying intention is to show that many freedom rights remain only formal, in that they cannot be exercised due to a lack of necessities such as food, clothing, shelter, clean air and water, and preventative health care. In Shue's language, in the absence of basic rights guarantees, merely formal freedoms fall short of the "fulfillment" of the right or the "actual enjoyment" of the "substance" (1980, 13) of the right, versus its mere "proclamation" or "promise" (1980, 15). The substance of a right is "whatever the right is a right to," and "enjoying a right" means "enjoying something or other," like "food or liberty" (1980, 15). So far, the enjoyment or substance of the right seems to mean actually eating the food or actually exercising the liberty by doing the sort of action that the right protects. Where he makes implicit reference to the optional aspect by using the word "capacity" or "ability," the word "enjoyment" is connected, not with this aspect of choice, but instead with actually taking up the option in the relevant physical activity. Shue states, for example, that "the point is that people should be able [have the option] to enjoy, or exercise, their other rights" (1980, 20), that his central concern is "the capacity [the option] to enjoy active rights" (19), and that no one can be said to "fully enjoy" a right if there is a threat of physical harm if "he or she tries to enjoy the alleged right" (21). According to this model, which is the most evident impression the reader gets, the use of "enjoyment" seems to stress the performance of the specific activity or consumption of the right.

This sense of the practice of a right is not, however, what we mean in ordinary language when an opposition is made between (a) having a right merely and solely in some constitutional document and not actually in practice, such as under some oppressive government regime, and (b) the right as actually possessed in, say, the democracies of North America or Europe. The latter refers to the right as a ready *option* of exercise or consumption of something, what could be called a "respected right" rather than the "exercise of a right." I can actually have a right in my community without exercising it often, or even ever, provided I have a *ready option* of engaging in the right-protected activity or actually possessing or consuming the right-protected value. This may require a preliminary course of action, like doing whatever is necessary to become a full member of an organization to exercise the right of free association, but that course of action must not, in a practical sense, be closed or unrealistic to me provided I am a member of the appropriate category it seeks to represent. When a right on the books is actually respected in society in this way, it could be called a "behavioral" or "operationalized" right. Real freedom of association means that I am free to choose among available alternatives that are significant to me, and not that I have actually chosen.

The distinction between Shue's enjoyment-as-exercise concept and this concept of operational option is not a minor one, but rather has implications for the whole direction that must be taken by any persuasive justification of the rights prerequisite to the development of full respect for human rights across the board. We shall first trace the consequent limitations of Shue's conceptualization, which essentially takes what I shall call a *logical provision* approach to prerequisite rights and their corresponding duties. Then I will lay out a more empirically realistic alternative which takes a *causal option* approach instead. We are led here to explore further the distinction between (a) providing, as basic right-values, the physical conditions necessary for action, and (b) providing for the ready options that are here called minimal prerequisite rights, whether of minimal significant choice (in the civil-political areas of expression and association) or of access (in the economic-social areas of food and minimal health) in order to start a steady, progressive development of the options that here are called operational human rights.

In contrast, Shue's primary stress is on the biological requirements for ordinary physical activity, entangling him in problems with our sense of rights in ordinary language. Certainly, to do well or conveniently the things that we take to be exercise of rights, good health is necessary; the question is whether good or effective action is necessary to our sense of having rights in practice. In ordinary language in a right-respecting society, we do not speak of physical limitations on our activity as detracting from our ability to exercise our rights, or as detracting from our rightly regarding society as respectful of rights in the civil-political area. If an extreme physical limitation preventing any expressive or associative action did occur, no one would ordinarily invoke the language of rights respect unless the tragedy followed from politically motivated crime.

Moreover, there is a further difficulty in the way Shue's argument would play out practically. Clearly, there *is* some physical threshold of disease, injury, or malnutrition below which action in the exercise of freedom rights actually is impossible, and which, according to Shue's argument, should be addressed by a corresponding duty to protect the rights. Someone inclined to minimize the need for aid, however, could argue that such a standard might be very low indeed. It could be much less than Shue's platform of physical security against all sorts of assault, the removal of air and water pollution, and the provision of "adequate" food, clothing, shelter, and minimal preventative health care. For example, the serious air pollution of Los Angeles, California, does not prevent its inhabitants there from engaging in free expression and association; indeed, it often tends to catalyze such action. The same can be said under certain conditions for malnutrition based on food shortage or a boost in food prices beyond the means of many poor, say as a result of the International Monetary Fund (IMF) mandating the elimination of food price subsidies. Only a degree of malnutrition or environmental poisoning so severe as to prevent all movement or coherent expression whatsoever would call for amelioration according to this view. That amelioration need proceed only up to a point enabling some sort of gestural communication and the capacity of, for example, being moved on a stretcher to a meeting.

Curiously, Shue seems to tacitly admit this point when he gives an example of malnutrition linked to failure to enjoy rights, which seems to require quite an extreme degree of malnutrition for one's capacity to exercise a right to be considered harmed.

Any form of malnutrition, or fever due to exposure, that causes severe and irreversible brain damage, for example, can effectively prevent the exercise of any right requiring clear thought and may, like brain injuries caused by assault, profoundly disturb personality. And obviously, any fatal deficiencies end all possibility of the enjoyment of rights as firmly as an arbitrary execution. (1980, 24–25)

Even at this extreme, brain-damaging level of malnutrition, there would be practical difficulties in interpreting when damage had occurred, to what degree, and to what extent a given degree of brain damage had affected one's ability simply to choose between alternatives. For vast numbers of people suffering from malnutrition, determining whether brain damage had occurred would not be easy. Problems in "thinking clearly" might be hard to distinguish from other common disadvantages in taking articulate action (e.g., practically nonexistent education), which are not directly tied to malnutrition. Even beatings (which deny the right of security against assault) can be administered without impairing brain function significantly. Since, by Shue's argument, it is the minimum level *for right-exercising action* that constitutes the basis for assessing the advantaged world's duties in providing physical well being, that duty target might appear to be very low indeed. The net of this main avenue of Shue's justificatory discussion may thus actually be cast much too narrowly, and almost every case in which the victim is still alive could be contested.

Shue is certainly under the impression that his line of justification of prerequisite rights aims much higher concerning the content of basic rights. His formulations, such as "adequate" food, clothing, and shelter, universal security against assault, and the absence of air and water pollution indeed seem directed at a rather robust sense of exercise of one's capacities. However, his stress on physical requirements for action in the exercise of rights does not strongly justify more than a drastically low physiological minimum. Conservative observers might even argue that the world's current famine-relief efforts already meet that standard.

What we need in order to accept a higher minimal standard of food and health is an understanding of the heightened health *risk* associated with levels of food access that are higher than the physiological minimum, but which nonetheless amount to a barrier to right-exercising action. Particularly with the typically limited access to health care that is characteristic of the third world, protein/energy malnutrition, as well as physical injury from assault, weaken resistance and renders people susceptible to potentially life-threatening infection and disease. This more fruitful line of justification is briefly initiated in Shue's argument but not followed up in its meaning and implications for rights implementation. At one point he went beyond the idea of actual health threat *directly* limiting right-exercising action, to that of the *threat* or *risk* of harm serving *indirectly* to suppress exercise of rights. On the civil-political side, the right to physical security against assault, Shue gave the example of the threat of getting beaten up following one's participation in a particular association (1980, 26–27). He then insightfully proceeded to parallel this with food threat, suggesting that "the same is true if taking part in the meeting would lead to dismissal by the only available employer when employment is the only source of income for the purchase of food" (1980, 26). Shue explicitly considers this a kind of parallel with limitation by physiological insufficiency hindering action; he says that the "credible threat" of deprivation of subsistence and security against assault can leave one "readily open to coercion and intimidation" so as to "paralyze a person and prevent the exercise of any other right as surely as actual beatings and protein/calorie deficiencies can" (1980, 26). Thus not only actual physiological harm but threatened harm can, via intimidation, prevent the exercise of rights and hence the enjoyment of them.

This is the trend in Shue on which I wish to build. As Shue presents it, however, we would have great difficulties identifying the target category of victims. The question of whether a threat is, in a particular instance, credible would be a difficult one, subject to both local cultural variability and individual perceptual subjectivity in each particular case. Poor peasant clients may be intimidated in a civil-political sense without any overt expression of a threat, whether demonstrably credible or not; this could even happen without any patron intention to intimidate, and just as a matter of client perception alone. Intimidation emerges from the situation of food insecurity, independently of whether there is a real aspect of patron culpability. By leaving the focus abstractly on those lacking the enjoyment or exercise of rights, Shue fails to go far enough in delineating the category of those who refrain from independent civil-political behavior for fear of losing crucial economic opportunities for which they depend on the discretion of a better-off individual or household.

I now focus on this avenue of risk, developing it in a different conceptual context which is more consistent, I believe, with the ordinary language of rights and the human rights tradition. It requires a new formulation that can both (a) justify a nutritional standard that is realistically above the near-death physiological minimum for physical action, and yet (b) justify a standard that is more realistic in the light of current development aid potentials, falling below the ambitious, full-fledged levels of provision of food, clothing, housing, and environmental protection that Shue seems to have thought his argument justifies, and for which the economic-social human rights documents do ultimately call. Furthermore, the formulation must be illustrated and operationalized by already available information about empirical cases, that can lay a foundation for agreement on the necessary action to address these minimal-prerequisite rights.

THE APPROACH TO DUTY: SECURITY AGAINST ASSAULT

Shue's approach to remedy may be described as a *logical value-provision* strategy. In the area of security against assault, his response to the problems of actual and threatened harm is to identify a separate basic right, the right to security against assault, whose enjoyment is necessary (but not sufficient, as it requires subsistence as well) if the right of free expression or association is to be enjoyed. His recipe describing the advantaged world's corresponding duty to take action to provide for the enjoyment of "all other rights" is to provide this basic right to everyone.

As in our discussion of subsistence-related duty, however, again Shue has proposed an extremely ambitious basic requirement of providing impartial protection against all kinds of unlawful assault to everyone the world over. Such a requirement can only discourage the practically minded and invite skepticism, rather than providing guidance as to the first steps to be undertaken toward such lofty goals. In third world countries it is just as much a fantasy to require that physical security be directly and impartially provided to all by governments as it is to require that adequate food and health be directly provided via guarantee by "social arrangements" to all. Anyone familiar with third world conditions, particularly in rural areas, where fully effective governmental police protection will often continue to require purchase by bribes for generations to come, would be skeptical of such a demand.

Where rural people achieve substantial security against assault, they do so in part by protecting themselves, whether individually or in informal peer groups or patron-client clusters. This is a necessary bottom-up complement to top-down governmentally provided security. To ask that progress in other human rights areas wait for Western-style impartial police protection as a critical basic prerequisite to progress in a wide range of other human rights areas is to ask people to wait for a very long time indeed. It is to try to lay on the world's advantaged humans a duty that presently cannot be met; again, in Joel Feinberg's formulation, this amounts at best to a "manifesto right" which, by currently being impossible in practice, cannot find dutyholders on which to lay the duty and must wait for some future time when the required resources become available (1975).

One can question, however, the necessity of such an ambitious move on the count of linguistic sense as well as practicality. We may see this by turning to the particular situation of intimidation of associative behavior by the threat of violence. The focus of ordinary language concerning human rights in this instance is not the violence as such, but rather the *social context,* which tends to fuse the physical harm with the suppression of the civil-political right involved.

Shue's approach is, in effect, to isolate the dimension of enforcement of physical protection from the context of civil-political right infringement. His view on this is reminiscent of that of David Lyons, that politically punitive violence does not call directly on a corresponding duty to protect the right of free association, but rather calls only on the duty on the part of the state to protect physical security (see Lyons 1970). Following publication of Lyons's article, however, David Braybrooke and Marcus Singer argued (persuasively, I think), that the civil right to free association was also, in fact, central to a discussion of corresponding duty in this sort of case.[2]

The causal nexus for feasibly laying the foundations, on which to build the wider and higher reaches of rights realization, requires not so much logical analysis as causal analysis. It is unlikely to prove either simple, direct, or elegantly clean. On the ground in the third world, bottom-up efforts to defend security against assault, whether by group self-defense and mutual support in court or by the presence of local police, tend to long precede the development of comprehensive modern law enforcement and protection. These autonomous efforts could open up a minimal degree of civil-political choice in expression and association, which in turn can contribute substantially to the coordination of such bottom-up security efforts by building local solidarities independently of (perhaps in spite of) official police involvement. In the American Old West, long before security against violence was widely operational, a minimal scope of free expression and association already operated and facilitated individuals' use of their own arms and efforts to protect themselves. From the point of view of the developmental causation of operational rights, the full-blown right of personal security against assault is best viewed as one of the ultimate *consequences* of the operational development of a prior, and more fundamental, causal nexus of four interdependent operational minimal-prerequisite rights—minimal significant choice of expression and association (from the freedom sector) and minimal access to food and health (from the well-being sector)—catalyzed by a critical fifth factor to allow the other four to develop, minimal significant choice of endeavor for food access.

THE LIMITATIONS OF A CONSERVATIVE ALTERNATIVE: FREDERICK HAYEK

An important preliminary point in Shue's argument had to do with vulnerability to coercion following from dependency on a single local employer for very scarce employment opportunity. This put the employer in a condition to undermine the employee's exercise of rights of free association or expression by threatening withdrawal of the job should the worker engage in the "wrong" sort of civil-political activity. We can understand this point better in its comparative context by turning to a much earlier discussion of vulnerability to coercion in a similar context, written in the 1950s by the important conservative scholar Frederick Hayek, in his book, *The Constitution of Liberty* (1960).

Hayek explicitly discussed the situation of a monopoly employer facing an employee with no food-viable alternative, conceding that it invited coercion. Hayek's underlying intention, of course, was to apply this approach to the Soviet Union. Indeed, he quoted Leon Trotsky on the dilemma that faced a Soviet opponent of Joseph Stalin in the early 1930s—obey or starve (Hayek 1960, 137). Hayek's discussion was ultimately crafted to try to insulate the context of economic dependency from any concerns to protect the victim's freedom; in so doing, he illustrates well, I think, the conservative approach to this issue and, along the way, its shortcomings.

Interestingly, in defining coercion, Hayek showed care and realism in making his model of infringement of liberty a realistically comprehensive one. He did not require as a condition of coercion that a direct order be given the victim; rather, he defined coercion as "such control of the environment or circumstances of a person by another" that the victim chooses to do what the coercer wants, "in order to avoid greater evil" (Hayek 1960, 20–21). In another briefer rendition, coercion was summed up as "the control of the essential data of an individual's action by another" (Hayek 1960, 139). Hayek thus located the operation of coercion in the victim's likely perception of the alternatives. Moreover, for Hayek, coercion "need not consist of any use of force or violence" (1958, 138). It can also include the withholding of any resource or service that is "crucial to my existence or the preservation of what I most value" (Hayek 1960, 136).

Hayek mentioned two relevant examples: (a) a monopoly of ownership of the only spring in an oasis, which serves as "an essential commodity on which people were completely dependent," and (b) the sort of employment example as we found in Shue's point about restriction of association, in which coercion exists "in periods of acute unemployment [when] the threat of dismissal may be used to enforce actions other than those originally contracted for" (Hayek 1960, 136–137). Conditions of acute unemployment thus create what Hayek called the "opportunity for true coercion" (1960, 136). Furthermore, Hayek did not limit the problem to the instance of getting someone to do some particular thing. He also included compelling someone *not* to do something, as in Shue's example of deterring someone from assembling for some purpose, such that:

infringements on liberty consist largely in people's being prevented from doing things, while "coercion" emphasizes their being made to do particular things. Both aspects are equally important; to be precise, we should probably define liberty as the absence of restraint and constraint. (Hayek, 1960, 16–17)

It is at this point that Hayek's conservative analysis stops short of Shue's basic needs approach. In his example of a monopoly on the available food-viable employment, for example, the situation of vulnerability to coercion was not cause for alarm unless there followed a particular act of coercion—with the employer actually requiring or prohibiting some sort of work beyond the job definition. Hayek says that if, for example, I am employed "in a distasteful job at a very low wage" for the only available employer, and under the threat of "starvation to me and perhaps to my family," nonetheless, my *arrival in this situation* does not involve coercion unless "the act that has placed me in my predicament [is] aimed at making me do or not do specific things" (Hayek 1960, 137). For Hayek, it is only actual coercion—intentionally forcing someone into vulnerability and, perhaps, subsequently into having to do specific things—that government must consider controlling. Moreover, in a different part of his discussion, he indicated that it is only "severe" coercion that government must act to alter (1960, 138–139); he conceded that some aspects of taxation and the military draft were coercive, but argued that they had noncoercive aspects (impartiality, limited and predictable impact, etc.) as well.

Hayek thus rejected applying the category of liberty infringement to the monopoly employment situation itself, refusing to render the poor victim open to coercion if coercion has not yet actually occurred. For Hayek there must be a specific human perpetrator with a specific intention of directing the behavior of the victim for the outcome to be properly labeled coercion. His view thus reflects a legalist view that I call the "individual-perpetrator" model of human rights infringement. That is, if you cannot identify a specific guilty party or parties that intended the outcome, there is no problem. For Hayek, the reality of the example of high unemployment paired with conditions potentially threatening to health and life for the unemployed—which I consider the sort of "choice structure" that is characterized by only one "significant alternative"—tends not to be the immediate outcome of the intention of any one (or a few) specific individuals to control the behavior of the poor. Rather, in Hayek's view it tends to be the result of certain market effects and other surrounding economic conditions, and thus does not fit the legalist individualism requirement of a particular perpetrator. According to Hayek, unless a situation presenting an "opportunity" for coercion (1960, 136)—equivalent to Shue's "vulnerability to coercion" (1980)—is actually acted upon by giving a specific directive to the victim, the latter remains free.

There are various perspectives, of course, from which this conservative view may be challenged. Hayek requires that the causal factor responsible for liberty infringement be human (rather than, say, natural, like the contours of a crevasse pinning a fallen mountain climber), and further, that the human causal agent have a particular intention to coerce the behavior of the victim. However, the condition of vulnerability itself, independently of whether specific directives have been issued, may be considered to be of human origin if it is caused by a particular pattern of local social practice and is *feasibly alterable* by humans, consistent with human rights. It seems that the causation of the situation of one-employer dependence and vulnerability, for example, is human insofar as it is feasibly addressable by humans. If public policy has the *capacity* to improve the employment situation by providing to the unemployed, at minimum, a second significant alternative for minimal well-being—such that the polity could, at a reasonably acceptable cost, provide the required alternative way of provision of minimal well-being—*human* responsibility for any one-alternative employment structure seems to be established. Here it would *not* be persuasive to call the situation the result of the impersonal market as if the market, like the weather, were not subject to human regulation—it is.

However, for calling the situation a deprivation of liberty, Hayek also required that there be a *particular intent* of forcing the victim into the situation of a monopoly of newly available employment. A conservative might plausibly accept that humans may indeed be responsible for governmental policy, which could include as feasible alternatives either stimulating the market provision of employment alternatives to the point where there are significantly different employment alternatives, or providing a solid welfare or unemployment compensation system as an alternative. Yet at the same time, our conservative might contend that the polity's failure to do so does not show a particular intent to force workers into situations wherein behavior outside the job description can be directed by the employer. Instead, the conservative might maintain that programs to alter the situation are simply perceived as too expensive for the level of tax burden that a democracy (with its perceptions of what is necessary to maintain prosperity) might accept.

Nonetheless, however, an absence of ameliorative public policy, and the resulting numbers of poor people who are forced to accept what is offered by an effective monopoly of new employment, also results in a generally more compliant workforce. Interests pressing against ameliorative public policy in the polity may indeed have in mind intentions that are not revealed in their overt behavior. They may be quietly appreciating greatly the benefits of a more compliant workforce, whether or not they have yet planned how they will use their increased power over vulnerable workers for whom that employment is the only means to well-being. Perhaps potential employers might be able to write into new employment contracts a far greater discretion in controlling employees, even to a point not easily distinguishable from slavery, as we find, for example, in the South Asian "bonded labor," or debt slavery. How do we know the real intention of those in a position to guide public policy? The contention of the conservative is utterly impossible to empirically verify in this situation.

Hayek's other condition for sufficiency for coercion that concerns the intent of the coercer is that the former must actually exercise his power over a vulnerable employee. The employer must direct behavior outside the job description, whether to do or not to do something (perhaps in the area of civil-political choice). The conclusion that there must be a specific exercise of power for there to be constraint, however, may also be challenged, from the direction of the theory of power in contemporary political science. According to Robert Dahl (1976, 30–31), one form power can take is power by "anticipated reaction." The behaviorally flavored concept suggests that someone (person B) who is aware of a possible threat from a potential controller (A), can be constrained to avoid doing certain things if B "anticipates" the feared negative "reaction" of A that would follow if B did those things that he or she believes to be contrary to A's preferences (Dahl 1976, 30–31). In this situation, as Dahl observes, the most inclusive immediate cause is not actually controller A, but rather B's perception of A's preferences, which can be independent of A's actual behavior or even A's actual preferences.

Applying this to constraint, we may define vulnerability to constraint as a general situation encountered by B, in which he or she knows that *if* A *does* have a preference for his or her behavior in some area of choice (e.g., political expression or association), A *could* readily structure B's alternatives so as to render the behavior A prefers the necessary lesser evil for B. Someone working for the only available employer to earn income for enough food for minimal subsistence—the situation with which Hayek and, later, Shue, were concerned—may see "no choice" but to follow whatever he or she understands to be the employer's preferences for his or her political activity (or lack of it), even without any specific directive to that effect.

HAYEK AND ALTERNATIVES FOR CHOICE

A further striking feature of Hayek's requirements for a predicament to be one of absence of freedom has to do with what is left out, which makes explicit another feature characteristic of conservative thinking on freedom. He rules out considering the extent or number of alternatives for choice as a factor in identifying failures of liberty and points out that criteria of freedom or unfreedom that involve measuring the number of alternatives for choice might serve to lead a definition of freedom into what he calls the "freedom as power" interpretation. The general identification of freedom with power to do particular things is regarded by Hayek as a dangerous misinterpretation, inasmuch as its proponents tend to focus on wealth as the key source of the power to greatly enlarge the range of alternatives for action, which requires a redistribution of wealth in order to do justice to the value of freedom for all:

This confusion of liberty as power with liberty in its original meaning inevitably leads to the identification of liberty with wealth; and this makes it possible to exploit all the appeal which the word "liberty" carries in the support for a demand for the redistribution of wealth. Yet, though freedom and wealth are both good things which most of us desire and though we often need both to obtain what we wish, they still remain different. Whether or not I am my own master and can follow my own choice and whether the possibilities from which I must choose are many or few are two entirely different questions. (Hayek 1960, 17)

Hayek explicitly linked the freedom-as-power interpretation with (among others) the social-democratic view of the American social and educational thinker John Dewey (Hayek 1960, 17) who, in his *Liberalism and Social Action,* rejected merely formal liberty in favor of the "effective liberty" to do concrete things (Dewey 1963). Dewey did argue for at least the social regulation of the market and enough redistribution to provide an economic floor adequate for the social and cultural self-development of the less advantaged majority.

To be sure, there is a grain of truth in Hayek's view, in that in ordinary language, the word *freedom* is not used to discriminate between having a few alternatives for some field of choice and having a great many. However, Hayek seems to push the point too far, because a certain *minimal* range of choice does seem to play a part in the ordinary language of freedom, such as in saying, "I did not feel free in the matter; I had no choice, no alternative" but to take a certain action. To make the point clearly, but trivially, the difference between four meaningful alternatives and nine does not seem to invoke the language of freedom as a value, but the difference between only one significant alternative and two or more, quite reasonably does.

What is curious about Hayek's discussion has to do with what he says when turning to *philosophical justification* of his rejection of any consideration of the extent of the range of alternatives for choice when arriving at criteria for freedom or absence of it. Strikingly, his foremost philosophical reason for ruling out *any* considerations of the extent of range of alternatives for choice was based on an example concerning limitation to *only one alternative* because of nonhuman forces. He says that considering the range of alternatives for choice might lead us astray into considering, under the rubric of loss of freedom, constraint due to merely natural or physical limitations, rather than human ones. "The rock climber on a difficult pitch who sees only one way out to save his life is unquestionably free, though we would hardly say he has any choice" (Hayek 1960, 12). He is quite right here, in that a discussion of freedom is unlikely to arise in this case. The reason, however, may have most to do with the fact that the constraint is physical, arising from nature; Hayek himself made much of the requirement, for the relevance of the concept of freedom, that constraint must come from a human direction rather than from physical or natural factors. When one is left "with no choice" in a situation as a result *of the policy of another human* (or humans), the likelihood of ordinary language mentioning freedom or freedom-related terms goes up sharply, without involving what philosophers call a "category mistake," or employment of a word out of its natural context and usage in ordinary language.

Hayck himself lapses into language concerning degrees of freedom in the political context of rejecting the freedom-as-wealth account when he points out that "the courtier living in the lap of luxury but at the beck and call of his prince may be much less free than a poor peasant or artisan, less able to live his own life and to choose his own opportunities for usefulness" (1960, 17). Here Hayek does call on his own criterion for freedom, which is the rather vague and subjective sense of being one's own master and following one's own intentions (1960, 17). Implicit in his example, however, is a reference to a choice of a deeper, more significant sort, falling at the low end of the spectrum of possible ranges of alternatives—the criterion of whether there are a few such alternatives or none at all. Implicitly, the courtier is less free because he has no alternative to obedience to his prince when the latter wishes such obedience, assuming that the courtier has no other skills and that being turned out in the Middle Ages could threaten the most basic requirements for life. In contrast, ordinary peasants and artisans do indeed, under normal social and market conditions and land availability (for the peasants), operate within the limits of their condition but without positive direction by anyone like a prince. More accurately, we might observe that one has a sense of being one's own master only when there is at least some *minimal range* of choice. Elsewhere in his book Hayek states that he considers the worker

free, despite the most detailed workplace rules and supervisory patterns, provided an alternative employer is available in the economy (a requirement he considers not to have been met in the Soviet Union, which he characterized as a
single employer). This whole discussion implicitly uses a minimal range of alternatives as a criterion for free choice.

Finally, Hayek makes implicit reference to the range of alternatives when he
includes under the rubric of liberty infringement a power holder *ruling out* some
behavior by the victim, alongside the positive coercion of getting the victim to
do a specific thing. He indeed conceded that what he calls "restraint" may be an
even more common form of liberty infringement than coercive "constraint," and
he explicitly accepts both as violations of liberty (Hayek 1960, 16–17). Conceptually, however, restraint by ruling out an alternative seems to raise the issue
of the extent of the range of alternatives for choice, which Hayek elsewhere
disavowed as irrelevant to either the presence or absence of freedom. Hayek's
reply might be that the issue is not raised here in the same way as it might be
when we compare, for example, a poor person's range of nine things to do on a
Saturday afternoon with an affluent person's 79 alternatives. Liberty infringement by restraint often merely removes one alternative—say, banning one political party but leaving six others for which to vote. What is central to loss of liberty through ruling out one of the alternatives is that what is ruled out often is an
alternative that is quite *significant* to the victims. For example, in South Africa
the hypothetical banning of a tiny political party espousing a strange foreign
religion is a different matter from banning the African National Congress party
while numerous other parties remain legal. What this highlights is the importance of the issue of significance of the alternatives, which is largely ignored in
Hayek's inquiry.

We may see a deeper fault line in Hayek's analysis, however, when we turn to
what he positively considers to be the key characteristic of individual freedom.
To take the place of the rejected number-of-alternatives criterion, Hayek adopts
as his central criterion for freedom, that of a *self-generated life plan*. The essential characteristic of coercion is that it removes the capacity of the victim to be
his or her "own master" in the sense of pursuing his or her own life plan. What is
involved, in Hayek's view, is the question of:

how far in acting he can follow his own plans and intentions, to what extent the pattern of
his conduct is of his own design, directed toward ends for which he has been persistently
striving rather than toward necessities created by others in order to make him do what
they want. (1960, 13)

It was this criterion that Hayek used to sort out the *degree of severity* of the coercion. For instance, he accepted as necessary the state's practice of imposing
both taxation and compulsory military service, even though he was willing to
explicitly call both coercion. Hayek explained this by pointing out, not only that
compulsory taxation and the draft are practically necessary to preserve freedom
generally, but also that taxation and the draft "restrict the possibility of shaping
one's own life less than would, for instance, a constant threat of arrest resorted

to by an arbitrary power to ensure what it regards as good behavior" (Hayek 1960, 143).

It is here, I think, that Hayek's treatment of the monopoly employment example fails him. Hayek argues that the situation of the employee working at a distasteful job, for the sole available employer, amid high unemployment in the community and the threat of lack of food for the unemployed, and in which the employer *may* coerce anytime he wishes, does *not* take away the worker's freedom unless the employer then takes the further step of ordering the worker to do something outside the job description. However, even absent such extracurricular commands by the employer, surely we would not consider such a situation to meet Hayek's positive criterion of partaking in a self-crafted life plan or course of endeavor. This distasteful job, under these conditions, would not be considered as significant an alternative to the worker *if* there were other alternatives in the field for choice that provided equal access to food and were significant in the light of the worker's life plan. The worker forced by the threat of starvation to accept the distasteful job in fact regards it as significant only because it is the *only* option for access to food.

Three cases can be imagined here. If the worker under these high unemployment conditions has *two* alternative employers or jobs, one providing survival and meaningful for his life plan and the other providing survival but distasteful, the latter alternative loses significance in the present. It can regain significance as an alternative only due to its minimal survival value, however insecure, as an option should the desirable outfit, household, or individual fire the worker or close. If, in a third imaginable case, there are three jobs available in a local community suffering from high unemployment, two of them meaningful and survival-providing and the third distasteful but also providing a minimum level of survival, the third would become insignificant to the worker. Only the first two could have significance as alternatives, yet simply having those two alternatives yields a sense that one has at least *minimal significant choice* (as long as they are significantly different from each other, rather than, for practical purposes, merely two labels for the same category of experience).

Hayek's emphasis on following one's own plans and intentions highlights the case in which the job offered by a monopoly employer amid acute unemployment is an attractive one to the worker well beyond its provision of mere survival; indeed, for example, it might pay much better than the minimum wage. Here, Hayek's emphasis on the pursuit of a desired life plan and his disregard, on principle, of the number-of-alternatives question would require him to judge such a worker to be free. However, such a worker would be likely *not* to consider him or herself free simply due to the fact that he or she is comparatively happy in the position. Hayek himself emphasizes that our judgment of the nature of liberty as a politically relevant value has nothing to do with what is good or makes us happy (1960, 18).

Furthermore, how could Hayek operationalize the distinction at work here between a single-alternative choice structure in which the alternative is life-plan desirable, and one in which the single alternative is accepted solely because it is minimally (though perhaps insecurely) survival-producing? The determination of whether such a single-alternative choice structure does provide significance to the worker beyond that of producing survival is too subjective for an observer to ascertain in the context of the worker's self-generated life plan. In the kinds of real-world situations of third world dependency examined here, if the worker said that it was meaningful in this way, could we be sure that he or she meant it under these circumstances? How it could be verified? Any certainty here would involve a paternalistic decision by the observer to believe what the worker says based on the observer's perception of the worker's real interests. It underlines the subjectivity of Hayek's key criterion of a self-generated life plan, making it difficult to behaviorally operationalize.

I wish to argue that there is an available criterion for determining with some confidence the rock-bottom minimum of free will in someone's course of endeavor. The criterion involves whether it was chosen over at least one other significant alternative. The key word I use to designate such an alternative is "significant." To limit the subjectivity and paternalism to which we are tempted in such a definition, we must reserve the judgment of significance of one's course of endeavor to the life-and-death realm of minimal food access and minimal health of the family. Ordinarily, we assume different people around us to consider very different alternatives to be significant, and an attempt to say something generally about the significance of alternatives as such would be questionable. However, the particular class of situation that we are considering here—that of, hypothetically, the poorest one-third to one-half of the population in a less-developed country—is an exception. There it is not a question of following one of a variety of options, but rather of securing the most minimal necessities for following any other options at all. Hayek articulates well the common opinion adopted here in taking as a standard the "normal, average person":

Whether or not attempts to coerce a particular person will be successful depends in a large measure on that person's inner strength: the threat of assassination may have less power to turn one man from his aim than the threat of some minor inconvenience in the case of another. But while we may pity the weak or the very sensitive person whom a mere frown may "compel" to do what he would not do otherwise, we are concerned with coercion that is likely to affect the normal, average person. Though this will usually be some threat of bodily harm to his person or his dear ones, or of damage to a valuable or cherished possession, it need not consist of any use of force or violence. (1960, 138)

Amid high unemployment in a third world rural area and a concomitant lack of food-viable alternatives, for example, we may say that working for a monopoly employer, as in the example used by both Hayek and Shue (1980), is the sole significant alternative. It is the only available way of providing the poor with whatever degree of food security can be had, and accordingly, with the degree of minimal good health associated with minimal nutrition. It is something that must be accepted by a normal responsible adult (often for the sake of the family as well), even if it has no connection with one's self-generated life plan.

The issue with which we are concerned here is not one of comparing many with few alternatives, as Hayek presents it in criticizing number-of-alternatives considerations as irrelevant. Rather, it is the very different issue at the minimalist end of the spectrum, between two minimally significant alternatives and only one. It is one thing to question whether middle-class incomes, which offer more alternatives as to what to do with an afternoon, serve to make one more "free" than lower-level incomes, with fewer alternatives, in any way relevant to a discussion of rights; this sort of comparison is what Hayek rejects. It is quite another contention, and much less reasonable, to say that in an important field for choice there is no significant difference (relevant to whether I am or feel "free" or might reasonably invoke the term in ordinary language) between having multiple significant alternatives and having only one. The latter difference suggests the lack of even the most *minimal* freedom when the factors involved in the choice structure are humanly caused and addressable.

Hayek's portrayal of the example of the well-off courtier as possibly less free than the ordinary peasant might be correct for certain courtiers, but in a way that Hayek seemed to overlook. The courtier may indeed be less free than the artisan despite the former's greater wealth, but to show this, we have to look further at another aspect of the situation; we have to show that the courtier does not realistically have the alternative of resigning his job with the prince and finding other food-viable employment, either due to massive unemployment or due to a capacity of the prince to blacklist anyone deemed disrespectful from any job providing nutritional security. If unemployment in the local situation will cause a debilitating food deficiency for the individual and/or dependent family member, then the courtier's current employment is the only significant alternative for choice, and any freedom is questionable. On the contrary, a peasant who owns some land and can meet the needs of his or her own family from it may indeed have more than one significant alternative. To show this, however, the analysis of the choice structure in terms of the number of safe and significant alternatives *at the minimal end of the range*, far from being irrelevant, is indeed the central question.

The other key word in the phrase *significant alternative* is, of course, "alternative." Curiously, although Hayek perceptively argues that in cases of coercion there can be a *sort* of choice, he lapses again into use of the term "alternatives," which he elsewhere forswore as irrelevant. He says that, for example, I still make a choice when doing what my coercer wants, but if coerced, I do so "because the alternatives before me have been so manipulated that the conduct that the coercer wants me to choose becomes for me the least painful one" (Hayek 1960, 133). While degree of painfulness is a highly subjective criterion and it fails to mention compensating values alongside the pain involved in the various alternatives, nonetheless, he is suggesting a point that is very telling for real-world situations—that often, an obviously disagreeable course of action is described as one's "only alternative," followed by a statement to the effect that "I was not really free to do what I wanted; anyone else would have had to do the same." The option remains the only significant alternative if its consequences provide a different and more adequate degree of some essential value than the other alternatives, which thereby become insignificant alongside it.

I want to say that an alternative in the economic endeavor field for choice can be regarded as minimally significant for the developing world's rural poor if either (a) it provides short-term access to minimal food (whether or not fairly consistently) and is significantly different from other alternatives, or (b) it provides subminimal access to food (again, whether or not fairly consistently) but is the most food-adequate strategy that is readily available. In this second, subminimal way in which an alternative can become significant, an assumption of the model will be that given two alternatives that *do not* provide adequate food access, the alternative that provides the least adequate food access is not likely to be considered survival significant. As Hayek suggested, the lesser evil is a *constrained* choice over the more evil alternatives; one has "no choice" but to accept the lesser evil when the evils are threats to one's basic existence.

CHOICE STRUCTURE ANALYSIS AND THE CONCEPT OF MINIMAL SIGNIFICANT CHOICE

On the civil-political side, then, I have defined "minimal significant choice," for purposes of human rights analysis, as the assurance of an available *option of choice* among two or more significant alternatives, and I focus on two key fields for civil-political choice: expression and association (Smith 1986a, 1986b), which correspond to two of the more important civil-political human rights. On the well-being side of human rights, an operational human right is an available *option of access* to, for example, minimal food and preventive health care. The word "option" in the definition is included to underline the distinction between having a ready opportunity for feasible access to an appropriate situation for exercising the right, on the one hand—what we mean operationally by a right— and, on the other hand, the right's actual exercise (or immediately present capacity to exercise the right in a given instance), as is emphasized by Shue's (1980) approach to justification. One can fail to take up the option, whether by choosing not to make one's way into the characteristic choice situation for the right, or by not exercising choice once in that situation, yet *still have the option feasibly available*. The latter is the ordinary language sense of "having a right" in practice.

In the latter case, one may have the right in the operational sense yet, not *immediately* be able to exercise it. Often overlooked in the discussion of rights is the distance, in time and effort, that can sometimes lie between having an option and being in a position to exercise it. Between the two points can lie an easy—or arduous—course of endeavor in order to put oneself in a position to exercise the right, such as the effort of going to the polls in order to vote, of formally joining an organization (perhaps paying dues) to engage in association, or of going to a hearing to express oneself on a political issue. In the economic-social area, it is exemplified by getting to a clinic in case of illness, by getting to a relief station if one's fields have been desolated by drought and food supplies have run out, or by cultivating a field in order to get a crop adequate to feed the family over the whole year (in the case of the right to food). It is this territory of rights implementation that autonomous societal self-provision occupies at the grass roots, in contrast to Shue's (1980) emphasis on the immediate exercise of rights, to which his model of rights fulfillment (relying primarily on top-down organizational distribution) was so well suited. Instead, the crucial contribution that can be made *from below,* to establish social practices of respect for rights, can provide a far steadier and more reliable foundation for choice than conventional dependence on top-down institutional channels in the third world. Some selective involvement of outside delivery channels may be necessary, but it must occur laterally at the ground level, independently of the society's own social and governmental structure, and have its effect by catalyzing bottom-up processes rather than by attempting top-down regulation.

Characteristic of a "human" right, I think, is that while the option of getting oneself into the situation to exercise the right might require time and effort, to have the option in practice (and thus to operationally have the right) means that the situation of exercise must be *feasibly available* to any ordinary human. The right cannot, for example, be merely a "special right" available only to members of a necessarily narrow category, it cannot demand superhuman or dangerous effort from a certain category of people, and it cannot be something of which the rightholder could not be aware.

We may sum up, then, the minimal requirements for an alternative to be considered significant. First, (a) it must be known to the subject; it cannot be claimed that a subject has an alternative to what is currently being pursued, and hence a minimal option of choice, if the alternative has not been adequately presented to the would-be right holder. (b) It must be significantly different from other alternatives; it must produce a likely outcome that is clearly different from the current one, such as (in the choice of economic endeavor) providing a different mix of short-term food access and a long-term promise of a reliable food supply and predictable amount of risk. It must not merely appear different while in reality it produces the same results. (c) It must be at least potentially effective for the desired goal (e.g., reliable access to food); it cannot be an unworkable option. Finally, (d) it must be feasible to try; for example, it makes no sense to say that a peasant has the option of trying a different approach to agricultural survival if it requires the purchase of an expensive team of oxen which the peasant cannot dream of affording.

A key field for choice in the case of the monopoly employer could be called "economic endeavor," a narrow form of which I shall call "food-access endeavor." Freedom of economic endeavor, however, is not included in the main internationally recognized human rights instruments, the Covenants of 1966 (in force 1976) and their forerunner, the Universal Declaration of 1948 (International Commission 1977). The desire by some conservatives to enshrine, under the rubric of human rights, rather expansive degrees of ranges of choice in economic endeavor may play a role in their wish that a right of property should be included. Some substantial range of choice of economic endeavor is closely connected with the concern, shared by many conservatives, for eco-

nomic rights against government regulation. Our concern here, however, is neither with full-blown freedom of economic endeavor (implying many different
alternatives) nor with property rights (which some interpret as necessary for it).
Instead, our concern is more minimalist. It involves the minimal significant
choice of viable economic endeavor recognizing that it may be interdependent
with other minimal-prerequisite rights: (a) minimal significant choice (among at
least two significant alternatives) as to association and expression, in the
civil-political sector, and (b) access to minimal levels of food and health care in
the economic-social sector.

Of the five minimal-prerequisite rights to be dealt with here, minimal choice
of economic endeavor is the only one that is not a minimalist form of a right
recognized in the Covenants' list of human rights. This is the field for choice
that underlies the monopoly-of-available-employment example used by both
Hayek (1960) and Shue (1980). Unfortunately, however, to limit ourselves to the
employment example overlooks the wide range of opportunities and resources
for which a poor peasant may depend on a better-off relative, neighbor, or fellow
villager. A poor peasant may need to borrow oxen at plowing time, get access to
water for irrigation, sharecrop a plot, or connect with a middleman to obtain a
price break on fertilizer. Several, or even all of these components may be necessary to produce a crop adequate to feed all members of the household over the
entire year, and the loss of even one of them may jeopardize minimal food access. Different geoclimatic or agricultural system contexts may characteristically
involve differing sorts of dependency. However, the predicament of clientelistic
dependency can nonetheless be generalized well beyond the employment and
share-tenancy examples to a wide range of types of dependency relationships in
which the third world poor may find themselves.

Noticeably, in third world political arenas the problem is seldom that there are
no alternatives at all for rights such as the freedom of association or of policy
preferences for permitted expression, and similar freedoms, but rather that the
range of alternatives permitted by the regime or by local economic or social conditions generally includes little of significance for the people and their real concerns, or in comparison to the range of interests and preferences afoot in the
Western democracies. In economic endeavor, what sometimes appears as an
array of alternatives actually coalesces, for the target group, into a single basic
strategy with varying components. For the poor, this tends to be a locally characteristic strategy combining different activities in particular local mixes designed to maximize the chances of assuring food and health for the household.
Commonly, none of these can be defined as a separate alternative in that no one
activity could, by itself, assure the goal of minimal viability. Thus, a single,
multicomponent strategy is, in effect, imposed on the target-group households.

The single-alternative choice structure for economic endeavor among the third
world rural poor typically involves clientelistic economic dependency on a better-off household (or more than one, in secondary ways). Generally, where such
a relationship is absent, there will be an unacceptable threat to health posed by
the resultant shortage of food, which tends to leave the victim in search of a pa-

tron for such a relationship. Our interest will be in those dependencies—or situations of need for a dependency relationship—that put holders of the survival-critical resources in a position to constrain the behavior of the poor client (or prospective client) in other fields for choice, leaving them only one (or no) significant alternative there also. What is required for actually having a human right in social practice on-the-ground is that the *option*, whether of getting oneself into a situation in which to safely and freely make significant economic or civil-political choice or of avoiding malnutrition and easily preventable health threats on the economic-social side of human rights, must be *readily available* to an ordinary person, whether or not effort is required to actually take up the option. We shall not aim at delivering all poor peasants from patron-client relationships, or even necessarily, in practice, from keeping an eye on patron preferences when considering civil-political behavior. Rather, we shall aim at providing some sort of optional alternative in the form of a readily available course of endeavor, that is capable of leading them to greater independence of any clientelistic influence. The key question (to which we now turn) is what combination of factors form the key to the most fundamental foundations for minimally providing the crucial options.

THE RELATIONSHIP OF MINIMAL-PREREQUISITE CIVIL-POLITICAL PROTECTIONS TO MINIMAL-PREREQUISITE ECONOMIC-SOCIAL ONES

Many empirical analysts who work in the areas touched on in this volume think of the economic situations of the third world rural poor primarily in terms of improving welfare, or satisfying "basic needs," largely in isolation from concerns about civil-political rights. Too often, however, this tradition limited itself to documenting failures of basic needs and (rightly, I think) demanding relief. Too few studies have taken up the vexing issues involved in realistic solutions and attempted to weigh the workability of both new and old, bottom-up and top-down components of strategies for aid in the light of the perceived limitations of the 1990s. On the economic-social side of human rights, I have argued (as part of a team of primarily Norwegian human rights researchers) for a strategic focus on crafting a short list of very minimally defined economic-social rights. This set of "minimal threshold" standards, as we called them, if assured in a way consistent with the other principles of human rights, could serve as a foundation for a reliable bottom-up momentum of progress over time toward realizing more fully those and other economic/social rights (Andreasson et al. 1988, 1992). A minimally defined combination of assured food, health care, education, and employment, we suggested, could lay the foundations for a causal sequence of gains in autonomous self-provision for the poor, enhancing the effectiveness of other sorts of aid in these and the other areas of economic-social rights.

The purpose of this volume, however, is to identify within that minimal set of economic-social rights an even smaller prerequisite subset of rights (focusing on

food and health and particular kinds of means to assuring minimal levels of food
and health care), alongside a similarly minimalist subset of crucial civil-political
rights, involving minimal significant choice in expression and association. The
four minimal-prerequisite protections, of access to food, health care, association,
and expression at the specified levels, stand in a crucial empirical *interdependence* with one another at the grass roots in the rural third world. As such, this
minimalist complex serves as a basis for bottom-up momentum toward, in the
longer term, the full realization of the complete lists in both the civil-political
and economic-social rights sectors.

Quite central to the prerequisite platform, of course, are minimalist versions of
two critical economic-social rights—food and health—which comprise much of
the basis for the importance of the option of minimal significant choice of economic endeavor. The peasant stratum discussed here lives at the margins of food
access, and the most powerful single threat to their minimal health stems from
intermittent or continuing malnutrition. As we have seen, malnutrition lowers
resistance to agents of infection and disease that are omnipresent in the poor
peasants' lives and are unlikely to be removed in the near term. While minimal
access to food is thus critical, the household's capacity for such access—
depending, as it often does on the capacity for doing effective agricultural
work—in turn requires minimal levels of good health (including small daily
quantities of clean water for drinking, washing skin injuries, etc.) and resistance
to infectious disease. Maintaining adequate health in turn requires minimal levels of food, creating a vicious circle. Minimal access and to food and health lie
in reciprocal interdependence with one another; without an assurance of one,
there can be no assurance of the other.

It is precisely to get *some degree* of access to food and health, though, that
poor peasants pursue available economic alternatives and enter into clientelistic
dependencies on their better-off friends, relatives, or acquaintances. However,
this in turn leaves the client vulnerable to constraint from the patron concerning
the former's expression, association, and economic endeavor to gain access to
food. With the opening up of a new feasible option of more independent endeavor for food access (even if so laborious that only a portion of the target
group adopts it), the option of minimal significant choice may follow in expression and association as well. Thus might be facilitated a whole range of associa-
tional activities at the ground level, which could, in turn, further improve the
access of the poorer strata to minimal levels of food and health care as well as
more secure options for voluntary civil-political action. More effective bottom-up pressure could build for the more impartial targeting of existing conventional aid programs, as well as for effective civil-political provision of justice
and security against assault. A mutually reinforcing dynamic of minimal
self-provision on the part of the poor (whether individual, household, or inter-
household mutual aid) in all these rights areas could thus begin to emerge. The
five options we have labeled minimal prerequisite rights—access to minimal
levels of food and health and to minimal significant choice as to expression,
association, and endeavor for food access, then, form an interdependent package

at the roots of human rights respect as a whole. We now turn to the question of whether and how there is human rights-based duty to facilitate this package, which requires that some practical avenue of impact can be found and that those responsible for implementing it can be identified.

DUTY

Analyses of minimalist forms of rights and how they interact are of only academic interest unless they bear on questions of possible practical duty. The following section is concerned with the philosophical and practical foundations of duty under the human rights rubric, and shows how they bear on the predicament of the third world rural poor. In particular, we must begin with conventional conceptions of our duty to enforce human rights and their relationships to the obligations of individuals and governments. Particularly through the cold war period, the governments of the developed northern countries of the world were used to thinking of freedom and needs satisfaction in zero-sum terms, whereby to pursue one of these values, one has to sacrifice the other. Furthermore, they were accustomed to viewing human rights-based obligation and action as the responsibility of governments only. Particularly popular in traditional legal opinion is recourse to the government of the national-territorial jurisdiction in which the victims live. Accordingly, only the most tentative international steps are taken by the world's most advantaged nations in the name of protecting civil-political rights in the third world (unless action coincides with national self-interest), and hardly any targeted steps are taken by Western nations in the name of observing economic-social human rights.

As to who potentially holds duties under the human rights rubric, the preamble to the Covenants does not limit itself to "considering" the duty of states under the UN Charter to "promote universal respect for, and observance of, human rights and freedoms." It also "realizes" that the *individual human being* "is under a responsibility to strive for the promotion and observance of the rights recognized" in each Covenant (International Commission 1977, 24, 34). While the "natural rights" of the seventeenth and eighteenth centuries, for example, were claimed against governments, nonetheless commentators such as Cranston, Raphael, Feinberg, and Wasserstrom, from their different perspectives, consider human rights to be claimed against all people, as well as their governments.[3] Practically speaking, there is no contradiction in this dual moral responsibility, as governments, with their special authority and capacity to extract resources, are, in reality, a necessary practical tool for individuals in discharging their human rights obligation.

Furthermore, where feasible, the *scope* of human rights duty seems to be international, as such thinkers as Beitz (1979) and Hoffman (1981) have maintained. To be sure, in the civil-political rights area, duty is immediately "undertaken" in the civil-political rights Covenant by "each State Party" to "respect and ensure" the rights to those only "within its territory" (International Commission 1977, 35). However, the Preamble speaks of "obligations of States" to promote "universal respect for, and observance of, human rights and free-doms" (International Commission 1977, 34). In sympathy with much recent commentary on issues such as the international provision of military aid to re-pressive governments, I do not see the special jurisdiction of a signatory gov-ernment over its own territory as inconsistent with any additional practical duty to contribute to civil-political rights observance internationally, where such duty is feasible to discharge, and as long as the mode of contribution is itself consis-tent with human rights. What is missing from the Covenants' formulation—and left to human ingenuity and determination—is guidance on the practical means of internationally influencing civil-political practices, in the direction of greater respect for human rights, in ways that are themselves consistent with human rights generally (including consistency with protection for national self-determination). The great difficulties in discovering realistic ways to dis-charge such a duty realistically remain a major barrier to recognition and action on this obligation toward civil-political rights observance. The following discus-sion aims to provide such guidance.

On the economic-social side, the relevant Covenant does not include clear language on territorial responsibility; it only obligates each state party to "take steps, individually and through international assistance and co-operation, espe-cially economic and technical, to the maximum of its available resources, with a view to achieving progressively the full realization" of economic-social rights such as those to adequate food, health, employment, and education (International Commission 1977, 25). There seems to be duty both to convey and to receive across national boundaries whatever economic and technical resources are real-istically available and effective in human rights-consistent ways. Once again, however, no guidance is offered by the legal instruments on just what sorts and amounts of international aid, delivered through what mechanisms, are practical and human rights–consistent; this is needed to make performance effective and to identify duty holders.

Empirically, at its best, the local social practice of respect for rights (e.g., as practiced in Western Europe), involves a *combination* of (a) restraint and pro-tection by private individuals with (b) law enforcement by government. While state enforcement can certainly make major contributions to voluntary respect for a right in society, in practice such enforcement remains just one of the cate-gories of causal contribution to respect for rights. The practical point of fostering observance of human rights is to establish respect for the option of having the right-protected value as a matter of ordinary, customary, and voluntary social practice at the ground level on the part of both private and governmental actors. It is worth noting here that some of the strongest institutional protection for hu-man rights is found in Western Europe, where key rights are already ordinarily respected and in little need of international or special governmental support.[4]

This empirical pattern is reflected as well in much of philosophical commen-tary on human rights. In its proper place as a right respected in practice, it be-comes, as McCloskey put it, "my own" (McCloskey 1976), or in the formulation of Wasserstrom, something I am entitled to enjoy "now," and "without securing the consent of another"; or "without further ado," and for which the exercise "needs no defense" (Wasserstrom 1964, 98–99). If it must be invoked, a bit of conversation normally does the job. Moreover, it seems possible to have rights operationally as a matter of custom, as Shue concedes (1980, 16–17), without the particularly Western forms of claim-making procedures, conceptions, and structures. While it certainly is a property of a right that it can be the basis, when necessary, for making claims on responsible parties for enforcements, the point of human rights that we must keep in sight is that of respect for the right in ordinary, conventional behavior. Conversely, without a prevailing social practice of respect for rights in customary behavior by ordinary citizens, government officials are in a very weak position to achieve much by laws and law enforcement alone. This latter situation characterizes rural areas in much of the third world.

Unfortunately, however, many commentators' conceptions of how to take action to promote human rights seem to emphasize only governmental enforcement or implement the protection of a right, rather than the right's customary observance in society. Feinberg, for example, defines a human right as a "valid claim" (1973), which connotes the exceptional case in which people must depend on government to resolve a dispute or supply a need, rather than the normal practice of respect for rights, in which governmental involvement need be only occasional and supplementary to that of society.[5] In the economic-social area, it is even more common to conceive of rights implementation in terms of the necessary, hierarchically administered aid to those in need (so well implemented by modern governments in northern Europe and Canada, for example), as opposed to the realm of autonomous societal self-provision which must be substantial enough that the remaining unmet need can be met by government.

Again, of course, I do not want to suggest that there can be a bona-fide human right operationally without the *availability* of some sort of claim-making and claim recognition mechanism; Feinberg's view is on target for an operational human right with regard to the necessity of such a route as an option when respect for the right in ordinary social interaction fails.[6] Nor, on the other side, do I want to suggest that every engagement in the activity protected by a right always qualifies as exercise of the right. What Donnelly calls "objective enjoyment of a right" (1989, 11) *often may not* qualify as the exercise of a right. Hypothetically (as Donnelly might point out), in a country observing an absolute right to food, one whose income is high is not, indeed, exercising a right to food when sitting down to a meal purchased with merely a tiny increment of his or her person's income for the day. However, a person in a definable target category of poverty who eats adequately without making a claim on anybody, but *consequent* to a program that is part of that country's pattern of arrangements to guarantee food security as a right, is exercising his or her right to food. This criterion requires that the activity or value would be threatened for the right holder, actually or potentially (in some comparatively immediate sense), in the absence of the pattern of respect for the right in local social practice. The general direction in which this requirement points is the possibility of informal lateral impacts of social arrangements that can, in practice, go far toward implementing a right, *without* involving continual direct dependency on governmental structure from above.

Henry Shue's approach to economic-social rights implementation leaves the matter of channels of implementation entirely abstract, taking the view that "it is not impractical to expect some level of social organization to protect the minimal cleanliness of air and water and to oversee the adequate production, or import, and the proper distribution of minimal food, clothing, shelter, and elementary health care" (1980, 25). The reader is left with the view that, for example, northern European standards in the relevant human rights documents must be met by intergovernmental distribution (perhaps using nongovernmental organizations as the delivery mechanisms), directly to the sufferers, of clean water, foodstuffs, clothing, a place to live, and so forth. Shue's use of the term "oversee" brings to mind governmental (or nongovernmental organization) top-down programs, as if, in the third world, governments or international organizations could be easily and cost-effectively turned to these tasks, getting laws and programs administered fairly at the local level were straightforward, corruption and clientelism at the intermediate and local levels were not a significant barrier, existing NGOs found it easy to circumvent such patron-client networks for effective impact on the target groups, and similar improbabilities.

In reality, many traditional programs that might appear on paper to be targeted at the poor, particularly those employing official channels of the third world government, tend often in practice to be diverted, whether systematically to some more or less middle-class constituency (often consisting of voters who are clients of local influentials), to ordinary corruption, or to some other form of diversion, often losing a major portion of the value to be distributed. From another point of view, most of these programs largely utilize current or modified patterns of continuing clientelistic dependency, which can bring with it civil-political constraint. To be freed of these drawbacks, programs would need to be accompanied by a very different—and lower-cost—strategy, which is outlined in chapter 5 of this volume. These problems *do not* justify withdrawal of such programs as are currently in place, as these remain a lifeline for many poor. The importance of these problems lies instead in the poor prospects they portend for any substantial expansion, in the near future, of the scope of existing top-down "social arrangements" to achieve the goals Shue has in mind.

METHODOLOGICAL BACKGROUND: PEASANTS AND POVERTY

In order to begin to identify the scope of the problem and suggest a remedy, the human rights analyst must be able to identify the actual or potential *sources* of independent minimal food capacity. Above all, this requires analysis that is interdisciplinary and practical. Each social science discipline tends to emphasize its own sort of resources. The economist, of whatever school, will emphasize abstract economic factors such as the presence or absence of income or land. Anthropologists tend to emphasize cultural linkages, or their absence. Geographers often emphasize position in the surrounding settlement or migration pattern, particularly in the light of natural resource limitations. The political scientist must consider influence in the local networks of political clientelism (which can differ from anthropological clientelism, with its more far-reaching and multisided cultural and economic dimensions). The human rights analyst must be open to all major conceptions of the resources relevant to poverty, choosing among them according to the criterion of significance for minimal choice and in accordance with each particular well-being, for country case and actual situation. A search for the locale-specific, key resource that proves most useful in identifying categories of suffering individuals for effective targeting of aid, must survey all of these aspects of the situation.

Traditionally, the subject of peasant inequality of wealth and influence under conditions of commercialization has been a field for contending empirical models too grand and abstract to yield practical recommendations. For example, a major early theoretical argument bearing on peasant autonomy and poverty was that of Lenin, which viewed the peasantry in terms of class polarization. On this model, real change for post-feudal peasantries meant accelerating commodity relations and a capitalistically flavored polarization of the rural inhabitants into landless laborer and agrarian "capitalist" categories. Individuals of both classes became wholly "free" of personalistic dependencies, which were associated with feudalism and were thought to fall away with the coming of the "free" market.[7]

This approach came under heavy criticism in the work of Chayanov, a retrospective analysis of the 1920s debate that centered on the Russian peasantry (and, by implication, what the Bolshevik regime should do about it), which at the time still farmed privately. Chayanov developed a model whereby the self-sufficient agrarian household, using predominantly family labor on its own farm, was itself a distinctive, somewhat autonomous, and stubbornly enduring formation.[8] A sympathizer with Chayonov was later to go so far as to refer to a "domestic" mode of production.[9] A step beyond the extremes of the theory-laden and somewhat parochial Lenin-Chayonov debate was taken by Shanin, who attempted to accommodate elements of both views in a list of diverse factors bearing on the social mobility of households amid rich-poor "differentiation" in the countryside.[10]

The theoretical debate about such questions, however, has largely failed to clearly identify differences in degrees of peasant *autonomy*. This latter issue has recently been raised in the quite different context of the dispersed East African peasantry. Hyden (1980) proposed an option of withdrawal from market involvement (and its aspects of dependency). He presented the image of the "uncaptured" African peasant who could withdraw into a more traditional "economy of affection," to meet his or her needs self-sufficiently by group self-provision and thereby preserve autonomy (Hyden 1980). However, Hyden's analysis on the Tanzanian case remained largely abstract, and careful local studies (e.g., Havenik 1983) have cast doubt on the breadth of applicability of the market-withdrawal option even in its presumed natural home of East Africa.

For Southeast Asia, a leading political scientist in the field of patron-client analysis, James Scott, has presented the decline of what he calls the "moral economy" of the peasant, referring to substantially the same phenomena as comprise Hyden's (1980) "economy of affection," which bear heavily on independent peasant viability (1976). Scott showed that in Southeast Asia, the village's substantial self-sufficiency in needs provision (and the attendant restraint on inequality) largely broke down through the late nineteenth and early twentieth centuries. It did so under the onslaughts of market penetration, local and worldwide financial crises, and the spread of fixed-rent tenancy and taxation. Scott shows that although peasant rebellions did occur, they largely failed to stem commercial penetration and rapidly developing inequalities. We are presented, then, with a second, contrasting picture of *loss* of both local autonomy and viable capacity for group self-provision of welfare, in this case exemplified by Southeast Asian concentrated and market-penetrated patterns of settlement, as compared to the East African image of more dispersed settlement with less market penetration. The key question is, of course, what independent variables are at work in producing local autonomy and welfare viability over the whole range between these two extremes of settlement patterns?

While the abstract contrast between "captured" and "uncaptured" peasant villages does say something about autonomy and poverty in the two regions, the real story must be told through closer inquiry into individual and group relationships within the village. How are degrees of autonomy related to degrees of poverty for the household and the extended kinship grouping (the size of which is itself a variable) amid gradual commercial penetration in different degrees? Here, the most sophisticated behavioral approach seems to be that of Barthian politico-economic anthropology, which fleshes out the investigation of structural inequalities with a close analysis of patterns of the exchange of scarce resources within and between patron-client clusters.[11] For Barth himself, patron client analysis gave rise to degrees of cluster *incorporation* as a key variable. The central contrast was between (a) traditional kinship-based "incorporated" patron-client clusters constraining peasant choice, which are associated with tight kinship ties and firm boundaries between kinship units, and (b) a more open, individualistic system of competitive exchange and bargaining between and among patrons and clients, which is, to some extent, correlated with commercial penetration.

As an analytical method, Barth's approach represented a useful turn away from the wholesale abstract characterizations of classes, regions, or eras (to which Hyden 1980 seems prone) and toward an empirically sophisticated study of variation in autonomy and welfare provision amid a single general process of encroaching commercial modernization and its attendant inequalities. As the Chayanov-Shanin approach recognized the durability of small kinship units (principally, the household itself) in relation to the issues of mobility, we can say that Barth's more empirical approach recognizes the durability of patron-client patterns in relation to the issues of autonomy and resource distribution. Furthermore, this approach does not presuppose any particular answers to empirical questions that may be yielded by its use in a particular case. Just as Shanin's somewhat more empirical, and less theory-laden approach to mobility did not *presuppose* a general answer to the question of how solid class boundaries and barriers became with commercialization and the rich-poor differentiation (leaving this question to empirical inquiry on a case-by-case basis), likewise, Barthian conceptualizations do not ultimately presuppose a particular answer to the question of whether encroaching commercial modernization in rural areas will bring about a more or less real autonomy or incorporation in patron-client patterns. Perhaps, new forms of the constraining incorporation of poorer clients (sometimes partially or wholly along kinship lines) can develop in the rich-poor differentiation process that occurs during commercialization and can, for some time at least, be as tight or tighter as in the older Barthian kinship-based incorporation model.

What has not been provided by debates so far is a theory specifically of the *poor* peasant, attuned to both of the interdependent factors of autonomy and welfare, and focused by the human rights rubric on the analysis of *minimal* autonomy (here called minimal significant choice) and well-being (here called minimal access to food and health). In this context, those lacking autonomy suffer a special penalty for choosing an alternative outside what they believe is expected by the patron. The penalty of unwise action or endeavor can be hunger, malnutrition-related disease, and a resultant threat to life rather than merely a temporary economic or social setback. In this case, finding and pleasing a patron who provides an opportunity for the family's survival is quite another matter from what it is for a peasant with an assured surplus, who can choose among patrons for the best deal, bargain over the terms of the patron-client relationship, or do without a patron altogether without a threat to life and health.

Here, the matter of exchange between unequals is not merely a possible basis for influence, as it is for middle-level peasants assured of making ends meet without malnutrition. We are instead dealing with exchange between unequals in which one party is less well-off than the other in a special way. It is a relation between a family whose survival is threatened (via starvation, malnutrition, and malnutrition-related disease for one or more family members), on one hand, and on the other, a member of a category of surplus resource-holders. The latter can possess what amounts to a local monopoly, whether direct or indirect, on a necessary component of the former's means of survival, food grain. Virtually all members of the surplus-resource category offer more or less the same deal to those dependent on them for opportunities for the self-provision of a minimal level of well-being. This context leads to an absence of significantly *different* alternatives, a social practice on a wide scale that puts the patrons generally *in a position to constrain* their dependents and candidate-dependents, rather than merely to influence them.

This is not a predicament that history leaves behind, as the Leninist theory would suggest. Marginal peasants do not rapidly collapse into a landless rural "proletariat," "freed" from old "feudal" chains and able to "freely" sell their labor as a commodity on the market. Instead, the smallholders prove, in fact, to be too smart to sell off their land any faster than absolutely necessary for survival, and the landless are not liberated from the need for patron-client dependencies, any more than are the marginal smallholders. This situation is found *both* in the relatively traditional (and generally, poorer) rural areas and to the relatively more modernized and more commercially penetrated rural areas.

WHAT TO DO?

Practically speaking, the track record of results of top-down structural strategies on the ground level, from legal tinkering to political revolution, indicates that such approaches are unlikely to do any more than modify these conditions of poor peasant vulnerability. Conventional development-oriented approaches have proved narrow and limited in their capacity for impact on minimal well-being for the third world rural poor. While the health and education components of the more intelligent integrated rural development programs at times do piecemeal good for segments of the poor, the components that improve agricultural production capacity mainly reach the "progressive" farmers, who were already better off. Many conventional advocates of equity or social justice in development in the end focus on the opportunities of "minorities" when they think of human rights. Such an approach results *in practice* in a conservative interpretation of "equality of opportunity" that accomplishes little more than the replacement of majority individuals with minorities in whatever structure of positional inequality is (still seen as) necessary for economic development.

However, the human rights instruments seem to call for concrete recommendations for feasible and cost-effective aid to foster the observance of human rights, in both the civil-political and economic-social sectors, and in the most reliable and human rights-sensitive way possible. Forms of intervention that involve coercion also have a track record of failing to eliminate clientelistic dependencies by the food-insecure poor, and thus may be ruled out. Noncoercive development aid strategies have been perceived as expensive and largely ineffective in penetrating far below the middle-income peasants who have the connections to participate in whatever opportunities are to be had. What shall be recommended here is a concrete lateral line of attack at the ground level that does not involve coercion or not rely on or bolster existing clientelistic dependencies, but rather opens up a new alternative route to independent minimal food security for those who want to take it.

This approach will involve, in the first instance, *giving* (not via credit) specified kinds of small-scale appropriate technology to peasants in the target category who enroll in the program, to be used for more intensive and productive food-crop farming on small plots. By itself, the idea of appropriate technology is far from new; a whole school of development strategy centers around it. The key here, however, is the particular adaptation of the idea to the rubric of human rights, the low-end, locale-specific sort of appropriate technology that must be employed, and the human rights–adapted requirements concerning how the aid must be delivered. The gift must be made without any of the obligations (such as debt) that traditionally turn aid relationships into clientelistic dependencies on local program agents or prove to be costly failures for the peasant and hence provoke suspicion and nonparticipation. The only obligation of the recipient country's government should be to provide protection for program participants. The only obligation on target group participants should be keeping and maintaining the received farming aids (without sale) for two years or more, upon penalty of forfeiture of future participation in the program for some appropriate period.

The idea is to open up a new alternative of economic endeavor that provides the option of much greater independence. Moreover, the aim in relation to those who do *not* choose to enter the program is to maintain for them the ready alternative of doing so, such that the *whole* target group, takers and nontakers of the technology alike, would now have the minimal two-alternative structure needed for significant choice. For the new alternative to have the feasibility and workability necessary to be considered a readily available option, would-be recipients of the appropriate technology must be able to entertain the *possibility* of cutting themselves off from their clientelistic relationships—with their access (albeit dependent and to some degree uncertain) to employment, tenancy, borrowing, or whatever other value for which they had depended on the patron—in favor of a new path, with all its uncertainties (especially in the initial period). They have to be ready as well to do without certain kinds of help in bad times, perhaps including emergency food access, that they may have had from the patron as part of the old relationship. All this means that an alternative survival source for desperate times of failure must be available if the peasants are to accept the new alternative as a serious option.

To provide a minimal sense of confidence in food security for those participating in the program and those considering doing so, while controlling the cost to donor, it would be necessary to provide small food-for-work projects in the lean seasons (e.g., in the weeks before the harvest), when employment is scarce and food-grain prices are high. There is now a strong literature on food for work in its own right in addressing the basic needs of the third world poor, independently of any role in interdependencies of minimalist forms of civil-political and economic-social human rights. While this is not the place to review the promising record of the food-for-work experience (see Alam 1986), we must note a couple of features that allow it to fit well into a recommended package of minimal and essential first steps in our duty to implement human rights. Unlike simple food or credit giveaways, food for work does not attract substantial numbers of middle-class households which are outside the target group. The program can remain limited to distress periods when other employment is not available, so that it will not compete directly with the local labor market and will not depress food prices in ways harmful to the overall incentive structure for agriculture. Furthermore, the food grains provided can be different, and hence lower in status, from those popular among the middle class in the locale (e.g., wheat in a South Asian rice-eating area), to help ward off those who do not really need it for minimal food access, hence controlling the cost. Finally, food for work allows implementation of certain small-scale projects that can directly support the productivity of the food and health care provision efforts for the poor, such as the digging of new wells for safe drinking water or irrigation channels serving several households' agricultural plots. The completion of such projects, alongside the appropriate technology contributions of the existing alternative system, could contribute to the necessary impression on the part of donor agencies and peoples that the aid is building a foundation for future self-provision as well as meeting a current need. Without this favorable impression, the aid flow stretching into the future could be perceived as too expensive to support.

Providing food for work, however, would not by itself provide the second significant alternative that is necessary for minimal significant choice. Certainly, a gain would be made in access to food, which, in my view, is morally justifiable on economic-social grounds alone. However, in a case where the aid approach included only food for work, peasants would continue to be dependent on their patrons for a major portion of the household's food-access package, with no significant alternative. Without the inclusion of another, more independent alternative in the choice structure, the poor household would remain unable to do without the employment, tenancy, implement or animal access, or other aid from the patron that is necessary to best provide minimal food over the whole year to all members of the household. Without the availability of a second significant alternative of autonomous self-provision (to be provided by new appropriate-technology inputs), the poor peasant's behavior in general would continue to be constrained even with aid in the form of food for work in the distress periods.

The autonomy-stimulating component of the program would also have consequences, I think, for the effectiveness of the food-for-work program itself. Without the feasible option of declaring independence from the patron, there might indeed be little bottom-up pressure to make the food-for-work program impartial (rather than client oriented in deference to the local elite), reliable, and hence secure for the target group. It might be hard for the donor agencies' local representatives to get information about what is happening on the ground vis-à-vis possible corrupt behavior or the diversion of food grain resources to the local elite. The aid might, as in many other programs, be vulnerable to capture by the local elite, whether private or governmental-bureaucratic (or both). Food-for-work programs could thus fall victim to the sort of costly diversion of resources away from the target group from which other development aid programs have suffered, and ultimately be perceived by donors as insufficiently cost-effective.

The first step to practical analysis is the identification of target groups. We must first focus on those individuals who lack assured access to minimal levels of food and health, including those with inadequate provision and those with minimal provision gained only very insecurely. We must identify clear indicators that reveal characteristics of the overall category by their linkage with poor and insecure nutrition and health, and that might be helpful in providing a remedy. We shall then explore the choice structure facing the target groups in the realms of economic endeavor and civil-political choice, with emphasis on the structuring of significant choice that results from relationships of dependency. Finally, we shall in each case explore paths of remedy. For each part of this inquiry, we shall examine three cases of rural poverty: Bangladesh, Botswana, and Tanzania.

NOTES

1. See p. 19, note 3. The initiative arose partly in the context of, and in places influenced, what was originally called the "Nordic" human rights yearbook project (which later also included non-Nordic human rights institutes such as those in the Netherlands, Canada, Austria, and Australia).

2. See the replies by Marcus Singer and David Braybrooke, both in *Nous* 4 (1970): 56–57; compare Singer's follow-up article, "The Basis of Rights and Duties," *Philosophical Studies* 23 (1972): 48–57; and that of Braybrooke, "The Firm but Untidy Correlativity of Rights and Obligations," *Canadian Journal of Philosophy* (1972): 351–363.

3. See Cranston 1962, 68–69; D. D. Raphael 1967, 65; Joel Feinberg, "Voluntary Euthanasia and the Inalienable Right to Life," *Philosophy and Public Affairs* 7: 96; Wasserstrom 1964, 61. Expressions of the view that human rights are directed only at governments may be found in Martin 1980, 391–403, and Wellman 1967, 68–80.

4. Cranston finds this fact "ironical" (1962, 24), and Henkin finds it "paradoxical" (1978, 104).

5. Feinberg does allow for a sort of *moral* "valid claim" independently of government, which "holds *now* whatever the positive law may say about it" (1973, 85). However, even there he requires justification in a court-like "enlightened moral discourse," that seems quite elevated and removed from the ordinary rights exercise of rights and conversation about it. Of course, what Feinberg says is useful for the exceptional hard case, but taking the hard case as the foundation of a definition can tend to divert us from the ordinary language of rights.

6. Human rights are widely agreed to be "claim-rights," rather than what Hohfeldt called "liberty" rights which, in their conservative form, maintain only that government should *not* do certain liberty-infringing things, rather than that the holder have the option of choice in a given field of choice. For a review of the Hohfeldt distinctions, see Perry 1977, 41–50.

7. See V. I. Lenin, "The Agricultural Question and the Critics of Marx," *Collected Works*, Vol. 5, 5th ed. (Moscow: Progress Publishers, 1975).

8. *The Theory of Peasant Economy*, edited by D. Thorner, B. Kerblay, and R. E. F. Smith (Homewood, Ill.: Richard C. Irwin for the American Economic Association, 1966).

9. M. Sahlins, *Stone Age Economics* (London: Tavistock, 1974), 74–99.

10. T. Shanin, *The Awkward Class* (London: Oxford, 1972).

11. Following his pathbreaking work on the Swat Pathans, Barth became a prolific writer with a deep influence on anthropology and, later, on political science. See *Selected Essays of Fredrik Barth*, Vols. 1, 2 (London and Boston: Routledge and Kegan Paul, 1981).

Chapter 3

Poverty, Clientelistic Dependency, and the Target Group Indicator in Bangladesh, Botswana, and Tanzania

Abstract conceptual models are not likely to be persuasive unless it is made clear how they can be operationalized. We must be able to see how its conceptual components look when fleshed out in the particularity of different individual cases. The following chapters of this book apply my theoretical model to common situations for the rural poor in three different third world cases with quite different circumstances: Bangladesh, Tanzania, and Botswana. Along the way, I present examples of the kinds of issues that are relevant in the exploration of any given area that is to become the focus of human rights-oriented research and action using the model presented here.

While the material covered here is largely empirical in nature, I take the standpoint not of a direct researcher, but rather of a human rights-oriented theorist and policy maker in search of an interpretation with both ethical and empirical validity. My treatment aims to process, into the analytical model, data gathered by other social science researchers from a variety of disciplines such as anthropology, development economics, political science, sociology, and interdisciplinary poverty studies. It is my view regarding the wealth of third world village studies that for such a valuable policy resource to bear fruit for important practical purposes a broad comparative synthesis must be made of their results. The scope of the perspective on rural poverty adopted here is only as wide as necessary for the particular human rights orientation that I adopt. It is fundamentally *practical* in its path of exploration; little is examined that does not have some bearing on the justification for, or practicalities of, the *action* that must be the goal of this research.

The first important part of such a demonstration is the specification of an *identifiable target category*. The unit of analysis will be the functional household rather than the individual. This is done most importantly for the sake of empirical realism, but also because statistics are available mainly on the household level. At the same time, however, I will be alert to the risk of overlooking

important dimensions of the choice and needs predicaments that may be rooted
in the often-unequal relationships between husbands and wives, as well as between sons and daughters. Where such intrahousehold relationships prove important in terms of the model, it will be applied to these interindividual patterns,
particularly in order to focus on the plight of women.

Of course, the category of the food-insecure poor is already in part the product
of various impacts of past development efforts and development-related trends.
Thus, the questions of just who is how poor and in what ways, as well as how
choice predicaments seem to be linked to the characteristic food insecurity
situations found in the various countries, implicitly raise contentious issues involving which factors, according to the particular theory, might have improved
the situation in the light of poverty-related goals. Some of the questions raised
and debates involved are old and familiar to researchers and theorists in the field
of development and equity. However, they must be glanced at critically along the
way from the distinctively human-rights-related point of view adopted here.
Some analysts would recommend the expansion of existing conventional development aid strategies in order to improve the choice and needs conditions of the
third world rural poor, while others no doubt would argue that further market-oriented modernization itself will pave the way to economic growth for the
lower sectors and thus will improve the situation.

A pessimistic view of poverty-oriented programs is that in practice, effective
targeting is impossible. Aid strategies that are unclear in their targeting or ineffective in reaching the target group turn readily into expensive mid-
dle-class-oriented programs with only paltry trickle-down benefits for the poor.
Expenditures on such programs are particularly difficult to sell these days.
Moreover, in the case of the sort of predicament addressed here, such trickle-
down benefits—whether from aid programs or commercial market expansion—
can actually *add* to the problem of choice-constraining clientelistic dependency,
even as they may marginally and temporarily improve the food security of a
small portion of the target group. By identifying as the target category people
who are not well reached by existing programs, in a way highlighting development possibilities uniquely crafted to reach those still in a condition of food insecurity, we may see our way to strategies that may (a) render existing conventional aid programs themselves much more effective in human rights terms than
they now are, and that may (b) give the poor a more reliable foundation for *bottom-up momentum* of progressive growth both in key economic-social needs
areas and in civil-political choice over the longer term.

In the following chapters, several dimensions of the predicament will be considered for each of three country cases: overall food insecurity and poverty, the
civil-political participation conditions for the poor, the target category indicator
of food insecurity, its choice structure amidst poverty-imposed clientelistic dependency (or the need for it), and the remedy, in the form of a particular kind of
development aid. Under each major topic, Bangladesh will be the case taken up
first and presented in greatest detail to flesh out the basic argument; the two African cases will then be used to show the capacities of the conceptual scheme for

diverse circumstances.

Our three cases provide more than merely a diversity of contexts quite different from traditionally discussed clientelism (e.g., Latin American *latifundia*-style
tenant farming). The cases are also interesting because of the different *possibilities* for the rural poor that are displayed for each. Bangladesh is an extreme case,
with huge numbers of people living in desperate poverty, but also with capacities
for very effective intensive cultivation of high-yielding varieties of food grains
on small plots, enabling the nation to support substantial population with a very
limited agricultural area. Botswana takes us to the very different case of a pastoral tradition and the independence that it traditionally offered, a currently very
favorable national resource situation (thanks to the government's diamond
mines), and a program initiated in the late 1980s to subsidize plowing, which
appeared on the surface (though less so in reality) to mesh well with the tradition
of small-peasant independence. Finally, Tanzania presents a case of the consequences and decline of a more radical approach with a distinctive development
impact aimed at the direct provision of services, villagization. Each case highlights different aspects of the model and ways of potentially filling in the variables. We begin with the general background of poverty and constrained participation (or nonparticipation) in the three countries.

THE SCOPE OF FOOD SUPPLY AND HEALTH CARE INSECURITY
IN BANGLADESH: CALORIC INTAKE AND MALNUTRITION

Bangladesh is a country with geo-climatic circumstances quite favorable to
agriculture. It is essentially a large flood-plain or delta at the mouth of great In-
dian rivers, whose seasonal floods, provided they come in moderation, provide a
periodic renewal of fertility for very productive rice agriculture. Cultivation with
the benefits of high yielding varieties of rice can be intense and very productive
on quite small plots, providing the potential for independence for very large
numbers of people on a limited agricultural area. On the other hand, however,
the case of rural Bangladesh also provides a look into the future of overpopula-
tion for areas that are geo-climatically favored for agriculture. There are periodic
ecological problems of excessive flooding and related agricultural disruption,
leading to what is referred to as an agricultural "bad year." In normal years, there
are seasonal pauses in agricultural activity (the "hunger season") that regularly
threaten the food security of the rural poor. Not surprisingly, the most pressing
problem for any humane look at Bangladesh is that of malnutrition and malnutrition-related illness due to lowered resistance to infection and disease. We must
begin by showing from available data that there really is a problem of basic protein-energy malnutrition due to poverty-caused insufficiency of food volume for
the poorer strata in Bangladesh.

We may begin to get a start on understanding the scope of the problem of rural
poverty and food insecurity with a look at daily caloric intake averages, which
are available for various years and which may be compared with the most minimal caloric and other dietary requirements. In this context, we need to view the

relationship of (a) average intakes from the *bad* crop year (of excessive or ir-regular flood or drought, occurring more or less every five years), which ad-versely impacts the whole agricultural sector, to (b) intakes in the comparatively good year of favorable agrarian conditions and robust rice output. A recognized minimum daily caloric requirement for Bangladesh, as a cutoff point for malnu-trition, seems to be 2,122 calories (Ghafur 1990, 73).[1] Some statistics prefer to use a "poverty-line" income, which can provide a daily caloric intake of around 2,200. Since these two levels are comparatively close, we consider data using them to be comparable. For comparison to this minimum range, official data from direct nutrition surveys and from household income and expenditure sur-veys (that may be correlated with nutritional intake levels) sometimes produce different results, which nonetheless yield useful ranges.

Bangladesh is 75 to 85 percent rural in its population and employment. We may look first to average food intake for the whole Bangladeshi population, taking both the rural and urban sectors together. Bad-year data range from 1,707 calories per day in 1976–1977, according to a Household Expenditure Survey (HES) of the official Bangladesh Bureau of Statistics (BBS), to 1,868–1,943 from other sources in 1981–1982.[2] In more normal years, we find 2,094 in 1975–1976 and 2,102 in 1983–1984 (Hossain 1989, 60). In the category of good year average intakes for Bangladesh overall, we find a 1962–1964 average of 2,251–2,301 and a 1985–1986 figure of 2,191 (Hossain 1989, 60). Some light is shed on trends for the rural sector by data on average rural food intakes in grams per day, which dropped from 886 in 1962–1964 to 807 in 1975–1976, and further, to 764–746, in 1981–1983 (Hossain 1992a, 75). From this rather low point in the early 1980s, there was improvement up to the good year of 1985–1986, followed by flood disruptions, which produced a bad year in 1987–1988 and a moderating of conditions into the early 1990s. The overall caloric average over the late 1980s appears to be around 2,000 calories (Khan and Hossain 1989, 52–53). An indication of what has occurred over the 1980s is given by comparing Bangla-desh Institute of Development Studies (BIDS) data on average rural food intakes (in grams) for the September–November lean period in normal-to-good years; lean period intake went from 663 grams in 1982–1983 to nearly 694 in the nor-mal year of 1990 (Hossain 1992a, 75), representing a slight gain in average rural caloric intake. Comparing these averages overall, the trends—downward over the 1960s and 1970s and mildly upward in the 1980s—seem less impressive than the tendency for normal-to-good years to fall into a common range when-ever they have occurred, and for bad years to do the same. Clearly, normal years do not bring the average out of the malnutrition range, remaining far below all internationally recognized minimum caloric intakes, while bad years drop na-tional average caloric intakes to ruinous levels.

Of particular interest to us in this context is the question of the degree of im-provement over the 1980s, a period of expansion of high-yielding variety (HYV) winter (*boro*) rice, and hence of increased overall agricultural production, which approached 20 million tons of rice nationally by the late 1980s into the early 1990s. Most notably, irrigated HYV *boro*, which is now grown in the previously dry and lean late-winter and early-spring seasons in many areas, has brought to many wage laborers and service providers enhanced employment opportunities and higher incomes than before for the same period. As to governmental policies, over these years there was a trend of withdrawal of some government-administered programs (in particular, subsidized access to fertilizer and shallow tubewells) that had been aimed at stimulating HYV, in favor of a more market-oriented approach. In the view of some optimistic analysts, these years saw a dent in the Bangladeshi poverty problem, with positive pro-market implications in the ideological debates between interventionist and market approaches. Other observers are more skeptical. We shall look now at both the before and after situation to identify the more enduring conditions affecting the poor.

To focus better on the target group, we must look to the percentages of the rural population existing *below* various poverty-linked dietary minima, in various years. Calculating incomes in the traditional way, in normal to good agricultural years, the percentage of the rural population living in poverty and unable to obtain as much as 2,122–2,200 calories a day seems to range from 47 percent to 62 percent, with the normal years of the 1980s falling between 47 percent and 57 percent (Sen 1992c, 34) and 1989–1990 at 55 percent (Hossain 1992c, 46).[3] Beginning in the mid 1980s, some surveys of the expenditures, consumption, and income of the poor began trying to factor in data or estimates for their informal "expenditure-saving" activities, such as kitchen gardening of low-prestige (and often low-nutrition) crops, fishing, gathering, and other informal-sector activities. When taking this into account and adjusting the old household expenditure data accordingly, it has been concluded that poverty had been a condition of 44 percent of the population in the early-to-middle 1960s and returned to that range in the better years of the middle-to-late 1980s; in the normal year of 1989–1990, a BIDS survey showed the proportion of the rural population in poverty, with expenditure saving factored in, had dropped to 38 percent (Sen 1992c, 36; Rahman and Hossain 1992, ii; Hossain 1992c, 46). Hence, the overall percentage for rural poverty for normal-to-good years appears to have declined by 6 percent under the introduction of HYV *boro*. In contrast, bad-year proportions calculated in this way are estimated at 65–72 percent in 1973–1974, 65–79 percent in 1976–1979, 65–79 percent in 1981–1982 (Sen 1992c, 34–37), and 60 percent in 1987–1988 (Hossain 1992c, 48). Clearly, bad years can take a terrible toll, and little real dent seems to have been made by the large HYV expansion of the 1980s.

Moreover, a major portion of individual caloric intakes remain *well below* the recognized Bangladeshi minima. In 1988–1989, a year of major recovery from the early 1988 floods, 30 percent of the Bangladeshi population fell below the "extreme" or "severe" poverty level of 1,800 calories (Parkinson and Syeduzzaman 1993, 6). In 1983–1984—the middle of the period of increasing impact of improved agricultural methods, and neither the best nor the worst year of the decade—37 percent of the rural sector had nutritional intakes under 1,800 (Hossain 1989, 60–61), with 32 percent of the rural sector (26.4 million people) below the extreme poverty income level obtaining only an 1,805 calorie average daily intake (HES reports and BBS, in Rahman and Hague 1988, 2). Normal-year (1989–1990) data from the BIDS survey indicate that when expenditure saving is factored in, 26–27.5 percent were in the "extreme" or "hard-core" poor category, with caloric intakes under 1,740 (Hossain 1992c, 46; Sen 1992b, 181). These data may be compared with the 44 percent below 1,800 calories in the bad year of 1973–1974 (Parkinson and Syeduzzaman 1993, 6) and 47 percent in the bad year of 1981–1982 (HES reports and BBS, in Rahman and Hague 1988, 2). Hence, we may say that in normal years, 26 to 32 percent of the population suffer extreme caloric undernutrition (in or below the 1,740–1,800 range). Moreover, the hard-core poor did not seem to share in the mild recovery experienced by the moderately poor between the 1987–1988 period of flood disruption and 1990; according to the BIDS survey data, the situation of the extremely poor worsened for categories such as those owning under 1.5 acres of land, wage laborers, and those reporting chronic food deficit (Hossain 1992c, 48), and the percentage living in hard-core poverty actually increased over the 1987–1990 period (Sen 1992b, 181), even as overall national rice production was increasing to new heights.

Recent data from the 1989–1990 BIDS survey of 62 representative villages seem to confirm that the two poverty categories—(a) overall poverty, including all degrees from severe to moderate, and (b) "extreme" or "hardcore" poverty—do indeed reflect conditions of food shortage, as income and expenditure data predict that they would. In the normal year of 1989–1990, which featured 37 percent of the rural population living in poverty and 26 percent in extreme poverty (with expenditure savings estimates included in income), 24 percent of the population fell into both the categories of extremely poor *and* those reporting at least an occasional food deficit (calculated from data in Hossain 1992c, 52). When we expand the target group to include the moderately poor, 46 percent of the population were classified both as poor (including both the extremely poor and the more moderately poor) *and* as reporting at least an occasional food deficit, and more than a third of these individuals reported being chronically in a state of food deficit (calculated from data in Hossain 1992c, 52). Including everyone reporting a deficit to BIDS data takers, it has been concluded that 68 percent of rural households faced seasonal deficits for two months or more (Rahman 1992a, 110). On the basis of this and the other data reviewed here, we may conclude that a *conservative* estimate of the size of the target population with which we are concerned here is, roughly speaking, 37–46 percent of the rural population of Bangladesh, though in truth the category may be much larger.

If we consider nutritional minima beyond mere caloric intake and look to the balance of the content of those calories, the situation takes on an even darker hue. Data indicate that only a quarter of rural households in Bangladesh consume an adequate amount of protein (Ahmed et al., 76). The Bangladeshi diet is dominated by cereals, which provide 86 percent of calories and 75 percent of protein, as opposed to the typical American diet of 17 percent of calories and 12 percent of protein from cereals (Quddus 1984, 7). What protein there is in rice (much less than in wheat or maize) is poorly assimilated due to the Bangladeshi diet's comparative lack of the amino acid lysine, which must, in Bangladesh, be made up by pulses (Quddus 1984, 7, 18). However, the spread of irrigated HYV agriculture over the last 25 years has tended to crowd out pulses, driving down the acreage grown and their consumption by the poor. Even in years when food grain consumption has stayed high, fish consumption—the protein source that compensates for the relative absence of meat and milk—has continued its decline from the early 1970s (Ahmad and Hossain 1983, 20, 22). Ominously, the BIDS study of the late 1980s encountered a prevailing opinion that fishing was worsening (Rahman 1992b, 245). Notably, by 1980 protein intake in grams per day had dropped from 58 in 1962–1964 and 58.5 in 1975–1976, to 48–50 in 1981–1983 and 49 in 1990 (Chowdhury 1992, 77). The increased production and availability of basic food grains in 1985–1986 may have occurred at the expense of availability of protein and other specific nutritional components necessary to an adequate diet; the availability to the poor of pulses, fish, meat, and milk may have worsened overall during the period, and it remains a third to half of requirements (Hossain 1989, 56–57).

There are clearly seasonal highs and lows in poverty and hunger. In Bangladesh, the main traditional crop of rice, referred to as *aman*, utilizes the rise and fall of the yearly delta flooding, and is harvested toward the end of the year. There is a slack season from September to mid-November (Ahmed et al. 1990, 65) leading up to the harvest, and just prior to that harvest is a time of widespread food shortages among the poor and the highest market prices for rice. Traditionally, there has been a second yearly lean period, in what was a lengthy dry season in the winter and early spring, including February, March, and April (Ahmed et al. 1990, 65), before labor opportunities arise in getting the next rice crop started (in addition to *aman*, a minor variety referred to as *aus* was grown in some areas in the summer). Since the 1960s an HYV rice referred to as *boro*, grown under irrigation, has spread for the winter dry season. Before irrigated winter *boro* cultivation spread, the dry season in winter increased poverty rates and hunger substantially in the early months of the year. Now owners with access to tubewell water for irrigation can grow a *boro* crop, and agricultural laborers have more widespread labor opportunities in the winter season (in some cases requiring seasonal migration). The other major slack season in September through December before the main *aman* harvest, however, remains a problem, along with less intense slack periods in March–April and June–July (Rahman 1992c, 111). In many areas shortages may be intensified because the new HYV *boro* crop has to some extent displaced acreage that used to bring in a minor *aus* harvest in the late summer. Data from 1989–1999, for example—for many, a good year of recovery from the 1988 flood disruptions—indicates the proportion of the rural population in poverty as rising from 44.5 percent in July-September to 51.1 percent in October–December, and receding again to 46.6 percent in January–March and then down to 33 percent in April–June (Sen 1992c, 37), after the *boro* harvest. The average rural daily calorie intake according to BIDS data, for the normal year of 1990, was 1,892 (Hossain 1992a, 70), well below the malnutrition cutoff of 2,122.

There remains a special malnutrition problem for women and children, which extends beyond the poorer stratum even to some middle-level households and persists for the poor even in agriculturally good years with strong overall rural output in the country. A 1981–1982 (bad year) direct survey of nutrition found 61 percent of all Bangladeshi children under age five suffering moderate to severe malnutrition by weight-for-age criteria (Mahmud 1987, 7). The BBS National Nutrition Survey for 1985–1986, a very good year for overall food production, still showed 60 percent of children under age six with "chronic malnutrition" of varying degrees (Miranda 1989, 4).

The upper portion of Bangladeshi households, however, seem to be doing better; the number of children under five considered normal by weight-for-age standards rose from around 20 percent in 1975 to 36–42 percent by 1981–1983, and then to 47.8 percent (BIDS data) in 1990 (Chowdhury 1992, 65). The rate of stunted height, a long-term indicator of malnutrition, has similarly declined, from 58–74 percent in 1975–1976 to 43–59 percent in the early-middle 1980s, and down to 40–45 percent in 1990 (Chowdhury 1992, 78). Furthermore, data on very extreme degrees of malnutrition have shown lower rates over the 1980s years of HYV-driven increases in overall rice production and food-for-work supplementation. Severe malnutrition (below 60 percent of normal weight-for-age), has also gone down from 26 percent in the bad year of 1975–1976 to around 7–10 percent in the 1980s. Notably, BIDS data show a decline for normal years in the lean-period rate of underweight (being under 80 percent of normal weight-for-height) from 18.6 percent in 1982–1983 to 12.1 percent in 1990 (Chowdhury 1992, 68). There are some indications, however, that most of the significant weight improvement in the 1980s has been for males (Chowdhury 1992, 63–64, 70). Husbands and eldest sons often eat first, before wives and younger children. Among children over age 1 and up to age 14, girls, on average, receive only 80 to 90 percent the caloric intake of boys. (Mahmud 1987, 10–13). Son preference, which is common in South and East Asia, seems to be a major factor here. There also remains a well-known problem of malnutrition among pregnant and lactating mothers.

Clearly, the most important effects of malnutrition on economic capacity occur via the crucial intermediate factor in the causal sequence, the risk of malnutrition to health. It is well known that malnutrition in children produces not only underweight and stunting but also heightened susceptibility to infections and the parasites that are omnipresent in the water and the damp housing of the poor. As a result, lengthened periods are often required for recovery. Diarrhea, dysentery, respiratory diseases, and tetanus are major killers, and 18 to 20 percent of children die before the age of five (Miranda 1989, 4). We do not have data on the degree of mental retardation caused by early childhood malnutrition, which impairs for life a person's capacity for the self-provision of food. For the bad agricultural period of 1988 in Bangladesh, estimates by the United Nations Children's Emergency Fund (UNICEF) indicate a high infant mortality rate of 118 per 1,000 and an under-five mortality rate of 188 per 1,000. In the mid-1980s it was estimated that half of all infants were born weighing under 2.5 kilograms (a weight at which Western babies are put in hospital intensive care), and by age four three-quarters suffer anemia; a mid-1980s BIDS survey showed one person in seven suffering from disease.[4]

Poor access to safe water has traditionally been a problem, but the spread of the availability of tubewell drinking water seems to have improved the situation. Such access has increased from around 50 percent early in the 1980s to 80–90 percent in 1990 (Sen 1992d, 90). With the exposure to diarrhea thus reduced somewhat, thus lessening diarrhea's own overall contribution to malnutrition, an even more significant role emerges for establishing basic resistance to respiratory and other infection and corresponding nutritional levels.

In the abstract, health weakened by malnutrition might be compensated for in part by health care, at least for the worst cases. However, there is little affordable health care actually available to the rural poor in Bangladesh. A major household expenditure is required for health treatment, for which the poor do not have the funds. Despite health care being theoretically free, the reality is that government-supplied health care is distant and in short supply (Ahmed et al. 1990, 58); recent data indicate that only 13 percent of rural inhabitants are treated in government health centers (Sen 1992d, 90). In practice, the majority still depend on private practitioners, from government doctors holding private practice hours to traditional healers of various types, and much is spent on drugs (Norbeye 1986, 186–187). Health care is even more expensive in urban areas, where modern private medical practice is becoming increasingly widespread. The continuing dependence of households on costly private medical care and medicines, the poor performance of Bangladesh on health indicators, and a figure for 1985–1987 of 55 percent of citizens (60 million people) lacking access to health services (UNDP 1990, 130, 132) suggest that the poorer strata among this massive population remain too poor to obtain viable health access. There has been no improvement in this situation over the 1980s.

As was the case with malnutrition, in health access there are differential effects within the household, and primary among the victims are the women. Female "overmortality" is striking. Within the under-five category, there remains a particular health risk to female children due to differential female malnutrition, and attendant higher death rates for females in the one-to-four age range, particularly for diarrheal diseases, which are extremely sensitive to malnutrition (Mahmud 1987, 10–13). Moreover, female children receive less medical attention than males; after an infant mortality rate favoring females at 104 to males at 113 per 1,000 live births, the age one-to-four death rate reverses this pattern, at 16 female deaths per 1,000, compared to 13 male deaths (Jahan 1989, 8). What with the prevalence of malnutrition (57 percent), anemia, frequent pregnancies, and the general absence of trained health personnel at births, the maternal mortality rate is 6 per 1,000, making it one of the world's highest (Jahan 1989, 9).

POLITICAL PARTICIPATION IN BANGLADESH

Perhaps understandably, given the great sensitivity of local politics and the difficulty in achieving forthcoming interview data on patterns of village-level political power (particularly in relation to economic inequalities), grass-roots politico-economic relationships have seldom been the central focus of detailed empirical studies in rural Bangladesh or in the third world generally. Nonetheless, we do know the general contours of rural Bangladeshi politics and how the poor are related to it.

For some time, Bangladesh as a whole has had party competition at the intermediate and local levels and, often, factional political competition at the village level (even in the periods of martial law). Despite the wretched conditions facing the poorer strata and the lack of serious governmental action to remedy their plight, for the most part the poor are silent or compliant supporters of better-off political participants. The latter contend for power, status, and wealth but fail to challenge the status quo with regard to basic socioeconomic conditions. While there are often palpable grievances of poor households against the local elite, there is little *independent* political participation by the poorer strata in Bangladeshi villages. When they do participate in village politics, the poor tend to follow their better-off economic patrons, whether neighbors or near or distant relatives, in choosing the factional alignment to support.

At the lowest level of relevant groupings, White aptly refers to a "cluster," meaning a group of neighboring or kin-linked households that are directly or indirectly dependent on a common rich patron for opportunities for labor, sharecropping, and/or credit; this cluster seems to function as the equivalent of a party or faction, with which people frequently identify (White 1991, 40). Most commonly, the wives in poor households do not participate openly in politics and are, in effect, represented by the husband's choices for the household unit. The unit mediating between this lowest level of cluster and kinship (from the *bari* or homestead family compound, to extended family and lineage linkages) on one hand, and the village as a whole and its leadership on the other, is a kind of society called the *shamaj*, which has its own customary court, the *shalish*, for maintaining its social norms. Members of a cluster are typically members of the same *shamaj*. Adnan's survey of village studies describes the *shamaj* as:

a group of member households, forming a distinct and exclusive group, which had reciprocal obligations to each other. . . . Households belonging to a given *shamaj* were required to help each other out at times of life-cycle rituals and crises, such as birth, marriage or death. In addition, the *shamaj* was the indigenous social institution through which villagers enacted and enforced the normative rules by which their social lives and moral codes were governed. The *shamaj* was also the premier arena for resolving conflicts between its members. . . . Over and above these functions, the *shamaj* organization was also overtly or covertly utilized by the rich and powerful of the village as a platform on which to launch their political aspirations in broader arenas. (1989, 111–112)

The *shamaj* usually coincides with a neighborhood, and may or may not be coterminous with a single kinship unit such as a patrilineage. Where the *shamaj* is larger, it seems typical that the wealthiest kinship group tends to lead and that wealth and influence are a requirement of the position of *shamaj* leader, or *shamajpradhan*; in smaller, kinship-based ones, seniority may rule (Adnan 1987, 86). While *shamajpradhans* may oppose one another in social and political matters, in disputes within the *shamaj*, poor clients are expected to support their patrons. All are to abide by the decisions of the *shalish* (*shamaj* court) and its *shalishkars* or judges (typically *shamajpradhans*), in places where the *shamaj* is a viable mechanism. In villages close to urban areas, where commercial modernization has had a major impact, there may be wealthy patrons with economic bases in the town who can afford to be independent of *shamaj* linkages; in most areas, however, the *shamaj* has retained a major political role (Adnan 1989, 114–115), even as commercial individualism and inequality within the kin group have weakened kinship solidarities. Jahangir (1979, 91–93) and Adnan (1989, 117–119) found that while the *shalish* was unlikely to be the determining factor in settling a dispute between richer peasants, it remained an effective means of dispute resolution when involving middle and poorer-stratum peasants, though the richer *shalishkars* could be partial when their own interests were involved.

Where presented with the opportunity, as Adnan has shown (1989), the secret ballot in parliamentary elections can yield widespread support for a candidate articulating the grievances of the poor. This is rare, however, and in such cases the candidate tends to be well-off, and there can also be special circumstances encouraging elitist tolerance. In the case of a group of villages studied by Adnan (1989), the "radical" candidate supporting the poor belonged to a very small party with no chance of victory nationally, which was likely to fade out locally after the election. The party's participation in the military regime's parliament was appreciated by its leadership at a time when the more powerful opposition parties were boycotting parliament; the candidate's success locally would weaken the positions of local elite members of more powerful opposition parties (Adnan 1987). In the rare cases when a village's leadership is gained by espousing to some extent the interests of the poorer strata, the leader steps into the traditional role of an intermediary controlling the flow of benefits from the outside (MacGregor 1989, 45–47). Most important politically for the poor are the power alignments in the village, in which the poor tend to support the preferences of their patrons. As has been recently observed, the rural poor tend to have little awareness of populist rhetorical programs at the national level: "A dramatic illustration of the preponderance of this patron-client politics is the near-total absence of any issue-based demands in the election manifestoes of candidates" (Rahman 1992, 293, 298).

THE POOR IN BOTSWANA

The case of Botswana includes a number of factors seemingly favorable to independent food security for the poorer peasantry. A large country with a comparatively small population, Botswana has extensive cultivable land, though much of it is characterized by poor soils, erratic rainfall, and shortages of surface water. This situation, however, makes for favorable pastoral conditions, with cattle serving as a source of milk and of draft power for plowing, as well as insurance for the bad agricultural years of low or ill-timed rainfall. The privileged access of Botswana beef to European markets provides a good commercial outlet for the cattle. There are extensive communal grazing areas, and in principle, unused land may be allocated by the land boards to those who need it for farming (Harvey and Lewis 1990, 69). There are many small cattle owners, along with a tradition called *mafisa* whereby (typically) larger owners lend out the care and use of some of their animals to smaller ones. Traditional Botswana norms included local community obligation to provide aid in adversity and extended kinship-based patterns of cooperation (Duggan 1983, 131; Solway 1980, 13–14). Additionally, the profitability of the diamond mines, swelling government spending (by comparative standards) and expanding formal-sector employment, and the proximity of Botswana to South Africa provide the option of profitable migrant labor for family members (particularly during the construction boom of 1987–1990). Starting in the early 1970s Botswana became an international favorite for development aid. Moreover, due to the government's diamond resources, Botswana has been able to avoid the overwhelming debt problems of so many third world countries.

Nonetheless, 70 to 80 percent of Botswana households live rurally and, especially following the drought of 1982–1987, which decimated the herds of small owners, a large proportion of the rural population have too few cattle for a viable pastoral living. Meanwhile, among the national cattle herd which at 3 million is now pressing the nation's carrying capacity, overgrazing has become a serious problem, particularly in the communal grazing areas, on which the smaller owners must rely. The larger owners have, over recent years, moved many cattle to the vicinity of the newer western boreholes under their private control, but they have actually used the new space to expand their herds, still leaving substantial numbers in the eastern communal areas and hence failing to relieve overgrazing there (Harvey and Lewis 1990, 86–87). Those with few or no animals must rely for a substantial component of their subsistence on often precarious agricultural conditions. They are often without adequate productive resources for cultivation, tending as they do to possess too few cattle to maintain a team of draft animals for plowing. Indeed, 30 percent of farms have no cattle at all (Oygard, Arntzen, and Selowane 1983, 8). Small herds were hit hard, and some were eliminated altogether, by the long drought of 1982–1987 and the shorter one of 1991–1992, thus weakening overall access to draft power.

There has also been a weakening of access to borrowed oxen and milk, of kinship obligations of the well off to the poor (whether kin or not), of availability of family labor for farming, and of access to outside mine employment that pays well enough to provide for adequate remittances home. The recently brightened employment prospects for migrants to urban areas have helped with remittances—of course, under the control (if not wholly at the discretion) of the migrant remitter—but for substantial numbers, employment is either low return or part time, and it has not made up for the barriers to economic security for the poorest. Years of drought not only dry up the chance to plow and harvest crops, but also harm informal employment opportunities in the rural areas (Harvey and Lewis 1990, 279). In the short but severe drought of 1991–1992, the planted area was reduced by a third and grain output was estimated at 15,000 tons, much below the annual average of 55,000 for the previous two crop years (EIU Report 1992/2, 29). The indications are that between the years in which major surveys were taken—1973, a comparatively good agricultural year, and 1986, at the end of the drought—while rural income distribution did not get substantially worse, the income levels of the poorer rural strata did drop in real terms despite a drought relief program, gradually rising urban employment prospects for migrants, and an increased average wage (Harvey and Lewis 1990, 281–282, 298).

An important special subcategory of the poor in Botswana is made up of the San, an ethnic minority of former Bushmen, who are the subject of open discrimination and often harsh conditions. A large proportion of the San fall into the category of remote area dwellers. As the term indicates, they live in the remotest areas, often far away from adequate social service facilities. Most have been either deprived of their traditional hunting territories or significantly restricted in their use.[5] In recent generations, in some areas cattleowners have made San work as serfs (Silberbauer and Kuper 1966). They tend to remain in a semifeudal dependency on the cattle owners on whose land they live, without being allowed to own cattle or possess any recognized land rights. While some can periodically leave the cattle post area for temporary labor opportunities elsewhere, in hard times they must return to the herd owner who is recognized locally as their master.

The latter situation renders the San vulnerable to expulsion, a situation to which Hitchcock and Totten (1988) have drawn attention in human rights terms. Often young boys must labor as herdboys, receiving little income or only food from the activity, while they are informally outlawed from other employment. In some areas, the availability of this serf labor was what made possible the outmigration of the males of cattle-owning households to the South African mines (Wilmsen 1982, 15). Such migration could, in turn, often allow even small herdowning households to gradually build up the herd until, on average around age 40, the miner would end his mining career and return permanently to rural Botswana (Gulbrandsen 1984).

It is difficult to combine herding with other income-generating activities, and many of the young San boys do not attend school. Elsewhere, many San work on freehold farms, of whom 72 percent were estimated in the mid-1970s to live below the poverty level (Granberg and Parkinson 1988, 62, 65). The freehold farmworkers work long and irregular hours for no extra pay, live in very bad housing and sanitary conditions, and sometimes get their whole income in the form of the food they eat. As with herdboy households, most of their children do not attend school.

Most recently, the San's loss of the traditional hunter-gatherer subsistence alternative has further accelerated due to the tribal grazing land policy (TGLP), under which large areas previously occupied by the San were turned into commercial farms. This policy tended to fail to recognize the existence of existing occupying populations and their traditional land allocations,[6] despite the rhetoric of the law in favor of the latter (Hitchcock 1982). Well-off individuals or syndicates drilled boreholes in dry areas outside their traditional villages (generally to the west of often overgrazed eastern Botswana). They henceforth effectively owned them, as they proceeded to claim the land around them under TGLP. This process apparently continued into the 1980s, despite the existence on paper of a freeze by the land boards (the local bodies supervising land policy) on the granting of new borehole rights (Gulbrandsen 1984).

Finally, there were about 8,500 destitute persons registered in the country in 1988. Only those individuals who are entirely without assets and without any close relatives to assist them are defined as destitute, including the handicapped. The idea is that the state should only intervene to assist persons in cases where there is no extended family network. In practice, people are not eligible for assistance if they have family members who ought to provide for them but do not. However, traditional Botswana norms of extended family obligation and voluntary community charity seem to be steadily eroding with so-called modernization (Granberg and Parkinson 1988, 56–57). There has been a flow to the larger towns of advantaged individuals, who thus abandon the villages and any sense of social obligation felt toward them. The number of needy people has been growing steadily, and many who would potentially qualify for support apparently do not get it (Granberg and Parkinson 1988, 58).

The result of the general situation of the poor, and these latter special situations of the subgroups, is undernutrition or malnutrition for many, particularly starting in October and November. Undernutrition renders especially large numbers vulnerable in drought periods (Vierich and Sheppard 1980, 60–62), with the rate of malnutrition among children under age five rising during the drought years of the 1980s to a peak of around 32 percent (Granberg and Parkinson 1988, 76) despite a widely respected drought monitoring and relief system. This figure, however, is roughly the same as that recorded in a major mid-1970s survey, which was taken in a *good* rainfall year,[7] probably reflecting mainly the improved effectiveness of drought-relief measures. The government distributes food aid to drought-stricken areas via clinics and health posts, and primary school children receive one daily meal. In the off-season, labor-based relief programs provide some employment for cash to buy food. The situation was well summed up by Harvey and Lewis, who explain that:

Monthly weighing of children at health posts, covering some 60 per cent of the age group, showed that the percentage of children below 80 per cent of their expected weight for age rose continuously in 1982, 1983 and 1984 but began to fall thereafter. The rise was limited, though; the under-weight percentage increased from a range of 24 per cent to 29 per cent in "normal" years, to a range of 27 per cent to 32 per cent in the drought years; there was also very much less seasonal variation in drought years than in non-drought years . . . because of the regular supply of the drought-relief food. (1990, 301–302)

The food ration system, however, was not without problems, which also play a role for the 40 percent of children who are outside the sample because they cannot travel to the health posts. The rations are handed out to all children under the age of five, pregnant and lactating mothers, children under ten not attending school, and tuberculosis patients—or at least those who can transport themselves to the health posts where the rations may be obtained. However, the monthly rations of food are set at only 21 percent of normal calorie requirements. Moreover, to get additional rations, the severely malnourished have to come to the local clinic daily, often involving a long walk and time that women cannot spare from the needs of other children and household chores. When enough rain falls to remove an area from the drought list, food rations are reduced and there can be a significant increase in malnutrition rates of children under five, as the effects of ongoing general poverty weigh in (Granberg and Parkinson 1988, 59). Especially in the small villages, which tend to be more remote and where the poor tend to be in the majority, the system for getting food to the needy in times of drought has at times been inefficient (Egner and Klausen 1980, 11–13).

Health access in Botswana remains limited. A much-cited figure is the 85 percent of rural dwellers said to be within 15 kilometers of one of the health posts built with Norwegian aid in the 1970s. However, the long distances, coupled with uncertainty about dates when qualified personnel will be present, result in low utilization by those most exposed to health risk due to undernutrition. Even near large villages, those most dependent on arable agriculture show a tendency to live more or less permanently "at the lands," adjacent their farmed fields often at a substantial distance from the home village. At the lands, access to water points during the dry season, as well as to other services, is worst (Silitshena 1983). Many of these households are de facto female-headed, as the husband may be working as a migrant laborer in a far away town and unable or unwilling to provide significant remittances. With the construction build-up in recent years, especially around Gaborone (where it was financed with revenues from government-owned diamond mining), this separation of males and females in the household is likely to increase.

POLITICAL NONPARTICIPATION OF THE RURAL POOR OF BOTSWANA

As to social and political independence, Botswana has a democratic tradition (though single-party dominant) in national politics, which is rare in Africa. It also has a tradition of local democracy in the *kgotla* (village council), which invites one and all to free expression, association, and political participation. Problems connected with poverty would seem to invite active political participation by the poor in efforts to adopt or adjust programs to address their needs. In civil-political fields for choice in rural Botswana, however, poor rural households tend to be inactive, with the exception of voting for their patron's party (usually the Botswana Democratic Party) in national elections, which are remote from the rural poor's knowledge and interest.

This political quietism of the poor is noted in a number of studies (e.g., Fort-mann 1983; Holm 1982, 92–98). There are typically between two and four factions in Botswana villages, and their leaders are usually wealthy. As Kuper showed, factional leaders are not in their positions solely because of their cattle wealth, and many wealthy are not particularly influential in village politics; status and clan connections and education-related ability are major factors as well (Kuper 1970, 87). However, no issues involving poverty could be found on the village political agenda by Kuper (1970, 90), and no factional leaders were poor. Factional political contests, such as between more modernizing leaders on the old Village Development Committees and the more traditional elders in the *kgotla*, continues to be an intraelite affair (Noppen 1982; Fortmann 1983, 22–23, 42–48).

In national politics, Botswana's multiparty parliamentary democracy has developed under the sway of the Botswana Democratic Party, which has been dominant in most rural areas. It can call on its clientelistic network to deliver large rural majorities for the government at election time, but its much-touted commitment of providing the services of a resource-laden government to rural development has not borne fruit for the rural poor. With the traditional local *kgotla* available as an outlet for protest, along with the need of the government party for the votes of the poor, there would seem to be good reasons for the poor to participate in the village political arena. However, the *kgotla* remains a field for elite activity only (Fortmann 1983, 22–23, 31, 43). Most rural political activists are herd owners, who receive substantial government livestock services (Holm 1982, 97). The all-important decisions on land allocation (Gulbrandsen 1984, 1990) tend to be made in consultation among the land boards, the headman, and local influentials, with no opportunity for mass influence in the headman's *kgotla* itself (Fortmann 1983, 43–44). Criticism of government development policies is unlikely insofar as government is the critical provider in times of drought (Holm 1982, 93).

A large and easily identifiable category among the nonparticipants in politics is rural women. Not surprisingly, the problem is often viewed in terms of their lot. The conventional view is that women's lack of time and men's view of women as inferior disadvantage peasant women in general. This view is presented in mainly cultural terms, without refinement and adjustment for the economic particulars of the food-vulnerable stratum. However, there are examples of comparatively better-off women (with the same family burdens) participating politically, as well as much evidence of males in the vulnerable households remaining as politically quiescent as the women. Gender-based cultural discrimination is surely a crucial factor in the lot of women generally, but as a comprehensive account of the problem of nonparticipation in politics, poverty measured by low or no cattle ownership seems a very powerful explanatory factor, with poor women, of course, making up a large portion of the vulnerable category (Hesselberg 1985).

Also among the nonparticipants are the San households. Whether cattlepost dependents (where they are not considered citizens or members of the village community), remote area dwellers in relocation settlements, or freehold farm-workers, the San remain without effective formal political representation as they lack representatives in the national assembly and the cabinet. Hitchcock and Totten (1988) do mention a few development schemes for groups of resettled San, offering land, water, and service facilities. By 1988, "most of the San communities in Botswana" had their own "headmen, councils, or Village Development Committees." As to significant political involvement, however, the authors go only so far as to say that these "institutions were beginning to press for recognition of the land and other rights of San groups" (Hitchcock and Totten 1988, 6).

The most prevalent pattern for the rural poor in Botswana, then, is nonparticipation amid elite dominance and widespread silence about the interests of the poor, despite available democratic procedures and aid workers willing to articulate their interests at various policy-making levels.

WHO ARE THE FOOD-INSECURE POOR IN RURAL TANZANIA?

In contrast to Botswana, the conventional picture of Tanzania is that of a macroeconomic basket case, which nonetheless provides minimal economic sustenance and at least rudimentary civil-political access to its rural poor. The government's policies of limiting rural inequality and providing access to land to all, together with comparatively favorable climatic conditions for agriculture, appear to provide minimal economic security for the rural poor. Village-level institutions on a democratic formal pattern and the comparative openness and democratic features of the one-party dominant political system are thought to provide civil-political access. While some aspects of this picture have validity, the situation of the rural dwellers is a complex one, with major potential limitations on the scope of exercise of both economic and civil-political rights by the poor.

Some 70 to 80 percent or more of Tanzanians live in rural areas (depending on how one defines "rural"), where the great majority of them farm with the hoe. Despite the low technology of most cultivators, however, there are positive things to be said about the Tanzanian agricultural context. In the southern highlands area, which has favorable conditions for maize growing, early on the combination of development aid and "panterritorial" official procurement pricing (evening out prices paid to farmers, in effect to subsidize transportation costs to such remote areas) made possible major output growth starting in the 1970s. A southern highlands program of credit to smallholder producers of maize for hybrid seeds, pesticides, and fertilizer was managed by the Tanzanian Rural Development Bank with money from the World Bank, the Danish International Development Agency (DANIDA), the Norwegian Agency for Development (NORAD), and other agencies (Havnevik et al. 1988, 36–37, 41). Agriculture was to some extent depressed by the economic crisis of the early 1980s, with its absence of the goods in the stores (that serve as an important incentive to agriculture), together with the low real prices offered by the centralized parastatal official procurement agencies, though many found outlets at better prices in the informal (and technically, illegal) "parallel market." Since then, the loosening of controls on officially marketed crops in the middle 1980s has provided improved incentives for surplus production. The 1992–1993 crop year, for example, yielded an overall national output of 2.8 million tons of maize, which on a per capita basis, contributed to 97 percent of "national self-sufficiency" in cereal grains (EIU 1993–1994, 13–14).

Moreover, in some areas many households own small cattle herds, allowing some pockets of mixed farming (Lindstrom 1986). Peasants with enough resources have in some places, where access allows, even adopted local versions of more modern methods to increase maize production, such as ox-plowing or biochemical inputs adjusted for local conditions of input access reliability, soils, risks, and so on (Rasmussen 1987). Reportedly, a few areas amenable to ox-plowing have seen a major increase in the use of animal draft power (communication, Finn Kjaerby 1989).

Overall national output figures, however, can be very misleading regarding the actual food sufficiency problems of members of the less advantaged strata. There are few indications of any gains in the nutrition situation of most poor Tanzanians (Havnevik and Skaarstein 1985, 11). A study in Iringa district showed that the poorer categories get 1–1.3 bags of maize per person kept for food, versus the estimated 2 bags needed for subsistence and 2.6 bags retained by the wealthier strata (Boesen and Ravnborg 1992, 73). Lacking the normal-year surpluses that are necessary for taking risks in cash cropping (Bryceson 1988, 39), the very large subsistence sector tends to market little grain. Consequently, the post-1984 increases in real official producer prices for marketed maize have had little effect on the majority of subsistence producers. Even if the newly plentiful "incentive goods" in the stores were priced low enough to be within their reach, the technology level of the poorer strata is too low to enable these prices to be a major factor. This latter category makes up the bulk of the malnourished population, and they are more likely to be suffering on the buying end of high food prices than to be gaining on the selling end. To make matters worse, particularly from 1992–1993, an explosion in fertilizer prices, the end of panterritorial pricing, the financial collapse of the cooperative union marketing structure, and the reluctance of the now-legal private marketers to go to remote locations in the southern highlands, have curbed the favorable circumstances for maize output growth there.

Even in the aggregate, nutritional levels for Tanzania are very low, despite continuing significant food aid. Projected for the early 1990s for Tanzania was a *per capita* caloric consumption of 2,076, well below the UN Food and Agriculture Organization (FAO) minimum requirement of 2,320, and about the same as was estimated for 1980 (Ames and Wojtkowski 1987–1988, 210). Of course, per capita indicators are crude and fail to stratify by economic level to let the real nutritional problems reveal themselves. The average Tanzanian diet of *ugali* (porridge, made usually from maize and, sometimes, a small amount of vegetable or pulse as relish), is well below recognized minimum standards, not only in overall caloric value, but also in protein, oils, and fats, as well as, most notably, in iron, iodine, and vitamin A. The clearest target group in the food security problem in Tanzania is the poorer stratum, consisting of the 30 to 50 percent of households which simply lack the means to produce enough food grains to set aside stocks for the most minimal nutrition required for active family members throughout the year, and also lack the income to make up the shortfall through purchases on the market.

The recent *Poverty Profile* used a weighted sample from representative areas, and concluded that in the rural sector 44 percent of people were "hard-core" poor, unable to meet an ILO-defined absolute minimum package of consumption requirements (with those considered the merely "poor" estimated at 59 percent) (Ferreira 1993, 23). The malnutrition figures that are most noticed are those of young children. If malnutrition is defined by the Harvard standard of weighing under 80 percent of the normal weight for a given age, various rural surveys in Tanzania have indicated average rates of malnutrition of between 40 percent and 60 percent (TFNC 1992, 13), and UNICEF figures for 1980–1987 showed 48 percent of Tanzanian children under five suffering from either moderate or severe malnutrition (6 percent severe) (UNICEF 1990, 78). In Dodoma region, one of the poorest agricultural regions in Tanzania, it was reported in March 1990 that on average, 65 percent of children under age five suffer from at least moderate malnutrition and 7 percent from severe malnutrition (compared with 3 to 5 percent in the severe category 20 years ago).[8] In a sample of different sorts of villages in Iringa district, Seshamani found an average of 40 percent of children to be underweight (1988, 35). At the more severe extreme, a recent survey indicated over 12 percent of sampled households to be consuming less than a disastrously low 1,500 calories per adult equivalent.[9] At these levels of malnutrition, energy intake from carbohydrates and fats is insufficient to the point of diverting what protein intake there is to energy instead of basic body maintenance (Seshamani 1981, 10, 18).

Such an extent of malnutrition has major effects promoting ill health and death. Malnutrition dangerously weakens the ability of children to resist the diarrhea, which is common in conditions of poor sanitation and water. It has been estimated that in Tanzania, 90 percent of detected illnesses among the children under age five are related to malnutrition (Omari 1986, 771). Malnutrition multiplies the risk of coming down with infectious diseases, ranging from diarrhea and respiratory infections to malaria, in a situation in which agents of disease are everywhere in the environment. The risk of death from common ailments is reportedly multiplied by between two to eight times for those who suffer malnutrition (TFNC 1992, 26). It has recently been estimated that 50 percent of the child mortality rate for Tanzania (167 per 1,000), is attributable, directly or indirectly, to malnutrition from lack of protein (Wagao 1993, 4).

How much of this situation is due to poverty-related food insufficiency and how much to lack of nutrition and health education and monitoring? An interesting light is cast by the program of the mid-1980s that started in Iringa under the auspices of the Joint Nutrition Support Program (JNSP), supported by

UNICEF and the Tanzania Food and Nutrition Center (TFNC 1992, 107–108), and succeeded in a wider range of communities by the Child Survival, Protection, and Development program (CSPD). Its activities range from nutrition education, general health consciousness raising, and child weight monitoring, to distributing a nutrient-bolstered weaning food base ("power flour") and, in some places, providing free feeding posts for severely malnourished children. In program areas, the under-five malnutrition rate appears to have dropped roughly from the 45–55 percent range of nonimpacted areas to 30–40 percent, and the severe malnutrition rate has dropped from 6–8 percent to under 2 percent (Kavishe 1993, 43–46). The problem is that the 30–40 percent rate in the favored areas has stubbornly resisted further progress (Kavishe 1993, 43). Some of the gain, particularly in the severe malnutrition category, may have come from the free feeding posts, which obviously would be beneficial to the poorest. On the other hand, many mothers of children with malnutrition, who are nonetheless aware of the campaign, may have stayed away from the clinics—and hence remained out of what is only a volunteer (rather than randomly representative) sample on which this data is based—in order to avoid the social stigma from the very public process of weighing the child, admonishing the parent, and so on,[10] which is done for consciousness-raising purposes. This contributes to the possibility of the data understating the actual remaining malnutrition rate.

As for older children, teens, and adults, fragmentary data show lower levels of malnutrition in rural Tanzanians aged 7 through 11, and then higher rates (up to 30–40 percent) at ages 12 and 13 (Kavishe 1993, 47). Among adults, in the late 1980s 30–40 percent suffered malnutrition as indicated by a Body Mass Index of under 20 (Kavishe 1993, 49). The consumption levels of pregnant women (of about 1,600 calories a day), are about what they burn in their work, which they must continue virtually up to the date of birth, contributing in turn to low birth weight (Kavishe 1993, 51–52; TFNC 1992, 9). Even many who are not actually experiencing malnutrition at a given time no doubt share with the victims the overall context of *food insecurity,* which characterizes daily life for the poorer strata in rural Tanzania.

As Holmboe-Ottesen puts it, "in Tanzania the size of food stocks was extremely important as a determinant of the level of consumption in the household (as indicated by the number of eating/feeding events and nutritional status)" (Holmboe-Ottesen 1992, 172). The situation seems to be particularly bad in the months of dampness, long and back-breaking labor, and exhausted grain stores prior to the time when the next harvest can begin. These are the early months of the year, from February through April, toward the end of which some "green" (unripe) maize is picked and eaten to survive. One survey of 21 villages indicated food-grain stocks lasting only six to eight months beyond the harvest, and local studies in Mtwara, Morogoro, and Rukwa in the late 1980s showed 60 percent to 74 percent of the sample households lacking sufficient food stocks (TFNC 1992, 49). A study in Sumbawanga district of Rukwa region showed that while a majority of the nutritionally vulnerable households may harvest a volume of grain that could theoretically suffice for a (very minimal) diet if there were no other necessary uses for it, in fact, the majority of the households exhausted their stores two or more months short of the next harvest (Holmboe-Ottesen and Wandel 1988, 13, 18, 31; Wandel and Holmboe-Ottesen 1992; Holmboe-Ottesen 1992). Of course, households must sell grain from their stocks for taxes, fees, essential purchases (cooking oil, salt, etc.) and other necessary cash needs, both at harvest and periodically over the year (Sosovele 1986, 15). Not surprisingly for these food-deficit households, consumption went down in the early months of the year before harvest, especially among the young children (Holmboe-Ottesen and Wandel 1988, 9). At this time the price of food on local markets is likely to be prohibitive (Schneider-Barthold et al. 1983, 47), and households having to buy maize experienced lowered meal frequency and also lowered weight-for-age nutritional status of the children (Wandel and Holmboe-Ottesen 1992, 101). During these hunger-ridden months of February to June, the highest numbers of illnesses and deaths are reported (Due et al. 1984, 6). Bantje's data on birth weight and maternal weight gain differences, along with other data on seasonal variation in the under-five mortality rate and malnutrition-related mortality, reinforce the common view of the hunger season in rural Tanzania (Kavishe 1993, 76–77; TFNC 1992, 22).

Especially for the women and children, meal frequency is a special problem in the five months prior to the harvest. The Tanzanian rural diet of mainly cereal (usually maize) is so low in energy density that much food must be eaten to supply the body with enough energy and nutrients for growth and tissue regeneration, particularly when there is much muscular exertion. In the first few months of the calendar year, the women work long hours in the fields, have little food stock left, and, if they are at all distant from the village, they are able to prepare for themselves and the children at most two or three meals a day of a thin maize porridge (*uji*), which, UNICEF says, requires at least four meals daily to provide the most minimal energy (Wandel and Holmboe-Ottesen 1992, 97; 1988, 10, 17). Even women impacted by the UNICEF-TFNC nutrition education program were unable to do better (Mbughuni 1988, 289), suggesting that a necessarily harsh shepherding of scarce resources is at least partially responsible for low meal frequency, as was indicated by Seshamani (1981, 7–8). Some Tanzanian women leave their children at home with siblings (when female elders or other wives are also in the fields), where attention to food needs will tend to be poor (Tobisson 1980, 53). Of course, this continuing disaster is much accentuated in a bad crop year due to irregular rainfall or pest infestations. These occurrences can delay the harvest and accentuate malnutrition both in this year and the next, when stores will run out weeks or months earlier. In contrast, where there is comparatively assured independent food sufficiency, peasants have a platform for market-oriented activities that can bolster their position, even in a bad crop year (Odgaard 1986, 220–221).

An often negative factor in the early exhaustion of food-crop stores has to do with gender, particularly husbands' periodic requests or demands that grain be sold to pay for their beer. At times this has been known to create conflict with the women, as the latter try to defend the stock (Wandel and Holmboe-Ottesen

1992, 91; Mbughuni 1988, 289; Mbilinyi 1989). When there is cash crop income for the household, the husband tends to control it, while providing food-grains to feed the family is often considered the sole responsibility of the wife. It appears that it is primarily women with an advantaged resource base, sufficient to make beer on a profitable scale, who are able to adequately regain this value from their husbands.

Our general account of the vulnerable category must be completed, however, with a return to the gender inequality problem in another context, that of middle- and upper-level households that would not generally be counted as in the vulnerable stratum. Gender inequality can, in a better-off household, render its rural women and children malnourished. Under the custom giving husbands control of most outside income, a man living in town may control sufficient income and be in an economic niche secure enough to fairly well assure minimal food access and significant choice to himself—and only to himself. Husbands of any stratum under Tanzanian rural conditions can limit the resources allowed to their wives on the land, in a way ruling out the latter's *assurance* of access to minimal significant choice and to food. I suggest that gender inequity in middle-level households that otherwise would not fall in the vulnerable category can indeed put women and children living on the farm into the vulnerable category. Here, the patron on whose good will the vulnerable depend is the husband in the household, not a well-off kin or nonkin unit outside the household, as in the case of the poorest households. Hence, the actual numbers of vulnerable individuals are likely to exceed the numbers of food-insecure people who receive most of my attention in this study (the 30 to 50 percent of poorer-stratum Tanzanian households in the sorts of conditions laid out here). In contrast, where resources of a middle- or upper-level household have been plowed back into making the rural locus of the women and children viable for relatively autonomous, food-effective farming, the entire household would remain out of the vulnerable category.

It might be suggested that for poor rural women in Tanzania, as elsewhere in black Africa, beer brewing provides an additional means of employment and an income supply that, in effect, supplements nutrition under the women's own control. This can certainly be so in middle-level households, but for the poor, beer brewing at best only helps them keep their heads above water. Often, much of the return from brewed beer has to be plowed back into grain, in the form of supplying beer parties to get labor for such intensive and time-sensitive labor as weeding. Moreover, women are responsible for supplying such necessities as the minimal needs of the children and the market-provided household essentials (e.g., cooking oil, salt, school fees), which tend to soak up any remaining proceeds of beer sales. The grain for brewing for these purposes must be subtracted directly from what is available for food needs, and the extra firewood needed requires extra long hours of labor gathering and hauling the larger logs needed for brewing. For women, beer brewing is just one component of the minimal survival package, and not a source of food security or independence.

This food security situation is interrelated and reinforced by a deplorable system of access to health care. To get feasible access to health care in the rural areas of a poor country like Tanzania, one must first have the minimal level of health and strength to transport oneself (or one's children) to a health care facility, and one's needs for health care help must not be too frequent. Hence, the foundation of the minimum threshold for real gains regarding the right to health must be enough food to eat, particularly in relation to the physical workload, to maintain natural resistance to infection and the underlying strength to travel to get help when necessary. Thus, the conditions relevant to minimalist food levels apply fundamentally to the right to health as well.

The other part of this prerequisite foundation for feasible minimal health has to do with access to healthy water, which is a frequent source of health problems, particularly for those already suffering some degree of malnutrition. A well-functioning village water supply close to the homesteads can reduce the number of diarrhea episodes (commonly, several cases a year for children under five). It can also save on the cumulative neck and back damage women suffer from headloading water and the precious time of often overburdened women. Clean and bacteriologically safe water supplies were a major promise of villagization in the mid-1970s, but they often didn't arrive, and those that did were often in disrepair by the time the economic crisis of the 1980s was in full swing. The original goal of having a regular supply of clean water within 400 to 500 meters was apparently reached in the early 1980s by only a quarter to a half of the rural population (McCall 1987, 202–203). With the crisis of the last decade, there was a disappearance of central government resources to maintain improved water supplies over time, leaving them to the resourceless local communities in the fashion of "self-reliance." UNICEF lists 42 percent of rural Tanzanians having access to safe water in 1985–1987, alongside 90 percent of urban dwellers (still, however, well ahead of the overall African average of 19 percent) (UNICEF 1990, 80). As to sanitation, following villagization, the use of traditional pit latrines became widespread, but sewer systems serve only a small portion of the urban population.

In aspiration, at least, Tanzania at the beginning of the 1980s looked like a standard-setter for poorer countries of Africa in achieving access to medical services. With much Nordic aid, the 1970s saw the establishment of a multilevel strategy. In each village there was to be a dispensary, where a village health worker and a rural medical aide could dispense medicines, administer first aid, and give health, sanitation, and nutrition information. The next step up, serving several villages at the divisional level, is a Rural Health Center, which does the same things with more personnel, plus providing a few beds for the sick. Of course, accessing real health care was, for those who could travel to the district or regional hospital, a formidable achievement for most rural Tanzanians. There was a comparatively high level of spending on health care up to 1980, and many facilities were constructed and numerous personnel brought on, with particular support from the Swedish International Development Agency (SIDA). Some impressive-sounding statistics could result for categories like numbers "served" by dispensaries, population within a certain distance from a health care facility, or medical personnel per 1,000 population (1.9 by 1984[11]).

In practice, however, the system was unevenly distributed and radically vulnerable to deficiencies in maintenance, supply, staffing at one level or another, and practical and timely accessibility. These difficulties set in with a vengeance in the 1980s, a period of crisis and resource scarcity, which affected the poorer strata adversely. Actual spending on maintained facilities was biased toward larger urban medical units and toward cure over prevention. This resulted in excessive demand on urban hospitals and their already-inadequate personnel and supplies (of drugs, bandages, etc.). The number of doctors remains very small. Meanwhile, in many areas, rural health centers, with numerous, but often poorly trained personnel, are poorly maintained, undersupplied, and underutilized, offering little more than village dispensaries. A study of SIDA-assisted rural health care centers revealed no maintenance, crumbling facilities, inadequate supplies, and unsanitary conditions; for example, among the surveyed areas that were considered underprivileged, no rural health care center was found to possess a working water supply.[12] At the village level, many areas suffer a scarcity of village health care workers (weakening the preventive side), and no maintenance of the dispensaries. Payment of the village health workers and dispensary maintenance were left to village governments, which lack resources, and both are done only irregularly and poorly. The erosion of health care workers' real incomes in many areas produced underemployment, as workers scavenged for other income and food sources to feed their families and sometimes responded especially to bribes.[13] In such circumstances, ordinary rural citizens hope for not much more than finding a unit where medicines are in supply.

However, for the practical purpose of exploring the immediate obligation of the world's affluent people to remedy the situation, the remedy must be targeted at the poorest category of vulnerable households. The cutoff point for key productive resources is the only criterion both (a) for targeting the conditions of those likely to be worst off and in the greatest immediate insecurity, and (b) for keeping the program cost at a level perceived by donor countries to be feasible. Poverty targeting of households, if successful in offering a significant alternative course of economic endeavor to the vulnerable category, could turn local social practices generally in a direction more respecting of significant choice and food access. By introducing an option for the future to those not choosing to take it up today, a human rights-sensitive, production-oriented aid strategy will increase the bargaining power of all, even those not taking it up. Its effect will be, not only on the vulnerable household category, but also somewhat on vulnerable individuals in households not classified as vulnerable, who will gain a source of economic hope outside their current household.

POLITICAL NONPARTICIPATION OF THE RURAL POOR IN TANZANIA

In Tanzania, as in the two other cases, there is a gap between the appearance of local democracy, with the poor having every reason to become involved and press for remedial governmental policies on the one hand, and the reality of non-participation by the poorest. Studies of political participation in Tanzanian rural areas indicate very low rates of participation by those outside the village elite, especially among the women. Again, however, studies are generally concerned with the low rates of participation by "the villagers," "the peasants," or "women," without a breakdown by economic level within these abstract categories. This makes it easier to reduce the causes to such factors as cultural discrimination against women in politics (assumptions that they are inferior, have no time for it anyway, etc.), the demoralization of villagers generally in the face of past frustrations at nonresponsiveness to village-generated development plans, the domination of the planning process by district authorities (the "bureaucratic bourgeoisie"), and so on. While these assumptions may certainly be reflected in some interviews and surveys of villagers, at the same time, they can mask other factors differentially affecting the lower socioeconomic strata, about which there is reason for poor villagers to remain consistently silent.

Village institutions in Tanzania tend to be dominated by the village or party chairman (locally elected), secretary (appointed from above), the better-off family heads who serve as heads of village "sections," and the more influential "ten-house cell" leaders (Madsen 1984, 24–25, 82). The outcome, according to Kauseni, is that "the leadership in most villages is made up by and large of individuals who happen to be the well-to-do and who had great influence in the society" (1985, 9). Formally, the village council is elected by the village assembly, but in practice the village assembly is rarely called except when a district or higher-level leader is visiting to explain a policy (Mhina 1987, 37). The village council rarely responds to pressure from below; it acts on its own or in response to higher authority. The chairman and secretary of the village council are automatically the chairman and secretary of the dominant political party, the *Chama Cha Mapinduzi* (CCM), and hence elected by the village's party members, typically 25 percent or less of the villagers. Party elections are freely manipulated from above via the screening of candidates by the district-level CCM to weed out independently popular locals (Mhina 1987, 38). When the cooperatives were revived in the early 1980s, there was some question as to whether their organization would coincide with village boundaries; this was resolved in the affirmative by the CCM National Executive Committee in 1985, consolidating the tendency for cooperative officials to overlap with other local party, government, and cooperative union offices in a single party-government-cooperative elite. Since so many benefits relating to agricultural production are channeled through the marketing cooperatives, the usual premium placed on clientelistic connections with party and government officials remained under the local government forms started in the early 1980s.

This is not to suggest any necessity that the upper stratum be always politically unified. Since village boundaries need not coincide with clan lines, contestation could occur between clans and between more modern CCM figures and older clan leaders. Factional conflict has, in fact, been discovered in some areas between more traditional and more modern categories of local influentials

(Thompson 1985). Sometimes, religious distinctions play a part, as Christian or Muslim factions tend to take the more modern and district-responsive roles (Thiele 1986a). However, studies suggest that whether or not politics at the village level in Tanzania has factional conflict, the active participants belong to the upper and middle strata which they represent (Kauzeni 1984, 39; Thiele 1986a, 345).

In the mid-1970s, the villagization program eliminated the earlier marketing cooperatives and concentrated authority in the village administration. One officially favored perspective on villagization presented the new system as breaking the hold of the rich *kulaks* (better off, more individualistic farmers[14]) on local power. Undoubtedly, the richer, "capitalist" farmers who lost some or all of their large farms did lose out, and undoubtedly, some smaller owners did take on ten-house cell leader roles, though not usually those from the lowest 30–40 percent stratum. The ten-house cell leaders were unpaid and tended to be more well-off (by Tanzanian rural standards), older, and male, than average villagers; they were often traditional clan leaders unless a perceived need for literacy in the cell leader seemed to require a younger man (Fortmann 1980, 42–44). However, the cell leaders seemed to function primarily for neighborhood dispute settlement and little more, and the rewards and influence pale in comparison with those attending the section leader and village administration roles. Even where they intended to make the system work the way it is laid out on paper, the cell leaders tended to be weak in their efforts to do so. They were commonly unable to get the village leadership and higher government layers to deliver on promises the cell leader had to announce to the villagers, and also unable to effectively mobilize the villagers to carry out self-help and other projects as directed by government. As intermediaries, they relayed messages that the audience was at least willing to hear, and otherwise adjusted and placated interests with primarily verbal behavior.

Collier et al., using a sample from 20 villages, compared the average income of "households" with a member serving either on the village council or as a cell leader to those without such a connection. He found the office-holding households average only 9 percent above the average incomes of those without a member holding office. From this result, Collier et al. concluded that "there is no powerful link between wealth and political participation and influence in rural Tanzania" (1986, 113). This use of averages for these offices and categories, however, does not give a reliable result in relation to the 30–40 percent who are the very poorest. Many with very high incomes will not have members in councilor or cell leader roles, since most of these roles are the ten-house cell leaders, who are saddled with the often unwanted responsibility of settling neighborhood disputes, and who may informally be clients of better-off non-office-holding households. These possibilities may serve to bring up the wealth averages for non-officeholder households. Furthermore, the authors admit explicitly that they "cannot distinguish between the influential and the less influential ten-cell leaders" (1986, 113). In fact, with many ten-cell leaders engaged in no more real leadership than dispute settling in their immediate neighborhoods or lineage segments, we cannot accord political influence as such to this office; going by "section" (the unit between ten-house groups and the village) in analyzing leader office holding would have served much better. Finally, inasmuch as "household" is not clearly defined, we cannot tell whether *extended family* connections to officeholders are reflected in the data, which would allow many very poor nuclear families to be included in the category of officeholder households, bringing down the income averages for the latter category. Such data may tell us that many middle-level households can participate in noninfluential offices, but it does not measure the involvement of the very lowest strata or the actual influence of the higher economic strata.

The village leadership is made up of a village council elected by the village assembly—whose chair and secretary, however, must usually be those of the party branch. Numerous studies indicate that the village leaders regularly tend to be wealthy, older, male, and literate (Fortmann 1980, 50–55). Such leaders are apparently elected in part for their instrumental capabilities as intermediaries with government, but some studies indicate that people also look to them also as a source of loans or other favors (Fortmann 1980, 51, 55). Village leaders often own shops or other businesses in town, and they are generally in a position to protect them when necessary. In short, while village leaders are at times in a position to defend the village against undue governmental demands, more continuously they use their institutional position to protect and adjust their interests and the interests of those linked to them in the village; as summed up by Fortmann:

The wealthy peasant (who in most instances is not all that wealthy) is likely to side with his fellow villagers against the alien (and indeed wealthy) bureaucrat when the chips are down. This is not to say that he will not work the system to his own advantage. Wealthier peasants are clear beneficiaries in peasant/bureaucrat patron-client systems. And wealthy leaders may subvert projects which are against their interests. (1980, 57)

The flow of resources relevant to the poorer strata have increasingly been "decentralized" to the village level, as in the case of Tanzania Rural Development Bank loans to small farmers, which are channeled through the village government, and the rare and uneven access to fertilizer, which is controlled by local cooperative officials, usually with close links to the village government. It is clear that the favor of village officials is necessary for gaining the peasant any advantages that might be had through the government.

All this is not to suggest that the village leaders are always unified behind the chairman and secretary, as one might conclude from the many studies and articles in the press that have described authoritarian rule by the top officialdom. There may be conflict within the elite—sometimes between factions that are interpreted to be modern versus traditional factions, as in cases where an accusation of witchcraft is leveled against a modern or aggressive farmer or bureaucrat. The early study of Van Hekken and Van Velzen (1972), which was made toward the end of the comparatively open period for social science research in Tanzania prior to villagization, focused on the lower-level dynamics of intra-village political conflict in one area, finding patron-client involvement on each side.

Outside of a type of dispute settlement that may draw poorer clients in to support their patrons, however, the usual pattern of poor peasant behavior in other areas of village politics is characterized by passive silence in public political arenas. There are two familiar interpretations, the first of which is the most common. It focuses on the ignorance and lack of skills of the poorer strata in making their participation effective, which is reinforced by the sense that key decisions, particularly in development-related matters, will be made by the higher-ups anyway. Indeed, by far the easiest and safest answer that an uninfluential peasant can give to any interviewer asking about nonparticipation is, "I don't understand these things." Such an answer can bring on trouble with no one. To accept it at face value, however, seems to underestimate the experience and capacity of judgment of peasants who have observed plenty of what goes on in their village. It also tends to overlook the whole dimension in village politics of informal and private resistance (both passive and active), which peasants have used from time immemorial to express their actual preferences and contend with encroachments by outsiders.[15] Fortmann's review of the literature by Tanzanian researchers lists some examples of how peasants go about opposing or avoiding having to respond to officials' directives, such as doing nothing, making only a token effort, managing to have "an unfortunate accident" preventing their carrying out a directive, seeming to misunderstand official instructions, or engaging in implicit or explicit bargaining (1980, 86–87). Of course, considering the political sensitivity of these matters and the difficulties of doing research that penetrates secrecy and the subjectivity of perceptions of them, existing studies are unable to reveal how much even these informal acts, when they involve poorer peasants, are done at the instigation of the patrons.

A second explanation of the public arena passivity and silence on the part of the poorer peasants is intimidation by the implicit threat of violence or incarceration by government officials. While many believe the government and party are willing to use, or at least to threaten, physical coercion in the rural areas (particularly selective, behind-the-scenes repression), the weight of this factor is impossible to fathom. The easing up of regime control at the end of the 1980s may have lessened the perception of this threat, but the advent of multiparty politics in 1992 and 1993 drew attention to it once again. Most notably, while parties other than the CCM are formally and technically free to organize gatherings in the rural areas, in fact, the bulk of the administrative and legal structure of single-party rule remains in effect, despite the urging of the official Nyalali Commission report of 1991 to abolish or revise the oppressive "40 Laws" (see Smith 1994). The district commissioner and divisional secretary (in charge of security matters below the district level) are empowered to use the police (or approve their use after the fact) to detain anyone, almost at will. Opposition parties complain that their local supporters are picked up and otherwise harassed and that district commissioners in rural areas routinely deny permission for open meetings and rallies unless the speaker is to be one of the party's better-known leaders (usually a lawyer) from Dar Es Salaam. It was reported in March 1993 by the Mara regional chairman of one of the opposition parties, NCCR-Mageuzi, that NCCR-Mageuzi members were being attacked by CCM people, with some whipping and property destruction, leading to 61 party members from two villages fleeing their homes to go into hiding in the bush[16]; additionally, according to the report, the party's Bunda district headquarters was broken into and property was stolen, all with no action by the police. This led to the party's national chairman, Mabere Marando, making an appeal to Prime Minister John Malecela to stop the attacks.

Arguably, however, for those with influence the official or private use of the threat of violent repression seems far more complicated than the easier and quieter use of threat of the withdrawal of economic benefits and opportunities under the control of private or governmental influentials. In one area, however, the threat of violence is clearly real; this concerns the participation of women. Women tend to be silent and nonparticipative in most public arenas, no doubt partly due to lack of time, energy, and skills, but also in some cases due to their husbands' use of intimidation and threat at home, including the men's threat of violence (Fortmann 1980, 61–63).

There have also appeared some very sweeping and abstract approaches to understanding these problems in Tanzania which tend to pass over the question of differential participation by the poorer 30 to 50 percent. Hyden (1980) argued that the party-government center aimed to "capture" the peasants, but that the latter were able to withdraw from control by the village authorities into an autonomous "economy of affection," whereby village- and kinship-based patterns of economic interaction substitute for larger market connections, in a degree of self-sufficiency. Villagization, according to this view, became a desperate attempt to take control of the peasants, which ultimately failed as they withdrew economically from the market into subsistence production, due to a lack of available products to buy. Arguably, however, the unofficial "parallel market" remained alive and well through the late 1970s and the crisis of the early 1980s, and Havnevik (1988) has argued persuasively that Tanzanian peasants remain rather thoroughly enmeshed in connections with, and dependencies on, the market economy. Available studies indicate that great variations and blends exist in the degree of state control, market dependency, and vitality of the economy of affection. Many among even the poorest peasants are involved, in one way or another, in commerce, crafts, and small-scale industry (where it exists), though usually only at a very low return and making a very small contribution to the farming household's survival package. Of course, those experiencing a yearly food deficit must normally buy food at high prices (by historical standards). In any case, whether involved in necessary dependencies on better-off kin (on the economy of affection model) or on non-kin economic relationships of all kinds, the situation of dependency caused by food insecurity still holds for the poorer sector of the rural economy.

The decentralization of the early 1980s gave greater authority to the district councils and new marketing cooperatives, which can only have increased the power of the rural wealthy and influential over against the administrative hierarchy (Holmquist 1983, 10). Doubtless the post-1983 relaxation of restrictions on movement must have further loosened the control of village governmental authorities (Havnevik 1988, 341). The very poor, of course, still had to depend on the village and higher authorities for the distribution of food in the bad or crisis year, but under the circumstances, their dependence on nongovernmental middle- and upper-level households seems as much, or more, important as the dependence on the village government.

While we cannot specifically generalize about whether the upper or the middle rural socioeconomic strata participate most, we still seem justified in concluding that the poorest 30 to 40 percent participate least, and when they do, probably as clientelistic supporters of others. It is the upper *and middle* strata, comprising individuals not moved by villagization, who were already best served by the pattern that villagization took (see, e.g., Kjaerby 1988, 39, 54). It is these households whose most crucial requirements for independent survival are met. Where there is participation by women, however, at best it involves a few middle- or upper-strata women with education or other advantages who participate (Bertell 1985, 59). Largely left out of the process are the concerns and potential involvement of the 30 to 50 percent of people who are very poor relative to the local context, a large proportion of which are women (Bertell 1985, 47–48). The poorest have (a) desperate needs, with yearly hunger over one or more months of the year, (b) a government ideology stressing meeting their needs and development requirements, respecting women as equals, and similar mandates, and (c) a government policy of local self-reliance that focuses attention on what happens in the local arenas. The poorest 30 to 50 percent would seem to have every reason to sacrifice time to participate, especially in slack periods in the agricultural cycle, and yet they do not. I will argue that in explaining this fact we cannot rule out, as a major factor, the economic dependencies in which the rural poorest must engage.

THE TARGET GROUP INDICATOR

This preliminary look at backgrounds of three cases with regard to poverty and political participation by the poor suggests only a general relationship between a group in a certain sort of poverty and a condition in the sociopolitical sphere. It generally indicates a connection between (a) a lower food-insecure of the population stratum and, in the context of local democratic institutions and many issues handled by political arenas that do, or might, affect the poor, (b) an *absence* of autonomous political involvement on the part of the poor themselves. It does not reveal specifically who the food-insecure poor are by any readily observable indicator or what sort of connection there may be between this category and the lack of independent democratic political participation in local arenas.

How are we to operationalize the classification of third world rural dwellers so as to distinguish better and worse conditions in a way relevant to food insecurity and choice constraint? Traditionally, social science has used various broad concepts through which to differentiate rural social and economic strata, most notably "class" and "inequality," and the literature on peasant economic "differentiation" is full of diverse criteria for classifying or measuring the relative positions on the spectrum from poverty to wealth. The Marxian use of the term "class" with regard to property ownership seems to crudely fit the relationship of landowner and landless, sharecropping tenant/laborer, for example, as in the case of the Latin American *latifundia*. However, it is of little help here, not least because the problems of food-choice vulnerability obviously extend beyond the category of "landless" (as to means of production), and well into the ranks of owners of small parcels of land.[17]

Some analysts have tried to better capture actual inequality with measures of, variously, operational land *holding* (including tenancies), income (in grain or currency), yearly surplus or deficit (in grain, money, or number of malnutrition or starvation months per year), caloric intake, or functional economic category (owner-cultivator, owner-cum-sharecropper, owner-cum-laborer, owner-employer, absentee owner, landless laborer, etc.). There is great variation in the availability and reliability of statistics for these factors at the macro and micro levels, and no one factor by itself is a wholly adequate measure of relative position for wealth or choice. The best combinations for indicating relative position are not available in macro-level data for third world countries; only long-term, in-depth, painstaking, micro-level study (exemplified by that of Jansen 1986 in Bangladesh) can reveal the distribution of all key resources. The complexity of the problem of accurately identifying the victims of poverty is in itself enough to discourage many people seeking practical ways of helping the poorest. Under these circumstances, however, what is needed is a comparatively *available* indicator, or pair of indicators, that tend, in the main, to be *best* linked with other telling indicators. For each of the three nation cases (with the heaviest emphasis on Bangladesh, for which the most information is available), we shall explore what the indicator might be and what it might have to do with the clientelist dependencies that serve to constrain choice.

THE TARGET GROUP IN BANGLADESH

Regarding the rural areas, where 80 to 85 percent of Bangladeshis live, the great majority of studies indicate that overall economic level for households is reliably and positively correlated with the amount of productive land owned. Observers and peasants alike generally classify rural economic positions according to how much cultivable land one owns, and virtually all sources on rural Bangladesh indicate the social and economic importance of owning land.[18] To be sure, some people hold niches in the trade and service economies that enable them to have a surplus food despite very low landownership levels, but even then, profit tends to be turned to buying land (often for renting out) in order to have at least a foothold in the agricultural economy. More immediately for our purposes here, land in rural Bangladesh remains the central resource for contending with hunger and malnutrition-related health threats, and it is the most important source of employment of family members and of surplus for starting up nonfarm activities.

Not surprisingly, there is a reliable link of various strata of landownership to common measures of poverty and nutritional adequacy. Statistics for caloric intake in rural Bangladesh indicate that ownership of less than an acre of agricultural land for an average family size of five is fairly reliably linked to poverty, economic insecurity, and protein-calorie insufficiency. Data gathered by BIDS teams from 1988–1989 show that while the poverty rate for those owning under a half acre of agricultural land is in the range of 71 to 79 percent, still, fully 61 percent of those in the ½– to 1½–acre range lived in poverty; above 1½ acres— which can nonetheless be entirely insufficient for a large family—the proportion in poverty drops to 44.5 percent (and it is much lower for larger land owners, of course) (Hossain 1992b, 170). That ½ to 1½ acres of land ownership is the key *transitional range* for poverty and malnutrition is also indicated by recent BIDS data on food deficits. The latter showed that while 44 percent of landless people and 39 percent of owners of up to ½ acre lived in *chronic* food deficit (roughly equal to the proportion in only occasional deficit), for owners of ½ to 1½ acres, the proportion in chronic deficit dropped to 12 percent, with 63 percent in occasional food deficit (Sen 1992a, 222). Moreover, the ownership of nonland assets jumps as we go from the landless through ½ acre category to owners of ½ to 1½ acres. BIDS data for 1989–1990 show that landless people and owners of up to ½ acre show 18–20 percent owning a cow, and 8–9 percent owning a bull; the proportions owning a cow jump to 40 percent and 47 percent, respectively, among the ½ to 1½ and 1½ to 2½ acre owners, respectively, and 29 percent and 48 percent, respectively, owning a bull (Sen 1992d, 224). Finally, of those people living in poverty in rural Bangladesh, 44 percent owned no cultivated land, 16 percent owned up to ½ an acre, and 21 percent owned ½ to 1½ acres (Hossain 1992b, 170). With the ½ to 1½ acre owners including such a substantial proportion of the poor yet remaining a mixed category in this respect, our choice of 1 acre as the minimum level of ownership seems justified, though necessarily a bit arbitrary and only a guidepost amid much variation in family and agricultural circumstances.

A further indication in this direction is found in somewhat older data about nutritional levels at various levels of landownership, which do use one acre as an ownership cutoff point in both good and bad years. Nutrition survey data for both the good year of 1975–1976 and the poor one of 1981–1982 indicated that per capita daily food intake was correlated with household landholding, with a significant dividing line for poverty lying somewhere between one and two acres for an average family size. The range from bad year (1981–1982) to good year (1975–1976) averages for one- to three-acre owners was 1,986 to 2,193, with the good year figure above the recognized Bangladeshi malnutrition level of 2,122; however, for half to one-acre owners, the range dropped to 1,775 in the bad year to 2,035 in the good year, and for zero to half an acre, the range fell to 1,672– 1,925.[19] Protein intake in the bad year rose above the absolute minimum only above one-acre ownership (Ahmed et al. 1990, 55). Only the one- to three-acre owners in the good year averaged over the absolute poverty level intake of 2,100–2,150 calories a day, and in the bad year, the averages for the categories under one acre were below the extreme poverty level of 1,800 calories of caloric intake a day. In the bad year, three-acre and larger households averaged 2,222 calories, putting them above both poverty lines. The death rate due to malnutrition for owners of land up to one acre is more than double that of owners of one to three acres, and seems to hold steady above one acre over all ownership levels (Ahmed et al. 1990, 59).

The category of landless to one acre owners appears to encompass half or more of the rural Bangladeshi population. In late 1970s data using a one-acre dividing point, 59 percent of rural Bangladeshi households (comprising 51 percent of the rural Bangladeshi population) owned under one acre (Jannuzi and Peach 1980, Tables D.1, D.2, E.1, E.2), while 61 percent of rural Bangladeshis fell below the acute poverty income level (Ahmad and Hossain 1983, 19). More recently, 1983–1984 BBS census data, using a half-acre cutoff, show 48.9 percent of households under half an acre, and BIDS data from January 1988 show 46 percent of households under half an acre (Rahman and Hossain 1992, 18). We may roughly conclude that dietary sufferers with direct threats to their health include the vast majority of rural residents owning under an acre (including most landless laborers) and many in the one to two-acre range (especially those with large families). This situation affects something like 55 to 65 percent of rural households and 45 to 55 percent of the rural Bangladeshi population.

It is important to get some sense of the qualitative situation of these households in reference to nutritional intake, which can be had from the micro-level village studies that have been done. The reasons for such a persistent linkage of landownership levels with nutritional risk are rooted in the economic context for households of around one acre or less. BIDS data gathered at the end of the 1980s indicate that 46 percent of the population were living both in poverty *and* in at least occasional food deficit, with more than a third of these reporting being chronically in food deficit (derived from data in Hossain 1992a, 52, Table 4.5). Of those owning under a half-acre, fully 88 percent were in the food deficit category (Sen 1992a, 222, Table 12.1). There is a high frequency of serious food deficit for such households over at least some weeks of the slack season every year and in some months of the bad crop year (expected to be at least one in five).[20] These land-poor individuals find themselves, either yearly or at least in bad years, unable to cover their minimal food needs year-round. The slack season, including the period prior to the main *aman* harvest, and in some areas including part of the post harvest dry season, is one of food insecurity and hunger for those without surplus food.

This food deficit must be covered by loans or other sorts of opportunities, which tend to exist on condition of one or more critical clientelistic relationships, which they must maintain. For example, Jansen's penetrating work focusing on patron-client aspects of the situation of the rural poor shows their characteristic reliance on clientelistic dependencies on better-off households (often relatives) from whom to borrow to cover their food deficits (see Jansen 1986).

As indicated in the recent BIDS study, a critical asset for a household is to link itself to a potential lender who knows the poor client's situation well enough and has enough control over it to be sure of repayment in some form (Sen 1992a, 215–216). Hence, the relevant economic context includes the clientelistic dependency relationships and choice structure facing this category of peasants in their often-desperate efforts to get enough to eat for their families. Without asset collateral, the poor often must pay prohibitively high rates to professional or semiprofessional lenders (Sen 1992a, 215).

Sources of such patronage for credit in times of distress can be quite diverse. Examples are "purchases on credit from shopkeepers-cum-lenders in times of acute shortage, *dadan* trade advances (i.e., loans against sales of output in advance), landlords' credit to tenants, employers' credit to wage labourers" (Sen 1992a, 216). Whatever the source, however, the relationship must be somewhat stable; as Sen puts it,

For such transactions to be effective, they must take place in the context of a *long-term* relationship between the two parties. The threat of credit cessation acts in these cases as an effective enforcement mechanism since poor borrowers expect repeated transactions in the future in times of unanticipated crisis-events and risks. (1992a, 216)

If they owe money to the patron at harvest, the peasants must sell (often to the patron) when prices are lowest and buy later in the slack season, when prices are highest. In such relationships the client whose fortunes are on the wane must periodically mortgage (and eventually sell) to the lending patron parcels of land to cover unpaid debts.

Households with a stronger resource and labor base are in a stronger position to secure patrons and the opportunities they offer than than those owning less land. White makes an interesting distinction, within a "lower" stratum owning under 1²/₃ acres, between (a) a "lower/strong" category tending "to have much stronger social networks and to maximize their labor through small business sidelines, and place a higher priority on sending their children to school" (1991, 39), and (b) a "lower-vulnerable" category of households, which lack these advantages. Of course, the advantages of clientelistic relationships depend also on overall market conditions to provide niches for intensive activity. A bad agricultural year tends to be a bad one for rural market activities generally; comparatively strong access to minimal food under these conditions is temporary, with the dependency becoming rather more stark in the bad year.

The very worst off have little or no land with which to interest a lender-patron. Data gathered in a 1984–1985 round-the-year survey sponsored by the United Nations Development Program (UNDP) of poor-stratum households in six villages in various parts of the country revealed an average daily intake of only 1,526 calories, with some households consuming much less; the worst off were the nonfarm workers, those self-employed in services, and farmers with under .3 acres as well as destitutes (Hossain 1987). Perhaps half the owners of less than an acre are completely landless, and hence, comparatively unattractive as clients to better-off households wishing to lend in hopes of eventually acquiring the

land of the borrower. Then, the incentive to lend can be at most to keep a reliably captive laborer on whom the patron can count at peak times when labor is
comparatively more scarce. Landless people who rely only on available labor
opportunities, without being able to count on a specific patron, are mainly dependent on the vicissitudes of seasonal agricultural activity and cannot ordinarily
count on having slack-season labor opportunities. These are likely to be constantly on the lookout for anyone who can provide short-term food security by
supplying credit or employment as needed to cover food deficits. As the work of
H. Z. Rahman makes clear, having exhausted their food stocks being and forced
to purchase food on the market at peak prices, those in distress often are forced
into "disadvantageous contracts such as forward sale of labour at much cheaper
rates, borrowing at very high levels of interest and distress sale of household
utensils and animal stocks" (1992c, 265). Thus, extreme degrees of current starvation may be averted, but the crisis will be extended by subsequent months of
essentially working without income to repay the credit (Rahman 1992c, 265). If
individuals have the connections to participate in a migrant labor gang, they may
be as dependent on the gang's leader as they would be on a patron.[21] Hence, very
low landownership succeeds here, too, in identifying the overall target group
four our purposes.

As indicated above, for the target households, cash crop income involves
selling at harvest, when the price is very low, only later to have to buy food in
slack season, when the price is high. Households owning a total of some part of
an acre (usually in multiple small plots) often undergo some starvation, if necessary, in order to minimize borrowing. This, in turn, can slow the consequent loss
of remaining land to mortgage and sale to the principal creditor. Keeping to a
minimum the borrowing needed to cover food deficits thus rationally stems or
postpones the approach to landlessness, which obviously would put the household into a more precarious situation with even less bargaining power. Such a
land-short condition is also related to much diminished capacity (a) to own and
maintain a viable team of cattle for plowing (and, hence, to sharecrop, as well),
and (b) to pay a controller of water—for example, from a mechanized tubewell,
whose owners may charge 25 percent of the crop or more (Khan and Hossain
1989, 55)—for enough irrigated acreage to grow a cost-effective, dry-season
boro rice crop.

Not surprisingly, those with some agricultural land but under half an acre experience a nutritional situation very little different from the landless. Owners of
up to half an acre actually have just below the food and calorie intake of the
landless, with 683 grams and 1,924 calories per person per day for the former
versus 694 grams and 1,925 calories for the latter; owners of half to one acre did
a bit better with 745 grams and 2,035 calories, but 1–3 acre owners move above
nutritional minima, with 785 grams and 2,193 calories (Rahman 1986, 43).

As can be gathered, the role of bad-year conditions—well known by heads of
rural households in Bangladesh today, especially from the famine year of 1974–
1975—is very great in the structuring of social practices affecting the poor in
Bangladesh. Even a very localized crop disruption can stimulate speculative

hoarding all over the country along with high prices for rice, affecting all who are in deficit. Peasant motivation in both borrowing and lending seems to be deeply tied to what will happen in that kind of year. In picking one-acre owner-ship as the upper limit of the vulnerable category, and in emphasizing one to one and a half acres as a threshold for viability in choice and needs provision, this inquiry has kept closely in mind the reality that the normal-year resource posi-tion is often quite inadequate to handle conditions in a bad year, and that bad year outcomes, in turn, can structure the conditions of families for many years hence (see Jahangir 1979, 196–197). It is primarily owned acreage—and access to the resources to make it productive (especially a pair of work animals and control of enough paddy straw to feed them)—that can make it possible for a Bangladesh smallholder to hold the line in a bad year, suffering no more than a few weeks of starvation or a few months of malnutrition, with no lost land and no impairment of productive functioning and choice making for the future.

How many are in the under-one-acre category that forms our target group? We have statistics for ownership of under less than a half-acre; and the number of landless and under-half-acre owners together increased 33 percent faster than rural population growth between 1960 and 1977, with the total share of popula-tion increasing from 35 percent in 1960 to 46 percent in 1977 (Ahmad and Hos-sain 1983, 31). This trend was not a steady one, however. Key indicators of landless and small-owning numbers had not increased greatly between 1961 and 1968.[22] It seemed that it was the period of the major beginning of commerciali-zation, the 1970s, that produced the data on land inequality that supported viewing it as a continuation—indeed, an acceleration—of the long-term histori-cal trend of impoverishment of an ever-larger "poor" proportion of the rural Bangladeshi population. The nutrition survey of the middle 1970s and the land-holding survey of 1977–1978 showed basically more of what earlier studies had revealed, which Van Schendel (1981) had also observed continuing in the same villages.

Clearly, the decline in land ownership over the 1970s was dramatic indeed. From 1974 to 1979, mean household ownership for the bottom 50 percent of landholders dropped from 1.2 acres to .5 acres (Hossain 1981, 95), indicating that a clear majority of rural cultivators dropped below the cutoff range for minimal choice and welfare that is emphasized here. Moreover, a 1976 ILO re-port indicated that in the 1970s under-one-acre owners sold "well over half of their remaining land in each year" (Khan 1976, 33). The central process afoot is one of steadily (or rapidly, in a bad year) mounting debt incurred to handle food deficits, resulting in the inevitable mortgage and eventual sale of the remaining land, as traced in detail by Jansen (1986).

Observers have taken different viewpoints on the degrees and ways in which economic inequality increased over the period of the 1970s. There was room for debate between (a) those viewing high-yielding variety (HYV) rice commer-cialization through the lenses of the "polarization" thesis, which stated that the rich were exploiting dependency amid HYV commercialization to drive the great majority to landlessness, and (b) those using a more complex "pauperization" model (e.g., Van Schendel 1981), which integrated the traditionally important factor of equal inheritance partitioning for all strata to yield a picture in which all but portions of the highest strata tended to sink to ever smaller landholdings. Adnan's perceptive review of village studies mentions his own 1986 study findings and proceeds to what is probably the safest conclusion:

For the Chittagong village of Shangkhomala . . . polarization had clearly increased during the 12 years from 1974 to 1986. The uppermost holding-size groups had increased their absolute and relative command over land, while almost all other intermediate and lower holding-size groups displayed corresponding declines.

The overall picture from [village studies], therefore, is complex. Long-run trends from the 1920s and the 1930s . . . are suggestive of alternate phases of polarization and pauperization (i.e., downward aggregate shifts), with the latter becoming increasingly dominant. However, studies which have followed the story into the 1980's have found polarization taking precedence in at least some parts of the country. The available evidence from [village studies] does not warrant more definitive conclusions. (1989, 48)

The 1980s, which saw a rapid expansion of both HYV rice and food-for-work projects, seem to have seen a stabilization in the factors that contribute to land loss, no doubt slowing it down. Data from the BIDS survey in the late 1980s show that among households reporting occasional or chronic food deficit, 9 percent reported "improved" land stability in recent years, 59 percent unchanged, and 32 percent with declining land stability; in contrast, 55 percent of food *surplus* households reporting improved land stability. Even those reporting improved land stability had their mobility "restricted to a narrow band with little prospects for escaping from the land-poverty trap" (Sen 1992a, 220). Upward mobility may be reported from chronic deficit to occasional deficit status, but rarely from deficit to surplus (Sen 1992a, 220). Hence, productivity increases and nonland opportunities permitting some mobility do not remove the limits set by lack of land (Sen 1992a, 220–221). Regarding the target group of an acre or less (to landless), Adnan's findings regarding the villages he studied are striking in that while there is significant upward mobility among owners of one to eight acres, those owning under one acre have experienced no upward mobility, only moving downward or sideways (Adnan 1987, 62). The indications are that conditions for this vulnerable category can at best be stable in normal years while worsening in bad years.

A related issue seems to be raised by data indicating that *nonfarm employment* increased over the mid-1980s, including among some of the landless, who do not have agricultural tasks to compete for their time with laboring for others. Certainly, the good-year agricultural economy provides greater incomes for the better-off, which trickle down in greater spending on services and draw more of the desperate, and not so desperate, into services (often self-employed). For example, White (1991) observed during this period that alongside the increased presence of rice mills, which displaced women's husking labor, there was an increase in "rice business" among women—buying paddy, transporting it to the mill for processing, and selling the rice. Furthermore, the Grameen Bank program has provided short-term loans to a small portion of the landless and near-landless, which can be reissued for those with a record of prompt repayment.

However, there are limitations on the possible impact of these developments. NGO credit programs reach only 10 percent of the landless and functionally landless households in the country, while only a few really target agricultural credit versus general education, training, and support services (Sen 1992a, 214). The Grameen Bank, for its part, seems to work mainly with trade, craft, or livestock opportunities, which serves as a limiting factor (Sen 1992a, 214). The number of such niches that can provide the rapid turnover for Grameen's 6-month loan repayment seems limited, and the program has not been a significant presence in agricultural production.[23] In general, most individuals shifting into services (e.g., rice processing or rickshaw pulling) seem to be achieving only part-time, low-return employment, usually at below the agricultural labor wage. They are often pushed into service roles by economic desperation and loss of land, rather than drawn in by positive incentives. Those doing significantly better in off-farm employment are likely to be those individuals already possessing the resources—usually from agriculture—to support family members in a trade or service niche on a scale sufficient to provide food-significant returns. Finally, people from households owning under an acre who are doing significantly better in a trade or processing niche—perhaps with Grameen Bank loans—may tend to be active on the required scale only with the backing of a patron, often a kinship connection who is in a position to informally guarantee the loan.

Of course, we are not claiming the criterion of household landownership of up to one acre to be an infallible indicator of the food deficit risk (and immediate health threat) discussed here. Particular household conditions, of course, vary significantly with diverse actual circumstances (in ways familiar to micro-level researchers). At one extreme, it is possible that a half-acre owner's clientelistic dependency could be on a very economically secure kin-linked household head who has made clear that he does not care about the social and political behavior of the client and whose character backs up that expectation. On the other hand, in a great variety of Bangladeshi rural situations, many households owning over an acre of agricultural land still lack assurance of having minimal food and health (by South Asian standards), possessing at best the short-term access provided by economic opportunities offered by a patron. The one-acre cutoff point used here is well below the figures of one and two-thirds or two acres, which are usually mentioned as "self-sufficiency" minima.[24] An acre or more of land is best not regarded as providing self-sufficiency alone (though it could conceivably under prime HYV conditions), but rather considered as a *base* for struggle, by choice of *further* efforts, toward attaining a minimally adequate diet for family members over all 12 months of the year.

Moreover, soil and water conditions vary between districts and among villages within districts. The often rich flood-plain agriculture found in much of Bangladesh is not within equal reach of all areas, and no more than 20 percent of cultivated land was irrigated in the early 1980s (Ahmad and Hossain 1983, 48). In relatively poor areas, the amount of land required for owner-cultivation to avoid food deficit over the whole year may be one and a half to two acres,[25] while in a richer context, with irrigated HYVs, in an average crop year, one acre can be sufficient. For our purposes, the latter possibility bolsters the choice of one acre as a minimal household survival base rather than amounts up to two acres, as it at least helps avoid overestimating the numbers of vulnerable households.

Additionally, there are variations in family size departing from the hypothetical average of five that is incorporated into the one-acre ownership figure. The *per capita* amount of land that is owned and owner-cultivated would be a better figure for making these distinctions; households with a larger family size can suffer months of starvation per year with as much as one and a quarter acres being owner-cultivated, while a three-member household with that amount under family cultivation might do quite well by rural Bangladeshi standards. Along with a variety of useful sorts of data other than household landownership (such as that on land that is mortgaged with a loss of usufruct), *per capita* land ownership is not widely available for generalization over the whole of Bangladesh.

Moreover, the age structure of the household (often measured via a "worker-consumer ratio") affects how well it can avail itself of the land it owns and its wage-labor opportunities at times of peak labor demand. A family with two labor-age sons but only a half-acre of owner-cultivated land has surplus labor (say, one of the sons), which can contribute a wage-labor income beyond the land base. Hence, again, the fact that 50 to 60 percent of rural Bangladeshi households own less than an acre is not intended to mean that all those families find themselves in an insecure situation—only that *most* will, and that on balance, the numbers in insecure households with slightly above one acre will, in all likelihood, outnumber those in exceptional viable households owning less than one acre.

Finally, there are differences among regions and districts regarding the availability of other ordinary income-earning opportunities (a) in and around agriculture, such as sharecropping, wage labor, and lower return activities such as husking, rice business, small scale petty trade (such as in wood), and begging, with which small holding households try to supplement returns from their own land, and (b) outside agriculture in trading niches, government jobs, or other informal positions. These latter roles can secure incomes high enough to be equivalent, for example, to that associated with owning one to three acres of farmed land (with incomes higher than this, rural Bangladeshis tend to invest in land, removing themselves from the low ownership category). While small numbers of landless and near landless people who do well from commercial or government undertakings do undoubtedly make their way into statistics of the group of those owning less than an acre, they appear not to number anywhere near the number of owners of between one and two acres who suffer health-threatening dietary poverty or the risk of it should they displease a patron.

The landless-to-one-acre ownership range, then, is meant as a conservatively crafted one, within which we can be *fairly sure* that a household will lack assured self-sufficiency in food production under its own control, and at the least will be uncertain of adequate food throughout the year. This cutoff point is low enough that the 50 to 60 percent figure of rural households owning less than an acre will probably *understate* the numbers in the vulnerable category. Because of its linkages to a whole range of important factors, this demarcator will, in turn, serve as a rough cutoff point for minimal independence in social, economic, and political clientelism—that is, for minimal significant choice in expression, association, and the food-productive endeavor.

In Bangladesh, smallholders living under these circumstances farm their land carefully and intensively in order to get every shred of return. The productivity of land increases in *inverse* proportion to household farm size right down to those owning only one-half to three quarters of an acre. A contributor to this productivity intensification on small plots is the otherwise underutilized labor supply that is often brought into play on smallholdings, with the willingness of small farmers to invest much meticulous labor in their own farms in order to get an incremental return. This is in part why, with available water and a reliable supply of other HYV inputs, family survival with a small surplus is possible with ownership of as little as an acre of cultivable land.

Finally, our identifying the key resource as agricultural land owned unencumbered, and the cutoff point as an acre of such clearly owned land, should not be taken to mean that *degrees* of food security or significant choice within the vulnerable stratum owning under one acre are measured by how much land is owned. Some landless laborers involved in migration north in the dry season may have years that are better than those of a household owning, say, half an acre that is unencumbered. It is only argued that those in the category demarcated by the land cutoff will characteristically be *vulnerable*, possessing only temporary food security at best and lacking the dual options of having assured food access and of significant choice. This long-term vulnerability will remain regardless of their situation at any given time in relation to these human rights values, which I regard as crucial to the foundations of respect for economic-social and civil-political human rights.

BOTSWANA: THE RESOURCE KEY AND ITS CUTOFF POINT

To identify the vulnerable category of food-insecure poor, we need to refine our conceptualization of the key scarce resource to fit the particular conditions affecting the target group. For the rural poor of Bangladesh, the most reliable indicator of the vulnerable category was free and clear possession (no part mortgaged) of an acre or less of paddy land for a household of five. In Botswana, the key predicting resource for food-effective agricultural capacity for the rural poor at present is cattle, primarily as draft power, supplemented where possible by food-viable labor opportunities as a back-up component. Beer brewing is a well-known after-harvest activity for the women, but the supply of grain for this, and hence the resultant income, often depend on the capacity to plow. Poor women derive small benefit from beer brewing other than turning some necessary food into necessary cash for nonfood household necessities (often directly at the expense of later weeks of inadequate nutrition).

The most pressing specific requirement within this category is traction for a plow under the household's own control. This normally involves the capacity for timely plowing of a subsistence-adequate field or fields with a household-owned plow-traction unit—a plow with whatever source of traction will pull it and the labor to operate it. Control over such a team ensures plowing with the first rains, once there is drinking water "at the lands" (in Botswana, at the fields which are often distant from the village) and the cattle have gained strength on the first green shoots, which is usually in November or early December. This makes possible a crop even if subsequent rain is irregular, and it permits a long enough growing season before the cold nights of June (and/or cattle grazing on the neighbors' stubble have a chance to destroy the crops).[26] The most common avenue to such a capacity is ownership of enough cattle—minimally, at least 10 to 15 animals in the herd overall (and at best up to 40) for ongoing use of 6 to 8 oxen at a time (Vierich and Sheppard 1980, 7, 18; Koojman 1978, 182–183). Unfortunately, drought occurs every so often and small herds suffer cattle mortality rates of two to three times more than average-size herds (Harvey and Lewis 1990, 75).

Additionally, draft oxen make possible transport (with a sledge or cart) of the harvest, water (in drums), firewood, and other requirements. Transport capacities are particularly important for women and households living at the lands some or all of the year while trying to maintain links with the village as well, with its better social, educational, health, and water availabilities during the dry, noncultivating season. Finally, households with the secure income to hire tractors at a premium—up-front money sufficient for timely plowing—may also be said to have the requisite capacity for independent, food-effective plowing.

Households who do not own a six-animal team of oxen (no doubt half or more of rural households in Botswana), must borrow or rent draft power, often from relatives. They normally achieve less than their full food needs from agriculture, and fall into our vulnerable category. The most common trade by the poor is of labor for the draft team owner's timely plowing, in return for late plowing on the laborer's field. This trade is absolutely necessary in the struggle of the poor household for survival—rendering it a very significant alternative indeed. However, its effectiveness is limited. As is well documented in the literature on this subject, the borrower's field will be plowed late—usually too late to take effective advantage of the first rains in October–November. This often means poor soil moisture when plowing is done and poor germination, as well as a shorter growing season and lower overall productivity. Most very poor individuals cannot afford the high rent for the use of a tractor and its driver to plow the eight to ten acres that are minimally necessary to bring in enough sorghum (and maize in some areas) for year-round food access for a family of five. Even if they could afford it, their small fields would be likely to give them low priority, usually making the plowing too late given the rate of tractor breakdown in the peak plowing weeks.

Additionally, this exchange of labor for draft power by those who do not own or control it is a costly one for the cattle-poor in terms of productive labor time on their own plots. Not only do they sacrifice timely plowing—the most strategic loss—but they may also be required to commit to labor later in the course of the growing season as well. A lack of timely weeding can be a key result in reducing food capacity, but a lack of effective bird scaring and harvesting can play a role too. In general, rural opportunities for labor for others are readily available only at the times when it is most needed by owners well-off enough to hire, at times of peak activity in the agricultural cycle, when it is drawn away from timely work on the poor peasant's own field and its productivity. In a bad rainfall year threatening crop failure, of course, such service opportunities related to agricultural production can be much reduced, with severe consequences even for those only partially dependent on them (Vierich and Sheppard 1980, 22, 37–43).

In sum, using the number of draft animals owned as a key indicator is fruitful because of the manifold consequences of the lack of control over plowing power for food insecurity. Households lacking the threshold number of five to six head find themselves in various sorts of clientelistic dependency that involve the gain of temporary food access but do not provide the much greater degree of security of food access that comes with an owned and owner-controlled draft team. We now turn to a case in which the intensity of cultivation tends to an intermediate range between that of Bangladesh and that of Botswana, and in which government has traditionally been a much more important actor in shaping the choice environment, and thus must be taken account of in identifying the indicator of the target group.

THE TARGET GROUP INDICATOR IN TANZANIA

In traditional black African land tenure, clan and tribal authorities played a powerful role in shaping the alternatives of economic endeavor, though that role was guided and limited by the earlier ease of movement for cultivation and pasturage that went with slash-and-burn techniques for renewing the fertility of the soil. Given comparatively plentiful land, the household could rely on the clan leaders and elders to assure what was needed in land access. While the market has eroded this guarantee, and in a few areas in Tanzania (e.g., around Ismani in Iringa in the early 1970s) even seemed to smash the old system, the option of moving out to currently unused land has remained in the background. Villagization (1974–1976) formally transferred land allocation from traditional clan-tribe authorities to the village government, but land remained, in principle, available in much of Tanzania for allocation to those in a position to farm it. The loosening of residence restrictions after 1983 (Havnevik 1988, 341) gave at least formal access to more distant plots (including plots that households used to farm before being moved by villagization), since they could now move part of the year to farm them more adequately. However, the capacity of the poor to farm additional land with the hoe provides only low food security. The five to six acres of food-effective land necessary to enable the normal five-to-seven person household to meet food needs very minimally throughout the year does not fully exist in workable form for the poorest 30 to 50 percent of the population of rural

Tanzania. Where there is cash crop income, the traditional male control of it (Holmboe-Ottesen and Wandel 1991), despite the women's provision of the lion's share of the labor on both food and cash crops, highlights gender as a factor in this predicament.

For the purposes of this human rights analysis, in Tanzania the lower-strata 30 to 50 percent in our food vulnerable category are indicated by low productive farm acreage possessed and by lack of means for transport or for plowing more extensive acreage. Whatever the men's advantages according to traditional practices of resource control, in the poorest strata they nonetheless join the rest of the household in lacking the *assurance* of food access. Where the husband lacks a securely viable subsistence foundation due to overall household poverty, his control over the cash crop does not assure access to food; a bad year will expose the males to a health risk as well. The male's economic activity, be it cash crop, wage labor, or entrepreneurial, will be so much a necessity for his own and the household's food access that he (and his family) will enter into a vulnerable clientelistic dependency on anyone whose favor he can gain to support his own niche. Nonetheless, the women's commonly worse-off position must be considered when it comes to the human rights-targeted remedy; labor-saving devices must be aimed particularly at food-crop assurance to benefit the poor women of rural Tanzania.

The particular way in which poverty brings limited household food capacity for so many in Tanzania seems to lie in a combination of the hoe technology and (post villagization) distances to the larger fields. In the land allotment that took place in the context of villagization, there was continuing reliance the informal influence of the elders and preceding customary allocations, and the extant land possession patterns for those not forced to move were not substantially disturbed (McCall and Sleutsch 1983, 6). It appears that the 30 to 40 percent of the peasants that had to be moved to other sites actually tended to get too little land close enough to the homestead for intensive and productive hoe cultivation. Increasing distance to fields throws more of the burden on women, who must go by foot and work in the hottest part of the day (Havnevik 1988, 170). Their larger old fields or newly assigned fields (where they could get such allotments from the village leadership, given their meager capacities to farm distant land), tended to be from 45 minutes to 2 to 3 hours away, making them too far from the homestead to receive good cultivation (Friis-Hansen 1987a).

Where distant plots are cultivated by the women of the household, a toll may be taken on the nutrition of children due to the difficulty of preparing a midday meal at the land plots.[27] Yields tended to decline over subsequent years, it is argued, for those without enough cattle for manuring and its transport to maintain soil fertility; this situation was often worsened by deforestation and erosion around the densely settled inner areas (see Mlay 1986, 102–104). Distances to potentially larger outlying plots were too great to allow effective weeding, fertilizing, or bird scaring (particularly necessary for crops like millet and sorghum, which are otherwise desirable due to greater drought resistance), and so these fields declined in fertility over the years as well (see Shao 1986, 232–236;

Thiele 1986, 249–253). Finally, for the poorer strata the food insecurity linked to all these circumstances has made it increasingly difficult to keep younger family members in the rural areas.

Among relocated households, in the main it was only those well-off enough to possess an ox-plow team or access to other means of carting and more extensive cultivation that avoided suffering a drop in well-being due to villagization (Friis-Hansen 1987a). Indeed, villagization served in some areas as a stimulus to ox-plow use in extensive cultivation (Havnevik and Skarstein 1985, 25; Kjaerby 1988) to help overcome the problem of the long distance to fields. However, the intensive techniques the government was urging on the peasants could only be practiced on the meager plots close by the homestead. Households were often removed from traditional water sources without the promised pumps at their new village by the road. The increased travel time for cultivation, and often for water and firewood transportation as well, greatly intensified the scarcity of labor time in the poor household, particularly for the women, the group most responsible for the food crops.

Until the middle 1980s, villagization restricted residence to the assigned villages, with the relocated peasants prevented from rebuilding their previous burnt-out or deteriorated huts close to their old fields. These residence restrictions have been loosened since 1983, and as Havnevik notes, "This may have relieved the pressure on the land adjacent to nucleated villages as well as on deforestation and erosion in village neighbourhoods" (1988, 341). However, the vulnerable situation of the poorer households (particularly those that were previously relocated) is likely to remain due to their lack of the means of transport and plowing. Poor households in the village are unable to take up high-yielding maize cultivation, not only due to the unaffordability of the seeds and inputs, but also to the difficulty in transporting more than small quantities of fertilizer to the distant fields. Notably, increased demands on labor time and the unaffordability of school costs have made a major contribution to a drastic drop in attendance rates of children in rural primary schools (Havnevik 1988, 171–172). We may thus identify the poor as those hoe cultivators who lack workable access to productive maize and beans fields, many—but by no means all—having been moved to strategically poor sites by the 1970s villagization program.

Villagization put the poor in a situation of great stress on scarce quantities of readily available resources, especially for those who had moved, but also for those whose villages they had joined. Kinship patterns of informal social redistribution were undoubtedly disrupted. There were indications that in some areas better off households were better able to engage in "double settlement" and invest in houses for rent, bus services, and so on (Havnevik 1988, 172–173), serving both to increase income and to hide wealth in order to shield it from social redistributive obligations to the poor (Havnevik 1988, 281–284). The economic crisis of the early and middle 1980s served generally to increase economic differentiation between upper-strata and lower-level households (Havnevik 1988, 283–284).

To identify the crucial resources that reveal the key lines of dependency for the food-insecure poor, we need to look to the situation in which they find themselves as presented in the available empirical literature. Over the long haul, households do seem to gain access to land; what they lack is the labor capacity and time (including labor-saving devices) for workable and productive cultivation of it. With villagization residence restrictions largely lifted now, the men are free to migrate to urban areas to work and the women are free to live part of the year in a hut closer to the distant fields. However, when the males abandon the village for work in a town, the hoeing household is left short of cultivating labor, and the pressure on the women (and their resultant vulnerability) increases. The double-settlement option of living seasonally in a hut at the field distant from the village adds an additional possibility, but taking advantage of it seems to further increase for women the time burdens of travel, seasonal migration, and access to services (Havnevik 1988, 170, 281–282).

When the poor household is able to keep one or more sons at home, a premium is placed on borrowing an additional plot close enough to the homestead to allow intensive cultivation. Friis-Hansen has observed the lending of close plots by individuals unaffected by villagization to those who were relocated (Friis-Hansen 1987b, 5). Naturally, cattle ownership (in those areas that can support cattle) became a premium factor in the postvillagization world. A plot too distant for effective cultivation by a household lacking the labor time and transport, could, in the hands of someone with draft power and a minimum of available labor, provide workable access to productive farming. Friis-Hansen found that villagers relocated by villagization who owned oxen did not suffer the drop in food production capacity experienced by their counterparts who owned no livestock (1987a; 1987b, 9).

Alternatively, access to more distant plots can be rendered workable by borrowing draft power for plowing in areas where there is some concentration of oxen. In such areas, substantial numbers of the resource-poor borrow oxen from cattle owners for the purpose of plowing, usually trading weeding labor or assistance in plowing to the team owner (Kjaerby 1988, 50, 77; Jorgensen et al. 1988, 17). Of course, many of these relationships will be based on kinship (Jorgensen et al. 1988, 17). As in Botswana, however, the borrower gets the use of the team after the prime time for plowing, which can cause major loss in productivity (Sosovele 1986, 12). The weeding labor owed in return comes at the expense of timely weeding on the borrower's own plots (Jorgensen et al. 1988, 23–24), and weeding labor remains a serious bottleneck even when oxplowing has removed the cultivating bottleneck (Boesen and Ravnborg 1992, 39). In the villages he studied, Kjaerby found one or two households in ongoing association with each of a number of ox-team owners in this sort of exchange relationship (1988, 77), leading him to conclude that "it is possible that some kind of patron-client relations have developed between ox-farmers and the middle-poor peasants" (Kjaerby 1988, 112). The cutoff point for independent plowing would be considered the ownership or full control of the two to four animals needed to pull a plow on most Tanzanian soils. As it stands now, the introduction of oxen into an area capable of making use of them generally leads to a shifting of patterns of dependency without providing minimal food security to the poor involved.

Less is known overall about patterns of clientelistic dependency in Tanzania than in Bangladesh and Botswana. However, the only direction of agricultural expansion for rural Tanzanian households (short of the land within reach given available resources) is to fields and huts that are distant from the village homestead, where greater fertility can be had without the unaffordable inputs of chemically supported farming. The key resource for this move is draft power, which for the poor must be borrowed in the context of a clientelistic relationship with either a kin or nonkin patron. Hence some level of draft power ownership is a key indicator of the target group in Tanzania, as it was in Botswana. For Botswana, we saw that the rural household's ownership of six draft animals served fairly adequately by itself as a resource cutoff point to delineate the target group of food-insecure poor households. For Tanzania, where the situation is more complex and less clear, to adapt the task to the local context, we would have to combine a two-oxen cutoff with a landownership factor. However, since distance from the village homestead is an important variable, the landownership level would have to be keyed to the proximity of the closest fields. In Tanzania, survival with the hoe is fairly secure with three acres of adequate agricultural land if it is close enough to the village; this minimum tends to be met much more often by households that were not relocated by villagization. Poorer households that were moved are much more likely to have had to find someone on whom to depend for borrowed resources to farm the more distant fields they have been allocated. Hence, we could target households without an ox team and owning less than three acres within five kilometers of the homestead to recognize, within the category, the problem of the poor who were relocated by villagization.

CONCLUSION

Clearly the target group indicator of those likely to need clientelistic dependency, and hence be vulnerable to choice constraint, will be different according to the local conditions and the local bases and reasons for clientelistic dependency. In Bangladesh, dependency tended to be based on a credit relationship with a primary creditor (often kin-linked), which is a requisite for survival in cases of ownership of less than an acre of agricultural land. The landownership figure proved a fairly good indicator of this kind of situation; people who own little land nonetheless do minimally well in trading, craft, or processing niches under a patron who backs them in bad times.

For Botswana as well there was a fairly reliable stand-alone indicator; ownership and household control of at least a team of six draft animals for plowing. The critical nature of plowing capacity and its timing for the comparatively dry, extensive cultivation of Botswana agriculture made draft borrowing the basis of clientelistic dependency for the target-group poor. It was not that land scarcity was failing to develop or that a minimum of land ownership is not also a necessity of food-viable farming for the poor, but rather that land is sufficiently accessible that we can reliably identify draft power ownership as an indicator. Tanzania, with less intensive cultivation than Bangladesh but more intensive cultivation than Botswana, allows us to combine measures of landownership with measures of draft ownership, provided we include proximity to the village homestead as a key factor, along with its access to other services. To prescribe a human rights-based aid strategy for simultaneously spreading minimalist versions of access to food, health care, and civil-political choice, however, we have to understand better the situation of the target group with respect to what I call its "choice structure" to which we turn in the following chapter.

NOTES

1. This is in the same range as the 2,150 calories estimated by Khan (1977, 4) for the International Labor Organization (ILO). It seems to be adjusted down to this level from the United Nations Food and Agriculture Organization (FAO) minima for Southeast Asia (of, variously, 2,273 to 2,332), to reflect the relative absence of milk, meat, and sugar from the Bangladeshi diet. See also Ahmad and Hossain 1983, 16–17).

2. See Shahabuddin 1989, 113; Ahmad and Hossain 1983, 16–17; INFS 1983, 28; Mahabub Hossain 1989, 60; Chowdhury 1992, 77.

3. In a good year for agricultural production, that of 1988–1989 (20 million tons total output), 48 percent of the rural population had a daily caloric intake under 2,122 calories (Parkinson and Syeduzzaman 1993, 6, citing World Bank figures), while in the subsequent normal year of 1989–1990, the poverty ratio by head count came in at 55 percent (Hossain 1992c, 46). In a midlevel year, 1983–1984, we find 62 percent below 2,200 calories and 50 percent of the rural population (41 million people) below the income level linked to it (HES reports and Bangladesh Bureau of Statistics [BBS], cited in Rahman and Haque 2). HES data for 1985–1986 show 55 percent of the rural population with a caloric intake under 2,200 (BBS, cited in Hossain 1989, 61). By household income, 47 percent had incomes under those fitting (according to the HES) a 2,200 calorie food basket (BBS, cited in Rahman and Haque 1988, 2).

4. Norbeye 1986, 62–63.

5. For an excellent brief history of Sarwa development, see Hitchcock 1987.

6. The issue of to what degree these land allocations can be referred to as "property" rights is a complex one; see Wilmsen 1982.

7. The RIDS survey figure is from a personal communication from Diana Callear, of the Government of Botswana, April 10, 1989.

8. "Dodoma tackles increasing malnutrition," *Daily News* (Dar es Salaam, Tanzania), March 13, 1990, p. 1.

9. "50 per cent Tanzanians live below poverty line," *Daily News*, November 11, 1993, p. 3.

10. Conversation, Ole Therkildsen, of the Center for Development Research, Copenhagen, Denmark, May 8, 1989.

11. Havnevik et al. 1988, 169.

12. Havnevik et al. 1988, 172–173.

13. "Nurses speak on corruption," *Daily News* (Dar es Salaam, Tanzania), March 4, 1990, p. 1.

14. The term originated in the Russian Debate of the 1920s over rural inequality.

15. This dimension is emphasized by James Scott in his *Weapons of the Weak: Everyday Forms of Peasant Resistance* (New Haven/London: Yale, 1980).

16. Concerning the attack, see "CCM accused of harassing opposition in Mara," *Family Mirror* 98 (March 1993): 7.

17. For thorough critical examinations of the capabilities of class analysis to provide answers for such problems in the case of Bangladesh, see Jansen 1986, 4–6, 300–304 and Van Schendel 1981, 37–39. For thoughtful arguments defending class analysis see, on the micro level Arens and van Beurden 1977, 71–88, and for a more macro-level and politically oriented emphasis, see Jahangir 1979.

18. Exemplary descriptions may be found in Faaland and Parkinson 1976, 124–125; USAID 1983, 14; Ahmad and Hossain 1983, 29; Hartmann and Boyce 1983, 86–87; and Ahmed et al. 1990, 24–26, 34–36.

19. INFS 1983, 64, 70; Ahmad and Hossain 1984, 21.

20. For an excellent village study combining development economics with Barthian anthropological approaches to deal with these topics, see Jansen 1983. Other thorough and extensive village studies in rural Bangladesh include White 1991, Adnan 1989, Hartmann and Boyce 1983, Van Schendel 1981, and Arens and van Beurden 1977.

21. See chapter 4.

22. Landless laborers as a percentage of total cultivators increased only from 17.5 percent in 1961 to 19.8 percent in 1967–1968, and the proportion of *operated* holdings of less than one acre among total holdings held steady over the period at around 25 percent (Khan 1977, 29, 40–41).

23. In 1982, for example, Grameen Bank loans went 43 percent for trading and shopkeeping, 24 percent for processing and manufacturing, 23 percent for livestock and poultry raising, and only 2 percent for agricultural production (Ahmad and Hossain 1985, 86).

24. Hossain (1981, 113) takes the figure of 1.67 acres (5 bighas), while Khan (1977, 33) and Jansen (1986, 162) employ 2 acres, which Van Schendel regards as the "arbitrary but generally accepted amount of land considered sufficient for an average household completely dependent on agriculture" (1981, 83). White takes $1^2/_3$ acres as the divider between the lower- and upper-stratum households, but she also classifies some of the lower-stratum households as "strong" and others as "vulnerable" (1991, 39).

25. Locales exemplifying the relatively poor areas are those of the Arens and van Beurden study (1977) and, to some extent, the village studied by Jansen (1983). These poorer villages (characteristic in northern Bengal) often show high percentages of sharecropping households, which is related to the low land productivity there and the relative scarcity of wage labor opportunities. Jansen found that cultivators possessing 1 crop-acre (either by owning a family-cultivated acre or, say, by owning ½ acre and sharecropping in 1 acre, which he counted as ½ crop-acre) had only a half year's food-effectiveness (1986, 162).

26. See Wikan 1981, 54, for a good brief description.

27. Personal communication from Jan Lindstrom, April 20, 1989.

Chapter 4

The Choice Structure

In the last chapter, our search for the best observable indicator of the food-insecure target group revealed the likelihood of clientelistic dependency in order to provide short-term survival. Clientelistic dependency is important because it structures the choice of the poor peasant in a certain way. While this may take a variety of particular forms in specific settings, in the choice of economic endeavor, a common characteristic is the presence, basically, of only one viable strategy or significant alternative. That path involves dependency (or the search for it) on one or more better-off figures in the peasant's life, be they kin or nonkin. With the risk or reality of subminimal food intakes for at least weeks or even months of the year (placing at risk the health of one or more family members), only the strategy providing the best short-term food access is significant; other imaginable alternatives that expose one or more family members to greater risk to their health and safety would rationally be considered unviable. They would not meet a key requirement of significance for an alternative; that it be feasible to try. Unable to risk losing whatever stability presently exists in their access to food the client is likely, in the most basic civil-political behavior—most critically, association and expression—to try to anticipate the reaction of the principal patrons by staying within the boundaries allowed by their preferences, as the client perceives them. This removes the option of significant choice, which is the operational meaning of a right. Of course, much of this analysis turns on just what is a significant alternative in what sort of situation, a question to which we now turn for each of the country cases.

In the following sections, choice structure analysis will be articulated in particular contexts, and key questions that arise from it will be explored. The basic argument will be applied with reference to situations common in rural Bangladesh; then, additional issues will be taken up more briefly for rural Botswana and Tanzania. Most important, we shall take up the question of what a significant alternative is in the light of common assumptions that poor peasants have options like sharecropping or off-farm employment as alternatives whereby to lift themselves up "by the bootstraps." It will be shown that these are really no more than component elements of a single multifaceted strategy that characteristically involves clientelistic dependency on better-off kin or nonkin contacts, leaving rural poor without minimal significant choice.

HOW VOLUNTARY IS CLIENTELISTIC DEPENDENCY IN BANGLADESH?

A common pattern observed in village studies for rural Bangladesh is for the comparatively poor to enter into one degree or another of clientelistic relationship with better-off villagers. Usually, one such patron is primary, being the main source of credit to cover periodic food deficits on the part of the poor household, though the poor borrower may depend on the patron for other critical opportunities as well, such as for employment or a small plot to sharecrop. Once the initial choice of patron has been made, the poor clients are directly vulnerable in their precarious food supply to the creditor's good will, and compliant social and political behavior tends to follow (Jansen 1990, 26–27). Local patrons seem periodically to avail themselves of such clients' vulnerability in requiring desired behavior. This happens regularly enough that we may consider local custom to have informally authorized such control in rural Bangladesh.

Of course, a portion of patrons in an area may not seek to control their poor clients' choices. Where this is the case, however, many of their clients will be apt to stay within the boundaries of their perceptions of patron preferences, anyway. In other cases lacking a patron's attempts at control, the scope of peasant choice as to association and expression exists only so long as the patron does not invoke the power that local custom authorizes. Hence, even in this most favored case (likely to apply to only a small portion of poor dependents), the civil-political choice that is enjoyed is not so secure as to approach the situation of an operational right.

Our conventional view of patron-client relationships amid the commercialization of agriculture is one of a voluntary exchange of values. Political support, occasional labor, and signs of deference are given by the client in return for access to sharecropping opportunities, short-term credit, and perhaps help in defraying unusual expenses such as a wedding and dowry. As presented by the economic anthropology of Fredrik Barth (used by Jansen 1986, for example, in his Bangladesh village study), each party pursues a strategy of managing and trying to capitalize on scarce resources in a competitive environment.[1] In this conventional picture of patron-client relationships, bargaining may take place, in that each party has the implicit option of looking elsewhere for a better deal. The value of the resources exchanged may be unequal, and the party yielding up the greater value to the other may be the one in a poorer resource position at the outset. This inequality in market-measured values, however, need not, on Barth's analysis, rule out longer-term "gains" by both parties, due to their respective particular positions which make the good received of importance for the particular strategy of each. The client may participate in the patron's political faction and have to consider what he or she says in public about an issue affecting the patron's interests. These constraints take on a voluntary character, however, due to the fundamental voluntariness of the choice of association in the first place, according to this conventional style of analysis. Many patron-client relationships in rural Bangladesh seem to fit this analysis.

Unfortunately for the conventional voluntary-exchange model of clientelism as a candidate for a comprehensive theory, however—or as a preconceived assumption, as some use it—many clientelistic relationships do not fit it. In Bangladesh, there are many relationships in which a voluntary, win-win characteristic is unclear, and they seem to cluster below the one-acre point of client landownership, though many client households in the 1–2 acre category may be long term losers, as well. Here the poor client is forced into a kind of relationship that eliminates several ordinary sorts of choice, and the "gain" is usually, at best, a temporary slowdown of loss by the client, with little hope of future turnaround.

First, the client must enter the relationship to have some central component of near-term assurance of family member survival—most commonly, an assured line of credit to cover family consumption deficits, perhaps with an opportunity of sharecropping a small plot, regular wage labor (especially in the slack-season), or even access to water for irrigation. There are seldom significant differences between the terms of one available dependency and those to be had from another advantaged patron-candidate who might offer such a relationship in hopes of eventually acquiring the client's remaining land upon failure of loan repayment. The client may, in a particular local context, have more than one interested patron-candidate, and thus may be in a position to make an initial choice as to which of them will be the primary lender to cover consumption deficits and to gain a mortgage in, and perhaps later purchase, the client's plots upon a subsequent accumulation of unpaid debt (Jansen 1990, 24–25). This is commonly the case when the client has the bargaining power to require of the patron, for example, sharecropping rights to land he or she may mortgage out to the patron in the future (Jansen 1986), or even a labor opportunity. However, this does not change the fact that the basic decision to enter into the relationship, with the standard term structure for the local area, was one that the peasant had to make.

Of course, the feeling of relief at having secured the household's survival over the near term (and perhaps, secondarily, having secured the patron's protection of the client against predatory raising of disputes to get land) must be as significant as the alternative itself. However, the voluntariness of a choice is measured, not by emotional affect, but rather by whether there was a significant alternative to the route chosen. Moreover, any relief will be qualified by the client's knowledge that the values given up to try to ensure the family members' survival will, over the long run, in all probability have quite high strategic costs—economic, social, and political—attached to them.

For our purposes here, a crucial consequence of successfully gaining such a relationship for a peasant with insufficient land to assure family survival autonomously is the consequent sacrifice of free choice in areas of expression and association that we in the developed world take for granted. The poor peasant characteristically becomes part of the faction of the patron for all purposes of village politics. In any dispute he or she must support the patron's position whenever such support is requested, perhaps even to the point of giving testimony (or refusing to do so) before either official or unofficial settlement proceedings. As such disputes are the essence of village politics in Bangladesh, this amounts to a loss of the freedom of ordinary political assembly and association.

As to association of a merely social sort, the poor client might have to be guided by the patron in choice of association on ceremonial and other occasions—perhaps even in the matter of marriage choice for the client's children. The latter coercion can occur even when following the patron's preference runs against the wishes of the peasant's closer relatives, at some social cost to the peasant client. Moreover, peasants know they may be called on at a moment's notice to put their life on the line serving as protection for the patron if the threat of violence or robbery to the latter arises.[2] Again, the peasant is, in a sense, quite willing to make these sacrifices of choice as part of a valued multidimensional relationship with the patron wherein the latter serves as a protector against at least the most immediate severe threats to life and health.[3]

The decisions behind this sacrifice of normal choice are indeed spread around among potential and actual patrons and clients to the point of being indistinguishably imbedded in an overall social practice at village level, making legal blame for the human rights situation impossible to attribute to specific individuals. While any given patron may choose not to extract obedience in these areas of freedom, the pervasiveness of patterns of constraint is such that we may certainly conclude that the patron in such a context is *in a position to constrain* the poor client. Thus, even should the patron choose not to make any attempt at control, patron preferences can carry great weight nonetheless, due to client anticipation of patron reaction.[4]

This pattern would apply throughout the whole range of our category of landless to one-acre owners, including those who are not at present fortunate enough to be in a multistranded, protective patron-client relationship. In the most common case of a primary creditor-patron relationship, the possibility of cutoff of credit, seizure of land (which is always at least the implicit collateral), or even merely a speeding up of the process of forced mortgage and sale upon mounting unpaid loans amount to threats quite sufficient to constrain behavior in expression and association. The range of benefits for which the client depends on the patron, such that the risk of withdrawal can constrain other behavior, can be wide:

Even if the poor would want to articulate some of their interests and discontent against the rich in a more jointly and systematic manner, they fear the sanctions they may face. Given the dyadic economic relationships which exist between poor and rich, there are several types of immediate sanctions with which a client may be confronted if he goes against the interests of his patron (withdrawal of the sharecropping contract, employment opportunities, credit on "good" terms, political protection). (Ahmed et al. 1990, 43)

Even those who are landless in the extreme sense of having no remaining homestead land to mortgage to a creditor are far from excluded from potentially coercive clientelism, and they will offer up compliant political behavior in the slack season (often one of starvation of one or more family members) in return for no more than an odd job or two for rice. Often landless household members will comply with the requests of a merely a *potential* patron in hopes of developing some sort of relationship or of maintaining a series of slack season labor opportunities, or even merely to maintain the flow of small gifts from relatives on ceremonial occasions. The bottom line for such households in poverty is the need for credit in immediate distress; it is critical for a food-insecure client household

to attach itself to a lender who has full information on its capacity to repay and who can control its member's lives sufficiently in order to minimize its risk of default. Such personalised relationship with lenders is indeed an asset for a poor household, particularly in times of risks. . . . For such transactions to be effective, they must take place in the context of a long-term relationship between the two parties. The threat of credit cessation acts in these cases as an effective enforcement mechanism since poor borrowers expect repeated transactions in future in times of unanticipated crisis-events and risks. (Sen 1992a, 215–216)

The end result for many in these situations would seem to be the view that Van Schendel found explictly prevalent among the members of a village, that those without enough food for the whole year "were ordered about by others," in contrast to "those who produced a surplus and could order others about" (1981, 243).

The situation is very different for the owner of at least an acre and a half, however. Being less dependent on any one economic path of association and endeavor for survival at a given time, this owner retains at least minimal choice as to expression and association (political, economic, and social) as well as economic endeavor. Such owners may behaviorally display similar compliance with the wishes of a patron, but unlike the poorer peasants, they can change patrons and bargain in their choice of a new patron, much better fitting the traditional patron-client model of a voluntary exchange of values. The landless and owners of less than one acre, on the other hand, can exercise such choice only when the patron has implicitly released the client by ending the survival-allowing opportunity or benefit. The owner of an acre and a half or more (who can go it alone if necessary) may indeed have several patrons, no one of which is important enough to family security to exact the control exercised by the primary patron of an owner of under one acre of land.

There are many indications of very high productivity and intensity of production on one- to two-acre total holdings. Bangladesh households prefer to put their labor into their own plots if they have a large enough reservoir of owned land to serve as a receptacle for all available family labor. At peak times they hire a laborer or two, and at other times they display the typical Chayanovian picture of "self-exploitation" by putting in the maximum of potentially useful family labor on their own plots, even to the point of very low marginal return. They can regulate their level of inputs according to their ability to purchase fertilizer and pesticide (crucial in HYV areas), which is an important sort of flexibility to have. Since they can get for themselves the full return on their intensively worked plots, they are often in a position to invest the proper input levels for HYV agriculture and obtain the doubled or tripled production made available by HYV. Moreover, such households are far better able to hold part of their crop off the market for a while after harvest in order to get a better price, and thus to stretch out, to some extent, their threshing and husking labor so as to take maximum advantage of their available labor time during the peak harvest period. As such a household can afford to keep aside as much as two-tenths of an acre or more as homestead land, it has more capacity for storage. Thus, these owners are far better able to take advantage of what they have than those who own less. The clear owner (no land mortgaged) of an acre and a half or more, then, tends to have a viable base of food and land on which to survive even a bad year without a catastrophic loss of land to repay. The owner is an independent choice maker who may switch patrons if unsatisfied with the terms. The clientelism exists but the vulnerability to coercion does not, and the minimalist option of choice among two or more significant alternatives in expression, association, and endeavor is comparatively certain.

An important factor in the capacity of such families to take advantage of their small surplus is their ability to support a team of cattle in sufficient strength and health (or one bullock to team with that of a neighbor, friend, or relative) for timely plowing and threshing.[5] Since such a household receives and husks the whole paddy from the land it cultivates, it can supply its bullocks with fodder from the husk, which is essential due to the scarcity of grazing land. A crucial result of this situation is that a major economic alternative for choice exists for the owner of an acre and a half or two acres that does not exist for the owner of less than an acre: the alternative of sharecropping at a cost low enough to get returns above those available from wage labor. We are thus led to the prevalent conception of the key alternative of economic endeavor for the supposed possibility of bootstrap recovery by poor peasants: sharecropping.

SHARECROPPING: A SIGNIFICANT ALTERNATIVE?

A common observation, among economists especially, is that measuring the size of the operational holding—the amount of land actually farmed, whether actually owned or sharecropped—remedies inaccuracies in assessments of the relative well-being that ownership figures suggest. The operational holding indicator is said to reveal what is actually a better-off position for marginal smallholders and landless laborers than landownership differentials show because it includes the returns of sharecropping land owned by others.[6] It is implied thus that extremely land-poor individuals indeed have the alternative of sharecropping others' land to the point of significantly improving their quality of life. As such, the sharecropping option would, in effect, render whatever impoverished or coerced position is suffered by poor peasants implicitly voluntary; hence, the logic might run, whatever victimizations they suffer need be of little interest, resulting as they do from a combination of the vicissitudes of an impersonal marketplace and the peasants' own lack of industriousness in failing to take up sharecropping alternatives. The operational holding indicator might thus be regarded as important for the identification of target groups whose human rights are in question.

In fact, the data seem to indicate that in the long run, the amount of land owned without mortgage *and owner cultivated* is more important for the poorest individuals than operational holding, including sharecropped acreage. For the category of marginal cultivators that is the focus of this inquiry, conventionally understood sharecropping is *not* a significant alternative for economic endeavor, but rather, where it exists, only a subordinate component of a labor-maximizing strategy. For under-one-acre owning peasants it is not feasible on a scale that would be sufficiently effective to render it a significant alternative in its own right.

One limiting factor for the poor is the lack of draft power. There is a low rate of cattle ownership among marginal owners of land (Sen 1992a, 208); they are unlikely to possess, or have the resources to support adequately, the draft animals needed for timely and affordable plowing and threshing (see Jansen 1986, 43–44; Van Schendel 1981, 86, 302). Access to draft animals can be costly as well, with as many as seven or eight plowings necessary (with more threshing to do, as well) for adequate output. In some areas, only those possessing a team of work animals are even allowed to sharecrop.[7]

Much of this also bears on the *potential effectiveness* of the sharecrop alternative for owners of less than an acre. Under the custom of having the sharecropper bear the input costs (Jannuzi and Peach 1980, 24), the returns (on a high volume of expended labor) are meager compared to those from owner-cultivated land. Sharecropping as a major alternative in itself becomes even more remote for the poorest in HYV-penetrated areas, despite the two to three times greater output. The high productivity is tied to bigger stakes, higher costs of agricultural inputs, and greater uncertainties. Cutbacks in fertilizer subsidies and increases in fertilizer prices by the end of the 1980s, by themselves, rendered the returns on sharecropping *negative* on average; according to the *Agricultural Sector Review* (*ASR*), low yields are a factor, connected to declines in fertilizer use due to increased fertilizer prices and "very low prices of *boro* paddy during harvest . . . when most [paddies] are sold by small and medium farmers" (Mandal 1989, 59). Moreover, HYV agriculture in its fully productive forms (winter *boro* cropping) depends on tubewell water, which in the case of deep tubewells means surrendering a share of the crop—normally 25 percent or more (Khan and Hossain 1989, 55; Lein 1989, 7–8)—to the water supplier; this again drops the return on labor back toward the level of wage labor, even for many of who are otherwise the most well endowed for taking on sharecrop land beyond their owner-cultivated plots.

With HYV agriculture, then, the gap between owner-cultivation return on labor and sharecropping return on labor, which is already great with traditional crops, really takes off (Hossain, 1991, 98–99). Many sharecroppers have been removed in favor of the more profitable owner-managed wage labor, cutting down on the number of sharecrop openings (Rahman 1983, 282–283; Arens and van Beurdon 1977, 124). Increasingly, moreover, owners who do sharecrop out require high input and output levels, whose costs are born by the sharecropper, so only the most productive get the few sharecrop slots. Under these circumstances, the operator may find it difficult to cut corners on fertilizer inputs, for example, to try to compensate himself for an unfavorable return on labor (Hossain 1981, 108).

White studied a village including a substantial number of smallholding sharecroppers, and regarding HYV winter *boro* cultivation, she found that for "lower-vulnerable" households (owning under 1½ acres and lacking other advantages), sharecropping was costly and only marginal in its profits; it mainly served to intensify household labor use with very low net returns, which "appear to be the rule, rather than the exception, across India and more widely" (1991, 60). Thus, even where the marginal peasant can feasibly sharecrop, it is often unclear whether the return will exceed the opportunity costs. In some cases the *timing* of return can be bad; while wage labor gives an immediate return during peak time after weeks of slack-season hunger, for the return on sharecropping, the peasant must wait until the paddy is divided. Hence, input costs also may include weeks of harvest-season malnutrition prior to marketing (not suffered by wage laborers), during which the worker's own caloric intake requirements may jump to as high as 5,000 per day of very hard work (Khan 1977, 9–10), adding to the pressure to borrow during this period. Moreover, a household may not have healthy male labor to spare from its own plots and from valued wage labor opportunities at times of peak activity (when very much must be done in the small time frame that nature provides during the monsoon cycle) to effectively farm sharecropped plots (see Jansen 1986, 47).[8]

Of course, many marginal peasants in Bangladesh do sharecrop small plots and enter the sharecropping statistics despite the low returns on labor, especially where wage labor opportunities are comparatively sparse (especially in the north and northwest). The meager return can still provide incentive when faced with weeks of hunger or starvation each year. If there is otherwise underutilized labor available in the household, a sharecropped plot is there as a receptacle for it, if wage labor opportunities are not reliable. Especially in non-HYV areas with lower land productivity and fewer owner specifications as to input levels, some corner-cutting on labor and its timeliness (both animal and human) can improve the return on labor with only a 10 percent drop in output.[9] Again, however, it is hard to imagine even this improvement occurring without some access to non-hired animal labor (perhaps pairing a cow with a neighbor's animal, both of which are likely to be weak and undernourished), which is characteristic more of owners of over one acre than those of less than the somewhat arbitrary demarcation point used as a rough indicator in this work. White found that in her area, where sharecropping is substantial in the overall village economy, even in the good year of 1985–1986 fully 69 percent of "lower/vulnerable" households did not participate in sharecropping (1991, 59).

Furthermore, accounts of sharecropping tend to leave out a major fact about many owners of an acre or less who are listed as sharecropping. The share-cropped portion often, in effect, *replaces owned land*, rather than supplementing it, as in the case of owners of an acre and a half or more. Here a food-deficient peasant sharecrops part or all of his or her own land because unpaid loans have led to mortgaging away usufruct of the portions to the patron, who in turn share-crops the land back to the same poor peasant due to the particular social relation-ship or to the patron's particular circumstances. We thus have an overlap be-tween owned acreage and sharecropped acreage. Only micro-level studies over a significant time period (allowing candor between peasants and observers) can bring this situation out, as does Jansen's careful study; he observes that:

In [the village] we found that many sharecropping relationships between well-to-do land-owners and poor tenants led to the result that the poor tenants through long credit rela-tionships had mortgaged and sold their own land to the landowners from whom they had sharecropped land. However, we also found in many cases that a sharecropping relation-ship had not preceded the mortgage of land, but followed after the mortgage. This is often an expression of the fact that the poor households mortgaging land have demanded a sharecropping contract on the plot they mortgage or more likely that the mortgagee has offered the plot for sharecropping, as he understands he otherwise will not be able to obtain the land. (1986, 167)

In this case, according to common social practice, the peasant is sharecropping the same half-acre, for example, that he or she used to own free and clear, but now he or she must provide all the inputs, with only half the output coming back; the food-effectiveness of the sharecropped acreage is significantly less than what is accorded the sharecropper in most calculations of economic posi-tion. Furthermore, sharecroppers are less able to maintain the health and strength of their human and animal labor, in the case of owners of an acre or less, be-cause of the reduced volume of paddy straw available for cows and bullocks as well as rice for family members. However, these peasants cannot make ends meet through a bad year, even with all the output of their land, and they are caught in the cycle of land loss so common among marginal smallholders in rural Bangladesh.[10]

For the landless and owners of up to one acre, then, the sharecropping alterna-tive lacks both the potential effectiveness, and the feasibility, that it must possess to be considered an alternative significantly different from wage labor in return for effort. Where it does aid in covering food deficits, it usually does so only marginally via the taking in of small, less productive plots (often in the context of sharecropping *out* other plots and mortgaging out land), producing a return little different from that of wage labor and often below it. It differs from wage labor primarily in that where it is most widely practiced it is there as a receptacle for otherwise underutilized family labor when wage labor is not available; and it is guaranteed over a whole crop season, rather than uncertainly from day to day or week to week, as in the case of wage labor generally.[11]

An incessant scramble for employment among the poor resulted in a great number of often temporary pursuits yielding the smallest of pay or profit in return for very hard and long work. The middle groups who could subsist on agriculture did not need to join the fight for additional income. What they earned was sufficient for their needs, but they could not invest in other pursuits (Van Schendel 1981, 170). Where there is HYV sharecropping by those owning under an acre, each sharecropped plot tends to be small but still represents "a strengthening of the traditional patron-client relationship, as the number of farmers depending on a few landowners will increase with the introduction of irrigation and the new rice" (Lein 1989, 6). It is thus important for these individuals mainly as one component of an overall household survival strategy. Even for owners of less than an acre who have unusually favored access to inputs, however, it is little better protection than wage labor against the occasional—and inevitable—bad crop year, as rice prices zoom well before the crop is in and marketed; the deck is thus stacked against the possibility of sharecropping making a difference as a matter of long-term endeavor, as any gains are wiped out by the bad year. The land-poor often decline to the point where it becomes attractive to sharecrop *out* some or all of their remaining plots because of a lack of resources to farm even these.

Among the various indicators of peasant position, then, operational holding statistics are helpful in indicating relative positions of owners over an acre and a half, who can make viable use of them at returns significantly different from those of ordinary wage labor. However, the operational holding indicator actually confuses comparisons of well-being concerning owners under an acre. The only case in the poorer category in which operational holding is more accurate than landownership acreage in indicating food effective acreage is one in which landownership *overstates* food-effective acreage (or understates poverty) while operational holding does not. This occurs when, due to lack of even the usual input availabilities for such cultivators, it is necessary for the household to sharecrop out one or more plots that it cannot feasibly farm. In each case the food-effectiveness of the affected owned land is cut (at least) in half.

ECONOMIC DIVERSITY AND CHOICE

Sharecropping is not the only activity that might look like a viable alternative strategy but, upon closer examination, lacks the potential effectiveness to qualify as a significant alternative in itself, and hence remains only a component of the single available path of endeavor. We may consider in the same fashion the various activities of household members, particularly women, that are ancillary components of the household survival package. Women in poor households use skills in seasonal crop processing, homestead vegetable production, husbandry of smallstock (goats, chickens, etc.), and such low-return crafts as sewing, basketmaking, and pottery. Since the demand for such services outside the *chula* (nuclear family) or *bari* (kin-based courtyard, often composing several *chula*) is so limited and the pay so low, such activities amount to supplementary survival package components; only the very poorest try to rely on any one of them primarily for survival (Feldman and McCarthy 1984, 122). For women, as the traditional mainstay of rice husking suffered under the impact of the spread of rice mills, the problem of the 1980s was less a lack of things to do than of generally depressed female wage rates in the context of continued dependency on personal relationships to secure whatever employment opportunities were to be had (White 1991, 87–88). When the price of rice on the market was unusually low, as in the circumstances of 1985–1986 (given high overall production totals with irrigated HYV rice spread and expanded food-for-work wheat availability in the dry season), the multiple components of the household survival package helped poor households do better, but when times returned to the normal- or bad-year conditions, the normal or bad outcomes returned as well.

Wherever cultivable land can be possessed and relied on, it is the core of household strategy; in the words of Feldman and McCarthy:

Control of cultivable land is defined as primary since it can be parlayed to increase access to other resources such as credit, other agricultural inputs, and livestock, poultry and fruit trees. People who own cultivable land also own household plots or the area surrounding and including the household compound. The absence of cultivable land excludes the need for agricultural inputs but may also exclude access to institutionalized credit since land usually serves as collateral for bank credit. (1984, 125)

Thus, the structure of alternatives of economic endeavor for poor peasants in this category is effectively unidimensional: owner-cultivation (where land is owned) supplemented by (a) scrambling for whatever low-return employment, craft, or petty trade opportunities can be found, including women's tending of poultry and small livestock (Feldman and McCarthy 1984, 129), and (b) consumption loans from a primary patron who, upon the accumulation of unpaid debts, may impose gradual mortgage and purchase of the peasant's remaining land.[12] The components of this alternative structure are not really themselves alternatives; they must all be pursued together if minimal welfare is to be achieved. It is lack of minimal choice in this realm of long-term economic endeavor—a sphere of freedom and opportunity much cherished in the Western tradition—that has the fundamental consequences for the absence of minimal choice in the conventional freedom-sector fields of expression, association, and economic action.

Again, it is important to be clear on what is *not* being claimed, and need not be claimed for the basic argument to remain valid. Not all landless and owners of an acre or less experience food-deficit conditions at a given time or even during an entire portion of a year. First, however, in such cases where survival seems assured over a whole year, this outcome for a given household does not assure anything for the long run, and usually results from precisely the kind of sacrifice of minimal significant choice in the patron-client relationship that we are emphasizing. Second, the majority who do not achieve such a successful client position as to protect against protein-energy malnutrition over all months of the year still tend to find themselves sacrificing ordinary sorts of minimal choice. That is, clientelistic dependency is not entered into solely to attain food security for any substantial period, but often only for partial steps toward it when nothing better can be had; the result may be not assurance of the client household's food maintenance even over the whole year, but only for a briefer period. Third, regarding the compliant social and political behavior that tends to attend clientelistic dependency, it is not asserted that obedience is always demanded by the patron. Rather, the key point is that such behavior is sufficiently pervasive in local social practice that the patron is *in a position to* require it, whether he or she does so in a given case or not, and that the poor client will be apt to comply with perceived patron preferences either with or without an explicit control attempt by the patron.

At this point, however, it may be objected that since the original choice of economic and political association was a voluntary one, all subsequent compliant client behavior is merely the performance of a kind of contract voluntarily entered into, and hence no absence of a right to freedom. However, the premises of this reasoning do not carry the weight it intends, and the inference from them is flawed for several reasons. First, while the choice of the *particular* primary lending patron (or wage labor or sharecrop opportunity offering) may have been voluntary in the case where more than one offer is made, only dubiously can it be claimed that this was a "free" choice of *political* association. In the perspective of the client-to-be, the choice was one of *economic* association, and only consequentially, not part of the original purpose of the association, does the customary *political* commitment follow, sacrificing ordinary liberties of association, expression, assembly, and movement in the face of the threat of greatly heightened health risk that follows malnutrition. Second, while again there may, under some circumstances, be an economic choice of the *particular* patron, the *nature* of the association—a patron-client relationship sacrificing minimal client choice in several areas of ordinary freedom—was not really chosen; it was an imperative of family survival. Moreover, the differences among the deals offered by patrons (when there is more than one there to make offers) are not significant in the long run. Regarding the central point of the arrangement, choice of economic endeavor, there is really only one viable significant alternative—the strategy itself—and even that proves to be significant only for alleviating immediate survival distress, and not for long-term economic endeavor. When only one offer is available, of course, there is not even the choice of a particular patron. Often the remaining client land to be eventually acquired by the patron is small or of poor quality, lessening the attractiveness of the client for potential patrons. Alternately, there may be no land at all, and political support or peak-season labor commitment may be the only benefit the patron is buying; the single offer must be accepted for the short-term assurance of family member survival.

The basic situation is not altered by the multiplicity of credit and employment dependencies that may coexist around the main line of dependency. These range from dependency of a woman of a poor household depending on a kin-linked woman of a middle-level household for tending a goat, on up to more significant values. Sources of credit as well as employment opportunity may be diverse (Feldman and McCarthy 1984, 139), as well. The overall situation is well described by Feldman and McCarthy's comments on rural women:

Restricted family resources and dependency on wage labor has resulted in women of landless and poor families developing complex subsistence strategies involving migration, petty trading, daily labor, loans, and sharecropping of poultry and small livestock. These activities require developing and maximizing social alliances with a series of power brokers and gatekeepers ranging from wealthy village families, Union Council Chairmen and thana officials, to established traders and businessmen. In this sense, the landless and poor replace dependence on family resources with a reliance on social networks. The networks tend to be contractual or wage based, flexible in design and temporary in duration. These networks, however, generate forms of obligation and indebtedness which generally inhibit the poor and landless from accumulating the means to substantially improve their conditions. In addition to individual and household level resources, the social connections and alliances of poor village families are essential in protecting them from increasing impoverishment. Among more secure families, social connections and alliances are mechanisms for increasing landholdings and power. (1984, 130)

Such multiple lines of dependency do not belie the tendency for there to be one main patron tied to the most important income opportunity and credit source, usually involving the male. It will be this primary patron's expectations, if any, that will be the first limit for the civil-political behavior of the household. The primary patron might *not* avail himself of the customary opportunity to limit the civil-political behavior of the clientelistic dependent. However, each of the multiple smaller dependencies are necessary with the household so close to the margin of malnutrition and its health risk, such that there will be one or more *other* patronlike figures in a position to constrain sociopolitical behavior in the direction of the small-scale patron's factional alignment. If there are two patrons, the more economically crucial one may not demand constraint, but a second- or third-ranking one, say a female supplier of employment and smaller loans to the wife, may have to be looked to. The chance of at least one component supplier having a preference is high.

   The frequency of this belies the orthodox Leninist claim (applying certain Marxist analyses of capitalist development to conditions of rural commercialization) that those who are wholly dispossessed of the means of production, the landless laborers, are correspondingly wholly liberated from all particularistic ties hanging over from the feudal era. The kernal of truth is that when they face immediate threat of starvation and have no significant ways of averting it over any time frame, they are indeed without such ties and must engage in starvation. The substantial fallacy, however, is that as soon as an increment of improvement is offered by a patron it becomes a quite significant alternative to enter into such a particularistic tie, removing the option of significant choice in the various key fields, however short or long the relationship lasts. The need for any such increment renders the peasants *vulnerable* to constraint even before a clientelistic avenue presents itself because they must please *potential* patrons even before one becomes available.

Finally, a larger question is raised by this objection; might the relationship involving coercive threat be voluntary in the sense that by taking up the alternative of economic endeavor the poor peasant could, *over time,* get out of the whole situation of vulnerability? If a short-term, compulsory economic route that involved the sacrifice of other sorts of choice itself led to future gains in well-being and the recovery of ordinary freedoms, our overall impression of an imposed failure of the assurance of minimal well-being and choice might be mitigated.

This analytical possibility, however, seldom exists empirically. Thus it fails to meet the requirement of potential effectiveness, which an alternative must have to be considered significant under the model worked with here. For the vast majority of peasants owning less than an acre and involved in the credit market, consumption loans are simply not signficant as the vehicle of a long-term course of endeavor to improve their situation of vulnerability. They know that this alternative has little chance of turning around the momentum of gradual land loss that they face in their own case, and that they see at various stages all around them among their poorer neighbors, kin, and fellow villagers.[13] They know that they will not be able to repay the more substantial loans extended by their principal creditor (even though they often do repay the small ones involving their equals among the poor), or will be able to repay only on terms so disadvantageous as to worsen their situation. Those still owning and cultivating land will repay what they can of what is borrowed in the slack season, but repayment is likely to be either by immediate sale at harvest, when the price is lowest, or in a commitment of labor to the creditor-patron at a point when the time given will be at the expense of either timely labor on the client's own land or better peak-time wages available elsewhere.[14] If full repayment is impossible and the unpaid balance accumulates, the poor client knows what can follow; the creditor may ask that a portion of the remaining owned land be mortgaged and its usufruct turned over to the patron's discretion.[15] Perhaps the use of the land will be dealt back to the client on a sharecropping basis, but that is not likely to forestall its eventual sale to the patron when the latter wishes, after a customary time interval of further debt accumulation. They know that their principal creditor is more or less publicly recognized as the future recipient of their land (Jansen 1986). What the consumption loan alternative buys is not choice or food security, but rather, more time before the poor householder arrives at a worse choice position.

THE KINSHIP FACTOR: A SIGNIFICANT ALTERNATIVE?

Social practices regarding the time sequence of land mortgage and sale do differ according to the area, according to events (especially the number and seriousness of bad years), and by type of relationship (such as whether it is between kin versus nonkin) to the patron, yielding different lengths of time that may be taken by the land transfer process.[16] It appears that the more land a household owns, the more likely sharecropping is to be kin-based; BIDS data indicate that for categories of owners of one-half to two and a half acres, 46 to 62 percent of rented in land is from relatives, while for landless and landless tenants, only 11 to 27 percent is from relatives (Sen 1992a, 212–213).

Kinship-based borrowing and mortgage ties, however, do not seem to consistently yield a greater scope for other sorts of transaction between patron and client (e.g., household employment of client family members, sharecropping, political protection, etc.); often, the nonkin route is better on this score (Jansen 1986, 124–126, 141–142). The poor peasant may have a "choice" between a higher resource return with a nonkin connection, on one hand, and, on the other, greater social proctection with a kin linkage. However, there is no significant difference in the sense of having an alternative that gives longer-term economic assurance, which is the highest priority; both alternatives are contingent on the good will and economic fortunes of the patron. Hence, the alternatives are significantly different only as to the short-term mix of factors of economic return and social protection amid ongoing insecurity. Second, the ground of the difference that is perceived in association is economic, not political. Whichever cluster they choose, the peasants cannot afford to make the choice on political grounds, but rather may have their political behavior regulated as a consequence. There is no assurance of an economic alternative or of being able to go back to the original cluster, and there is a possibility of being left without economic or political protection against health threat or predators.

Hence, the process of land loss for a vulnerable household without an unusual connection (e.g., to a government job, a patron to bankroll a venture in trade, or favorable off-farm employment) seems inevitable. A significant exception for agrarian households may occur in the small number of cases in which the land loss process begins at or above the one acre ownership level and is due to the presence of too many male children to feed. There, the several males may eventually attain an age making full wage labor possible (e.g., around 12 years) before the household has gone under, or one of them may land a government job or a good commercial niche (the possibilities of which are usually dim). The household, then, if it has been able to stay together over the tough years, may again be able to balance its rice budget and perhaps in good harvest years achieve a surplus sufficient to do some repayment and stem further land loss if any land is left. Even here, however, viability is not assured, as their recouped position is now reliant primarily on the labor market, which in a bad year will go sour on even the most labor-rich households.

Again, especially in the bad years, the situation differs little whether the main credit patron is kin or nonkin. A patron who is a brother or fellow patrilineage member may try harder to provide extra labor opportunities after all the peasant's land has been lost, while the nonkin patron will operate the land acquisition business in a more impersonal way, perhaps cutting off all help and lending once the last available plot of land has been sold. However, the difference in regard to *loss of choice* is negligible. The kin borrower's key decision making remains socially, economically, and politically according to the wishes of the patron creditor. When both sorts of client-creditor relationships come to an end due to the peasant running out of land, the latter will be even more ready than before to trade choice for survival, with even less return. For the borrower with some remaining land who cannot find within the patrilineage a patron capable of lending the money while a nonkin lender may be had, the peasant must commit to selling land outside the kin unit and thereby sacrifice the socially important goodwill of the patrilineage for the future. When this peasant finally runs out of his tiny plots to mortgage and sell, he or she will be especially ready to trade choice for the barest chance at family survival, having alienated the patrilineage and lost any patronage potential it might have offered in the future.

While kinship links seem important to owners of 1½ acres or more, they are much less so for the poor marginals. Investigators generally have not sought data on kin versus nonkin creditor relationships, but in the village Jansen studied, among owner-cultivators of less than one acre, only a small portion of mortgages were out to kinship-linked creditors, whereas this category amounted to almost half for one- to two-acre owners (1986, 123). The number of plots mortgaged dropped off considerably for owners of over two acres; for them, mortgaging usually is only short term, to cover a temporary expense such as the wedding of a daughter. For the poorest owners this may reflect the general tendency of weakening of lineage ties among the poorest (Arens and van Beurden 1977, 91–93), a lack of well-off lineage members to whom to turn, or perhaps the inability of the poor to afford the financially less favorable terms that often accompany kin-based mortgage and sale. In any case, for them the alternative lacks significant potential effectiveness (even as it may be preferable, all else being equal, for psychological reasons) and often feasibility, two key requirements for a realistic significant alternative for choice.

A final possible vestige of traditional kinship arrangements that we might be tempted to see as adding significance to a distinct kinship borrowing alternative is the reward the selling peasant might get from better-off lineage members for keeping land within the *gusti;* care for him and his wife in old age (Jansen 1986, 115–116). This vestige of the traditional communal solidarity seems to be dying with the spread of commercialization, but data on its current relevance across Bangladesh is as yet lacking. One thing, however, is clear; that the problem of the bad years intercedes. When starvation and malnutrition-related disease stalk everywhere, children and wage earners (actual or potential) must claim first priority at the expense of others. Moreover, patrilineal solidarity itself suffers as nearly the whole patrilineage falls into poverty. Strong segments within such units may disavow lineage or family ties, splitting a communally functioning extended family for the sake of the better survival chances of going it alone (Hartmann and Boyce 1981, 162; Jansen 1986, 112–116).

LANDLESSNESS AND WAGE LABOR

The situation of the landless household dependent on the labor market is complex, but it is not fundamentally different from that of owners of small parcels regarding the search for, or dependency on, clientelistic relationships. An assessment of poverty-alleviating programs in Bangladesh sees the two categories together in the same overall context:

Because of the predominance of the family based holdings the size of the labour market is small and labour is usually hired on a daily basis as and when required. The small size of the labour market, the casual nature of employment and large seasonal fluctuations in employment and wage rate render the vast pool of the landless extremely vulnerable to economic pressures. Hence, most of them have to depend for their existence on personal contacts with a few large landholders. Similarly, the scarcity of land and the insecurity of tenancy place marginal and small landowners at the mercy of the land-rich who rent out small parcels of land. The patron-client relationship is also created through the non-institutional credit markets, because the incomes of the poor cultivators who operate at the subsistence level depend very much on the vagaries of nature, and it is the land-rich who extend consumption loans to them to tide over the difficult times. Control over tenancy, labour and credit markets gives considerable social and political power to the land-rich, which they use for controlling the channnels of distribution of public services for rural development. Consequently, the poor also gain very little from the resources supplied by the government for rural development. (Ahmad and Hossain 1983, 72–73)

The numbers of households who lack any crop acreage owned at all, and of those owning only up to one acre, have increased rapidly in recent years. In 1977–1978 those with no agricultural land left numbered 29 to 33 percent of the households and 23 to 27 percent of the rural population, and those without even homestead land left numbered 11 to 15 percent of households and 8 percent of the population (Jannuzi and Peach 1980, Tables D.1, D.2, E.1, E.2). Except for the tiny proportion who have been set up in a viable trading niche, the bulk of the landless face yearly food deficits that produce periods of starvation and dietary malnutrition. The periods of having no food or only a meager one meal of rice a day may vary from several weeks in normal crop years to two to five months for many landless peasants in bad years. At any point, a starvation- and malnutrition-weakened worker can become ill, especially with the poor drinking water available to those without access to tubewell water (Friedkin, et al. 1983, 19, 23), bringing about a real risk of what mobility students call family "extinction."[17] This is a situation Bangladeshi smallholders and landless laborers are constantly aware of, on which they know that they must act, if they can.

In good crop years, the situation of many landless laborers is little worse than that of many owners of up to an acre of land. Landless laborers, who may be sure of many days of full-wage work at peak times (harvesting, weeding, Aman transplanting in the rainy season, etc.), receive their pay immediately; income from owned land, on the other hand, comes only at harvest time, and then with much uncertainty over how low market prices will drop then (especially when part or all of the crop has been precommitted to a patron or moneylender). At peak times, when wage labor opportunities are available at full rates, the small owning household with a third of an acre or more of land faces substantial opportunity costs, whichever choice of emphasis they make between working their own land at the right time and working for a well-to-do peasant at full wage, and thus getting a return then and there. In crafting the mixture the peasants may sacrifice timely harvesting or weeding on their own plots in favor of some full-wage labor opportunity; the badly timed work on their own plots reduces their productivity. This is especially tempting if the employer offers a chance at slack-time labor in the future as part of an informal commitment to be on call for the patron at peak times. As we have seen from the dietary data for landless laborers and owners of a half acre or less, the basic dietary situation for the landless laborers and the smallest owners are, on the average, roughly the same.[18] The laborer who has under three-tenths of an acre of homestead land left does not suffer the opportunity cost of labor commitment at peak times because there is little home cultivation to do beyond the vegetable gardening, which is nutritionally crucial (Dumont 1973b, 51–52) but less a contender with rice for timely work in this situation. Moreover, for those who lack agricultural land, recent indications are that even tiny increments of remaining homestead land have become of sufficient value that they may be the basis for clientelistic relationships with patrons out to gain land through mortgage and purchase, and hence for consumption loans from them (Jansen 1990, 23).

The other side of this coin, however, is that as remaining land dwindles toward zero, landless peasants eventually have less to offer a potential patron in return for consumption loans (Arens and van Beurden 1977, 113–114) and are much more at the mercy of slack times, fluctuations in rice prices, incidental personal difficulties (e.g., a family member in ill health), and—more disastrously—bad years (e.g., of flood disruption) (Van Schendel 1981, 68). Related to this, there is a vast difference between the small owner and the landless in the bad year which comes along every few years. The owner of agricultural land knows at least that it provides a receptacle for family labor and will get some return, perhaps at higher prices (see Van Schendel 1981, 180). Furthermore, he knows he has collateral for consumption loans to cover his shortfall. The landless laborer, on the other hand, may face a shortened   ak labor demand with the consequent widened food deficit (meaning   rvation or at least near-starvation malnutrition for the children). He has   , any collateral for consumption loans other than the small homestead plot that provides the nutritionally crucial vegetable component of the diet. The owner's worry is over how much land he will have to mortgage or sell as a result of accelerated borrowing, and perhaps—if his household has recently dropped from a higher ownership level—the loss of honor (izzat) of having to allow female household members to work in the households of others (i.e., to give up purdah). The landless laborer's worry is over life itself for family members, and he will even more readily trade choice for better probabilities for food security via the labor opportunities that the patron has to offer (Jansen 1986, 147–148, 193–194; Arens and van Beurden 1977, 99). What the marginal owner and the landless have in common, however, is central to our purposes here; they share the fear of the acute distress suffered more directly by the latter, toward whose desperate situation the former knows he is sliding. This whole situation of the recurring bad years serves to structure, for the whole spectrum with which we are concerned here, the relinquishing of choice to patron preference, even in normal years when food balance may be achievable.

Even in periods for which some aggregate statistics show a reduction in the numbers in the poorest rural category, the surrounding context weakens the statistical impression. A case in point is the situation of the poor in the 1980s period of improvement in overall food-grain output. Statistics from the Household Expenditure Survey (HES) for that period show a big reduction in the rural numbers at the severe, under 1,800-calorie poverty level, from 37 percent in 1983–1984 to 26 percent in 1985–1986 (Hossain 1989, 60–61). Methodological difficulties in the gathering and use of data have led to controversy and skepticism about these statistics, but even critics agree that the real (rice-equivalent) wage rate did rise toward the end of this period and the bottom 40 percent did better.[19] Rahman and Haque suggest that the gains in the real wage rate that they see as primarily responsible for the appearance of a 1984–1986 poverty alleviation were due to a transient drop in the price of rice rather than to gains in productivity or agricultural employment (1988, 27, 31, 38). Moreover, the preceeding, 1978–1983, period seems to have seen a distress-pushed rural-to-urban migration of up to a million landless households (Hossain 1989, 58–59), which would tend to improve rural statistics while actually doing no more than shifting part of the worst poverty to the urban Bangladeshi scene. The overall improvement for the lower strata may indeed have been less than meets the eye.

To be sure, the increased irrigated HYV acreage over the middle 1980s placed greater demands on the labor supply in peak periods. Higher wage rates amid lower rice prices would have helped landless laborers but have harmed the situation of some small producers. Only a portion of the landless laboring households, however, may have gotten improved food security from the higher peak-season market wages. Employers with clientelistic connections to the laborer (credit, sharecrop, slack-season labor), would have been able to continue to lock in lower-than-market peak-season wages.[20]

Some of those who benefited from the high peak-season market wage rates were members of labor groups who migrated under contract during the dry, slack season in their home area with weak development of irrigated HYV *boro*, to distant areas of concentrated irrigated HYV development (Jansen 1990; Adnan 1987), for whom the same period was a peak season demanding more labor. Thus comparatively assured of food security during the home-area (slack) dry season, they could fill far more of their year with peak or near-peak wage labor, and could in some cases more or less do without patrons. Jansen observed in 1986–1987 that increased demand for casual peak-season labor has led to more of the landless grouping together for migrant or home-area labor in peak periods, both for securing labor contracts and for demanding higher wages than those bound to their employer by clientelistic connections (1990, 30). White also calls attention to this development, in which the introduction of HYV rice has brought such a peak of labor damand at harvest that even local laborers, as well as migrants, work in groups performing all harvesting tasks (from cutting and threshing to sacking) in a system she calls "sharecutting," for 12.5 percent of the paddy

(1991, 62). In the Daripalla villages studied by Adnan, this demand for migrant groups came at the peak periods of June–July and November–December (1987, 259).

Jansen is careful to point out that dry-season migration in gangs to northern Bangladesh—in effect breaking the connection of dependency within the local area—is the crucial social foundation for such labor groupings (1990, 30–31). Insofar as this migration provides an often-lacking food source for a slack period of the year for at least the laborer himself, this can be a meaningful addition to the household's food access. Members of such groups, often having burned bridges to support in hard times from better-off households in their home areas, seem to feel they depend more on each other for crisis support. Jansen goes on to observe that at least some of these laborers make a point of ignoring traditions of deference, and have at times acted against landowners who were unwilling to offer the wage rates demanded (1990, 30–32). Jansen even observed that in local courts, poor people without patrons "on a number of occasions backed fellow poor people who were in trouble with the well-to-do" (1990, 32).

For the purposes of this analysis, however, even this most favorable situation for the landless does not meet the test of assurance of minimal food security over the whole year. These labor groups temporarily earning a comparatively good wage rate enjoy employment only in peak times of demand high enough to out-strip the supply of local clients, who get labor opportunities first (whether or not at lower wages as a part of the clientelistic relationship). Jansen is careful to point out that even the niches for such informal labor organization that do exist depend, not only on the choice to organize, but also "very much on the demand of agricultural wage labourers and employment possibilities outside agriculture" (1990, 30). In periods of comparative prosperity, and particularly in areas in close proximity to urban areas, demand for laborers in peak times can be intense, encouraging a tolerance of activities of worker solidarity provided the employer can be assured of a workforce for a key task (Jansen 1990). In agriculture, it seems to be mainly the richest landowners who employ the gangs; they are better able to afford higher wage rates and more likely to have land beyond what can be farmed by their clients.

There are significant disadvantages to even these laborers' situation, however, which enhance their vulnerability. Adnan notes that in the villages he studied, visiting migrant labor groups in peak periods experienced longer hours, inferior working conditions, and complete dependency for their needs on the employer (1987, 259). At the same time, the laborers enjoy no commitment for employment, credit, or other support in the employer area's slack season; even in 1985–1986, White observed in the area she studied that wage levels dropped in the slack season to little more than half their peak season levels (1991, 63–64), not to speak of the bad years when hardly any employment is available. While such households can have good food access years, comparative assurance is not there. Furthermore, migrating groups seem to encompass as yet only a small portion of the landless laboring subset of the vulnerable category.

Moreover, there are partially hidden clientelistic dependency aspects to the organizational behavior of these labor groups. Notably, the associative behavior that does go on is controlled by the labor gang leader, who makes all the key decisions (Jansen 1990, 31), possibly amounting to a replacement of one style of intermediate patronage with another. White points out regarding this "new" development of work gangs that, in the case of migrant gangs,

It is clear . . . that personal linkages are again very important in these relationships—they are the means through which a gang comes to a particular area, and they often strengthen during the period of stay. The class significance of migrant workers clearly differs in different contexts. In Kumirpur, their social backgrounds and the tendency to develop personal links clearly cautions against identifying them . . . as "proletarian elements" in the countryside. . . . [As to local, home-area groups,] the state of the market in general is only part of the story: in practice much depends on the nature of the relationship between employer and employee and how the two parties can manipulate this to serve their own interests. While there is no doubt that vertical ties through labour are more mobile than they used to be, this does not mean that labour is fully "free." Labour is often part of a wider cluster relationship. It is very common for labourers to be pledged to work for one particular landowner first, and for the landowner in return to be bound to offer any work first to them. While labourers may perceive these links to be chiefly beneficial to the landowner, they also recognise the value of the security they give. (1991, 62–64)

The necessary allegiance to the leader could extend to political behavior as well; Adnan notes two cases of wage worker groups that were each mobilized by their leader to vote for the candidate of the power structure in their villages (1987, 361). However, it must be said regarding the leaders of Adnan's groups, at least, that they did not get commissions (as with other labor intermediaries) and they seemed to allocate work in the interest of the whole group rather than the employer or the better-off workers in it (Adnan 1987, 266–268). Facilitating this degree of independence on the part of labor group leaders in Adnan's villages was the fact that at least some of them were better off than other group members, perhaps possessing land that competed for their time with group employment (Adnan 1987, 268).

As to the future, Jansen suggests that larger numbers of the landless may abandon attempts to find a quasiclientelistic relationship with one owner for reliable employment even if at a lower rate, and turn instead to this labor union–style bargaining behavior (1990, 32). However, if this did occur, competition among labor groups for the few opportunities offered by the richest would seem to lower rates and render employment for them even less assured than it is now. Rather than finding increasing landlessness bringing about more such solidarity out of necessity, the future may instead bring ever greater scarcity of food access–providing labor opportunities. Quite possibly, even the "single-stranded" employment relationship will become so highly prized by the landless laborer that, on one hand, such informal labor organization as that discussed by Jansen will decline, and on the other, those privileged with jobs may experience even greater vulnerability to coercion than what multistranded clients experience now. It remains Jansen's belief that "the great majority of the rural population are part of patron-client relationships which hinders confrontations between rich and poor" (1990, 32).

Of course, there are other sources of employment whereby a family member may earn something in the slack season, particularly for those rural areas that are close to urban ones. Indeed, overall statistics indicate that the farm sector has been unable to absorb growth in the rural labor force; between 1974 and 1985, the labor force occupied in agriculture remained basically the same in absolute numbers, so that the whole addition of 5.5 million to the rural labor force over the period had to go into nonagricultural labor, over a period of low growth in gross domestic product *per capita*—only 0.4 percent per annum (Parthasarathy 1989, 115). While the agricultural labor growth related to the the HYV-spurred 1980s has been heavily concentrated at certain peak periods in the year, the 1985–1986 peak in output certainly trickled down to more overall niches available in off-farm employment and self-employment, particularly for women in rice businesses. While White notes that poorer-stratum households able to take advantage of these opportunities may achieve "some independence of village patronage," she goes on to conclude that such independence "is far from complete: businesses are typically supplementary to other economic activities, profits may be marginal and are subject to severe seasonal fluctuations" (1991, 73). Indeed, recent increases in rural off-farm employment has been at very low returns, especially for new entrants, and such increases were greatest in the poorest villages, where the distress-push of agricultural employment was greatest (Parthasarathy 1989, 115).

Nor is migration to urban areas for a family member a significant alternative in itself for household food access. In urban areas the poor do traditionally have better real incomes on average than the rural poor. For 1984, data indicate that in urban areas the incomes of the lowest 40 percent remained 25 percent higher than those of the lowest 40 percent in rural areas (Rahman, Mahmud, and Haque 1988, 32), and 49 percent had a caloric intake below the national average of 1975, as opposed to 61 percent in rural areas (Shahabuddin 1989, 112). Furthermore, the urban poor seem to have access to a wider range of nutritional components in their diet than the rural poor. Perhaps partially as a result of mid-1980s distress-pushed rural-to-urban migration, however, in 1986, the statistically optimistic HES survey showed 56 percent of urban dwellers earning incomes that were not sufficient for the absolute poverty-level food intake of 2,122 calories a day (Ghafur 1990, 73).

The urban employment scene seems to be segmented, with huge numbers underemployed. Beyond the 300,000 to 500,000 employed as guest workers in the Middle East and elsewhere (who can send back good remittances), significant real wages and more secure employment are limited to a few industries, often calling into full or more intensive employment those already employed in those areas or with connections in them. Three-fourths of the urban employed are migrant workers, with the most common entry point the construction sector, most of whose wages are generally among the lowest for the unskilled (Mahmud, Rahman, and Haque 1988, 62–63, 65, 83). While the numbers employed can always be increased by starting more new construction projects, budgetary austerities render this uncertain as a long-term solution. There remains a large and growing mass of informal sector urban poor (e.g., unskilled construction workers, servants, rickshaw pullers, petty traders, and vagrants of various sorts) whose labor can neither support households nor provide entrée to anything better. The urban sector seems incapable of providing viable employment to the steady influx of unskilled would-be laborers escaping rural poverty. Urban migration usually amounts to no more than a detachment of part of the rural problem, and it does not give rise to remittances sufficient to make it a solution.

The employment situation is especially distressing for women, in both rural and urban sectors. Rural women's participation in the labor force outside the home would seem to be low, as the social value of purdah has traditionally kept outside-home labor by women concentrated among the distressed poor. However, some earlier surveys may have significantly underreported women's work outside the home; a recent *Agricultural Sector Review* survey indicates that rural sector participation, mainly in agriculture, may run as high as 42.6 percent, and rural labor force participation overall, as high as 54.4 percent (Safilios-Rothschild and Mahmud 1989, 2). As this is mainly poverty induced, it does not indicate real progress in women's education or training. Women in both rural and urban sectors work longer hours, commonly receive less than half the pay men get, and no relief from the burdens of household responsibilities. Adnan (1990) notes that in the 1980s the shift of some women out of agriculture has been mainly pushed by household subsistence needs rather than pulled by attractive returns; both respect and incomes from the urban garment industry (with long hours and bad working conditions) and other sorts of employment for women have been extremely low, suggesting at best only a component contribution to family food access. Women seem to have been accepted on more equal terms, however, at the slack season food-for-work sites and in the women's small-loan programs by Grameen Bank and other NGOs for small trade and processing activities (Adnan 1990, 36–38, 45–46). Nonetheless, only a small number of rural women have been reached by the latter.

Women in poor smallholding households owning up to an acre are comparatively underemployed in their traditional roles (i.e., rice husking, animal husbandry, vegetable growing on the homestead plot) due to a lack of crops and livestock, if they try to maintain *purdah*, the Muslim custom of sequestering women in the home economically. The return for nonagricultural in-home cottage industry work or petty trade is insufficient. The increasing mechanization of postharvest milling by the better-off is likely to reduce casual labor opportunities for poor women over the long term, even though it opens up a smaller segment of niches related to the "rice business" of buying, transporting to and from the mill, purchasing the milling services, and selling the end product (White 1991). Nonfarm income-earning activities are significant primarily for women of the better-off households who have the resources to get into them on a viable scale, and the elite are often exempt from the ostracism that can follow from breaking purdah. In urban areas, the garment industry has provided some growth in formal-sector employment. Apparently, however, the benefits have mainly gone to a small long-resident segment of urban women, as the sector remains insecure due to market fluctuations and more or less closed to more recent migrants to the city (Mahmud, Rahman, and Hague 1988, 68–70). Women's urban employment remains 60 percent in the service sector, mainly in domestic service. Women's participation in professional, managerial, or technical fields remains no more than 5 percent, and no more than 7 percent work in the civil service, three-quarters of whom are in education and health (Jahan 1989, 4, 5, 10).

To sum up, it is necessary for poorer-stratum rural households to parcel household labor in a combined farming, wage laboring, and borrowing strategy. This strategy is constrained, however, as prized wage labor opportunities in the slack season are often tied to labor commitments to the patron at peak times at lower than peak-market wage levels. Even more important, peak-period labor commitments come at the expense of delaying crucial work on one's own land (for those who are not landless). The owner of less than one acre cannot readily exit the relationship without a sharp drop in the level of temporary food security and is, for all practical purposes, confined to the current track of economic endeavor. Under current conditions, the slide into mounting debt, mortgage, and the sale of land toward landlessness seems inevitable for vast numbers.

This inevitably insecure existence is tied to characteristic limitations in the choice structure faced, amounting to less than an option of minimal signficant choice. First, in rural Bangladesh, the choice of economic endeavor is constrained to focus, first and foremost, on food access before any other sort of concern can be entertained. This in turn requires dependency on a primary patron creditor, sometimes one owning as little as two acres. The choice is not limited to well-off members of the household's own kinship group, as nonkin owners are also on the lookout for opportunities to gradually secure the land of food-deficit households. However, the initial choice of who the *particular* patron lender will be, including whether kin or nonkin, seldom makes a significant long-term difference in the outcomes about which the poor household is most worried— eating and the encroaching debt and land loss. While there are some short-term differences in the customary terms of kin and nonkin borrowing, the outcomes for pursued values do not significantly differ.

The confinement to this path of endeavor tends to result in the absence of minimal significant choice in other fields for choice as well. The dependent will often serve as part of the faction in village politics of the patron or the patron's patron, at times as part of the latter's informal security force, or even as part of a labor force commandeered at peak times, when the need for timely labor on the client's own land or seasonally high wages for labor make the opportunity cost of compliance very high. Loans may be customarily linked to a commitment to labor on the patron's land for particular types of peak period, like *aman*-transplanting (White 1991, 61). The patron may even influence the marriage choices of household sons and daughters.

Whether to seek such a patron and enter the relationship if one is available is itself not really in doubt. It is the only short-term alternative providing survival where there is a willing lender available, and the only significant alternative in the economic field of choice. Where there is not such a lender available—as in the case of many households who lack land for a creditor to acquire—they must seek one, in hopes at least of securing a slack-season labor opportunity and way to cover the deficit periods when wage labor is not available. They must bear in mind whatever they perceive to be the preferences of the whole category of candidate-patrons in advance. They are not really "free laborers" as the Leninists suggest, because of the imperative to seek a patron. Here clientelism is not merely a feudal vestige, but is rather an imperative of the new pattern of commercial penetration.

Again, one must keep in mind the limits of the argument here: that, for a definable poor category in a specific national situation of rural poverty and on ordinary assumptions about human motivation, a general choice structure is in place that involves a human rights problem calling for feasible, human rights-sensitive action. In no way does this argument involve an empirical prediction that *all* members of the category will display nonparticipation or single-alternative, coerced participation. It is only that the choice structure will not provide the *assurance* of two or more significant alternatives for choice of, for example, an economic course of endeavor or civil-political expression or association.

The attitudes of Bangladeshi patrons, clients, and unattached landless laborers, may, in particular times and places, allow for freer client behavior. In the anonymity of the crowd at a political rally, peasants might openly support a candidate representing their own interests (Adnan 1987, 451). Moreover, Adnan (1987) presented a case of substantial oppositional activity by poor rickshaw pullers supporting a candidate, Panjab (of a small party) who distinctively sought to represent the interests of the poor in some of the Daripalla villages. The rickshaw pullers canvassed for Panjab while, at the same time, conveying Awami League supporters to the polls in the hire of a wealthy and powerful supporter of a rival of Panjab (Adnan 1987, 434). However, the rickshaw pullers' support for Panjab at Daripalla indicated to Adnan only that the poor in general can "under conducive conditions" act in a way liberated from economic dependencies, so as to underline the fragility of such a situation and undercut any long-term conclusions about free political opposition by the poor:

The incident did, however, serve to reveal that the very poor rickshaw-wallahs led by Fatik did not feel obliged to support the AL electorally, even though they had been hired to provide a certain "service" by the latter. In other words, the economic/market contract did not, and was not seen to, tie their political freedom and rights. It would thus appear that, under conducive conditions, the poor and the powerless were perfectly capable of asserting themselves politically, notwithstanding any economic ties of dependency to which they might be simultaneously subject. However, such potentialities were unlikely to prove sustainable over time unless harnessed under the protective and directed command of an organizational structure capable of coping with the pressures and reactive sanctions likely to be forthcoming. (1987, 434)

Notably, Panjab's small political party, because of its willingness to participate in the military government's parliament while the country was under martial law—while the much larger Awami league boycotted parliament in protest of martial law—was actually officially protected at high levels of the political system. This scope of choice is not really assured in the way that alternatives are assured by the social practice of observing a right.

Unfortunately, Adnan does not distinguish, among the poor, different degrees and kinds of poverty (e.g., as measured by landownership among peasants), with their different consequences for the degree and kind of vulnerability that exists in the clientelistic dependencies. He gives no specific examples of *agrarians* among the poor engaging in overt oppositional political behavior (such as was displayed by the market-enmeshed rickshaw pullers) elsewhere except in cases where *shamajpradhans* (*shamaj* leaders) decided not to force the votes of their followers among the *shamaj* members, or even supported Panjab (Adnan 1989, 389).[21] Adnan states that "it was reported to us that many of the poorer peasants of Nandigram did not dare to work openly on behalf of Panjab, or express their support for him in public, because they were afraid of antagonizing Mokhtar" (who had not made threats in canvassing), in contrast to a "middle peasant" in Mokhtar's *shamaj* who voted for another candidate than Mokhtar's (1987, 396–397). In another area, Adnan states that

the factor *common* to all these cases was that those amongst the poor of Rajbari who expressed their support for JI openly were also among those who were not economically dependent for their survival on members of the Sultan Group. It was this crucial consideration which distinguished them from those others amongst the poor who did not actually support the AL, but maintained that they did so in public (particularly in the presence of Sultan's men). (1987, 394)

In another village, Adnan points out that:

what enabled Osman and the rest of Rahim's band of JI supporters to stand up to the *shamajpradhans* of KT in the first place was the fact that they were not particularly dependent on the latter's patronage and had independent means of survival of their own. (1987, 395)

In sum, in Adnan's account, oppositional behavior was observable among the poor as a whole only in the nonpublic phenomenon of the substantial numbers of them who had to have used the "protective cover and silence of the *secret ballot*" to support Panjab on election day (1987, 417). Moreover, where the intimidation of poor clients was through the threat of violence, the temporary cessation of such overt acts of intimidation need not rule out withdrawal or denial of *economic opportunities*, whether now or in the future, that provide critical components of poor households' minimal food strategy.[22]

In short, the number of unusual niches for a wider range of choice is small. The choice structure facing the vast majority of rural Bangladeshis owning under an acre, is unidimensional. They have no significant alternative to the household strategy they are following, of small plot farming (if available) cum credit-based clientelistic dependency and supplementary wage labor where possible. The strategy has a combination of components in some degree of trade-off with one another, which may be weighted differently for different households but is essentially the same for most owners of less than one acre. Thus the challenge is to open up a second significant alternative of economic endeavor, to be taken up only voluntarily, so as to render minimally voluntary whatever route is chosen, the present or the new.

HIGH YIELDING VARIETY PRODUCTION: A CURRENT SIGNIFICANT ALTERNATIVE?

Finally, it might be thought that small-owning peasants have the option of taking up high-yielding variety rice agriculture in order to double or triple their crop yields from owned or sharecropped acreage and thus reverse their situation. However, much that has already been covered here contributes to a negative answer about this option under current conditions. First, this is no help to the landless, for they do not have the resources to sharecrop or gain land. Moreover, HYV agriculture involves high costs (most significantly in the form of controlled irrigation water), particularly to make possible a winter "*boro*" crop, that those without irrigation access simply cannot produce. Significantly, from the 1970s, electric and diesel-powered deep and intermediate-depth tubewells, substantially subsidized by government and aid programs, have fueled an expansion of HYV output. Vis-à-vis poor peasants, however, this development has amounted at best to a modification of clientelistic dependency.

It seems clear to most that deep tubewell water programs have substantially benfited primarily the patrons and their clients.[23] The early formal "cooperatives," which got credit from development aid programs to obtain the diesel or electric tubewells, tended to be dominated by one or a few well-off landowners who had the contacts and paid the bribes to get the tubewell in the first place, and who often had the influence in the local elite structure to evade repayment of credit; they seem to typically use their control over water and its price to extend their control over land and strengthen their economic and sociopolitical position as patrons.[24] The picture emerges of clienteles who pay a quarter to a third of their crop to this tubewell "owner." These large tubewells, with their 50-acre-plus potential command areas, typically provide water for only 15 to 25 acres, due to difficulties in building (and sparing land for) water distribution channels and coping with the frequent breakdowns that can cause loss of a crop in which expensive fertilizer and insecticide (not to speak of labor) have been invested. Needless to say, even the least well-off among the clients receiving deep tubewell water for irrigation are normally above the level of an acre and a half ownership if they are primarily cultivating households.[25] The pattern of clientelistic dependency may thus develop around the water market, which may be "interlocked" with credit access, just as sharecropping may be (Jansen 1979); Adnan notes that in the Daripalla villages, waterlord sharecropping and fixed rent in kind replaced conventional sharecropping for irrigated land over the period of the introduction of the deep tubewells (1987, 220–222, 235). For owners of less than one acre and the landless, a much more inexpensive and decentralized access to water, under the poor peasants' own control, must be provided (among other things) for irrigated HYV production to become a significant alternative to the current situation of clientelistic dependency. Before exploring a more hopeful route of remedy, we turn to briefer examinations of very similar choice structure limitations in two very different cases, Botswana and Tanzania.

THE CHOICE STRUCTURE FOR RURAL BOTSWANA

We saw regarding rural Bangladesh that the rural poor owning very small acreages (or none) of agricultural land found themselves with only one significant alternative of economic endeavor, a dependency on a primary creditor patron (kin or not), with consequences of sharply constrained choice in the civil-political fields of action. In rural Botswana, we see again a dependency arising, here from the need for access to draft power to plow. The most common type of access to borrowed ox teams, requiring "putting in hands" (labor by the borrower on the ox lender's fields), tends to involve long-term dependence on the relative or neighbor whose ox-team did the plowing essential for household survival. A mid-1980 study of a village showed that such relationships tend to be maintained with the same household (usually kin-related) from year to year (ATIP 1986, 126). A secondary component of the single strategy, of course, was employment opportunities for family members, whether in the agricultural sector for the draft-lending patron or elsewhere.

The single alternative of economic endeavor was significant in making a crucial contribution to food access, whether or not that contribution was fully adequate nutritionally or relatively secure from year to year. In the case of year-round control over the oxen of others in the traditional *mafisa* relationship (a longer-term loan of an animal), food access could approach the comparative assurance (assuming some effectiveness for government drought relief feeding programs in the worst years) achieved by those who owned their own draft team. In the middle part of the spectrum were the varying degrees of nutritional inadequacy of those plowing late with some sort of draft borrowing. At the extreme, a shortage of plowing labor (usually due to male migration to unskilled labor elsewhere, able to feed only the laborer without significant remittance) can cause very poor or no plowing capacity, further reducing nutritional adequacy for the women and children. Throughout the spectrum, however, the amount of food access depended on the owner of most of the oxen used to plow and the labor opportunity offered.

To be sure, there are borderline situations that may be analyzed. For example, the owner of most of an ox team (say, four to five oxen) may come close to independently meeting food needs from agriculture. Those already owning part of an ox team might "*mafisa* in" some animals (particularly from relatives) to make a team under their own control for timely, first-in-line plowing. Nonetheless, the cultivator is still dependent on the owner of whatever plowing input must be borrowed. There is also a kind of *mafisa* in which labor-short households (female, migrant laborer, or old) owning a few animals may *mafisa* them *out* to a labor-possessing household (again, often kin-linked) holding part of a plow team (Koojman 1978, 182–183, 228–232). With this sort of lending, the owner of the majority of the team is likely to have the option of plowing his or her field first, preserving the rule of thumb that the household owning the least cattle is normally the more disadvantaged and dependent. Botswana is a dry country, and a crucial part in agriculture is played by the proper timing of plowing after the early rains.

A small portion of Western "sandveld" cattlepost dependents have customary access to timely plowing by borrowing cattle from the herd that are not used by their owner for plowing, if they own a plow (Hitchcock 1978, 323–324, 346–348, 354).[26] Many must borrow a plow, wherein the owner of the plow may require that his field be plowed first, and the crucial timeliness of plowing will be lost. However, having a favorable situation without ownership of draft animals is dependent on the continuation of the relationship to the well-off herd-owner, at the latter's discretion, and hence remains a vulnerably dependent one.

At the extreme, a cattle-short or cattleless household's productive viability may have dropped below the capacity to do any plowing on their own land at all (usually this is female headed). This may be temporary, as in drought, or permanent, as in the absence of family labor. Here the household members will have to hire themselves out for part or all of the agricultural season in what is called *majako*, often with poor security of payment according to agreed-to terms.[27] Being forced into the extreme dependency of a servant relationship with a rich household seems to be associated with shame and is much feared (Koojman 1978, 243).

Following the decimation of small herds during the drought of the 1980s, and the increasingly prevalent commercial attitudes toward cattle—making owners reluctant to reduce the value of their beef by the stress of plowing—lending and *mafisaing* animals for plowing from rich owner to poor holder seems to be on the decline. Access by the poor to borrowed draft oxen and milk, often involving extended kinship cooperation, has eroded rapidly (Solway 1986, 9–11; Farrington and Marsh 1987, 2–4). Silmultaneously, the erosion of broad kinship obligation has been observable starting from the 1970s (Koojman 1978; Gulbrandsen 1984b, 32). Also weakening has been the availability of family labor—the only resource the poorer strata have with which to contend with their lack of other resources—with the flight of many young men to the cities. Opportunities in both rural and urban areas (and in South Africa), for employment paying well enough for family members to remit money to the rural household to buy food and plowing power, grow ever more scarce in relation to the numbers seeking them.

As has been argued above in the case of Bangladesh, there is no evidence in the empirical literature surveyed here that dwindling numbers of attractive dependency relationships offering food access toward the adequate end of the nutritional spectrum in any way "free" the food-insecure poor from the dependency. Indeed, there is likely to be ever greater pressure on the poor to gain or keep scarce dependencies on better-off households around them. Such relationships are necessary for the meager economic opportunities for borrowing plowing power or for employment particularly in drought years, which allow them to get by (although in a state of undernutrition). For assuring mere survival, they must pursue them all the more avidly, and perhaps be ready to sacrifice ever more choices. With the comparatively favorable arrangements becoming ever more scarce and prized, the good will of the lender will be increasingly more critical. The favored situations of *mafisaing* oxen or holding a good remittance-capable urban job renders the holder ever more vulnerably dependent. For those lacking such a situation, choice constraint would extend to anticipating the limiting preferences even of any would-be patrons on the horizon, to some extent locking in significant choice constraint for even those without ongoing economic dependencies.

We may say of the whole category that their fragile minimal well-being in normal crop years, often characterized by undernutrition for one or more family members over one or more months of the year, involves dependency on a better-off household (be it kin or nonkin) for the survival-critical resource of plowing capacity. In a bad crop year, when even the owners of draft power might suffer substantial cattle losses or crop failure, the vulnerable households' dependency becomes stark indeed. The favor of the better-off household with which the poor has, or might have, a connection becomes "the only game in town." The need of those who have such relationships to maintain them, and of those poor without them to get them, can only bring the vulnerable category to attend ever more closely to the preferences of the possessors of potentially borrowable cattle when it comes to participation, or nonparticipation, in village politics.

The plowing aspect, of course, does not make up the whole single-alternative choice structure facing the vulnerable category in rural Botswana. A secondary, but still important, component of their food access strategies is employment, temporary or otherwise. Economists often talk simply of "jobs" or "job growth," principally in the urban sector, calling them the savior of outmoded "peasantries." This implies that what is called "economic growth" in macro-economic statistics means opening up rural or urban labor for others as a significant alternative route to rural subsistence. Also implied is the comparative "freedom" of differentiated urban economies and seemingly wide range of job choice, in the impersonal "modernized" world, without interpersonal vulnerability to civil-political constraint. However, what this conventional impression leaves out is the whole realm of the particulars of the job, and the urban cost of living if the job is urban.

In reality, the Botswanan urban sector is not sufficient to support more than a small portion of poor households that might be desirous of moving. There are few or no trading niches available (Gulbrandsen 1990), and those who do participate in the urban sector do so by temporary or permanent household division (i.e., the seasonal or permanent migration of one or more family members, usually male). Seldom, however, is this alternative capable of making a significant difference in the level of living of the household left in the rural area (Wikan 1981, 57, 74). Poor migrants characteristically lack modern education, and hence are limited to urban wage levels that are too low to allow sufficient remittances to improve the food capacity of the women, children, and elders back in the rural areas (Kossoudji and Mueller 1983, 842–844; Arntzen 1984, 11–13; Gulbrandsen 1990). Most such migration is undertaken by able young men, "disproportionately from the relatively privileged large villages" and possessing the "more employable skills" (Jones 1982, 321). Even households wealthy enough to provide modern education to their sons are now experiencing greater difficulty in turning the degree into a good job (Gulbrandsen 1990).

By far the most important consequence for the poor is loss of the labor that cattle-poor families used to trade for late plowing access (Egner and Klausen 1980, 11–12). Their food capacity vulnerability is thus made worse in many cases by the migration of family members to the urban areas, and they are still locked into the economic strategy of seeking access to borrowed plowing capacity. Often it was precisely because of draft insufficiency that the males had to migrate to town employment in the first place (Noppen 1982, 149–150; Koojman 1978, 228). As Hesselberg argues, the persistent gap between urban jobs and would-be rural applicants will keep the rest of the family rural where minimal survival can at least be had (1982, 323).

There might seem to be a major exception to this pattern in the pattern of migrant labor in South African mines. Gulbrandsen (1980) has argued persuasively that for many households, a long period of mine labor can provide enough remittances for small herds to be built up back home for the miner's eventual retirement (around 40, usually). However, the late-1970s limits placed on Botswanan migration to South Africa, cutting it off at less than half the 1970s peak levels, have curtailed this alternative. The result has been significantly increased economic marginalization (Gulbrandsen 1990), while pasture degradation has cut down on a small herd's potential.

A relevant government effort is the Labor-Based Relief section of the drought relief program, under which unemployed people who are reached by the program may receive jobs on development projects in return for pay. Usually work may only be provided for two weeks a month per laborer, but the rate of pay has been increased to keep pace with inflation. The projects are limited to times of year that are not periods of peak labor demand in the agricultural cycle, to avoid competing with farm owners for labor. Under these limitations it is unlikely that labor-based relief can amount to more than a small component in a survival strategy, however. Furthermore, participation remains dependent on the favor of the local bureaucrats administering it.

As one might suspect, a large portion of the vulnerable category are women and their children. Over half of all rural households are either formally or de facto female headed (Kerven 1979). The migrants to distant labor tend to be husbands and grown sons, leaving the wives as de facto heads of households. There are many de jure female-headed households, which are dependent on their brothers, fathers, or uncles for (late) plowing capacity and poorly equipped to weed effectively enough to farm many acres productively. The males work in the towns, earning subsistence wages for themselves, often including some for beer (which has some nutritional benefit for them), and possibly saved from having to have to suffer the privations of the women and children in the field to the same degree in the hunger months of hard agricultural work before harvest. Female-headed households that fail in this strategy may be forced into full dependency on a better-off household for *majako* work (Vierich and Sheppard 1980) over the whole season or, moving into town, a mixture of work commitment to an employer with farming a small amount of borrowed land from the employer (Hesselberg 1981, 44–45). These are but variations on a single strategy, with different prioritized components receiving different emphases as imposed by the circumstances. They involve economic dependency on a better-off household, be it kin or nonkin, that would seem to require sensitivity to the preferences of actual or would-be dispensers of access to draft power, labor opportunities, and so forth.

If, on the other hand, a household owns a team of animals for a plow and its traction, it can survive without fully food-viable slack-season jobs for the family members. Such households can often afford to send a child to a town for a good enough education to provide credentials for a chance at a formal-sector job. Such a household is likely to be able to survive even a drought year on the proceeds of good years, or the sale of an animal, with the chance of recouping to previous herd size in the better years following. We may conclude that the household with an owned traction unit actually has a foundation for *choosing between significantly different courses of economic endeavor*. Under these circumstances, constraint on civil-political choice is lifted.

CHOICE STRUCTURE IN TANZANIA

Tanzania is a country that for some time has been comparatively less open to objective social science research than the others considered here. It is also one in which the local party-government bureaucracy has been a comparatively stronger player in structuring the environment of average-to-poorer-strata peasants. Further, Tanzania's village setting has been profoundly affected by the villagization program, which sought to have government concentrate people in villages in order to (with donor aid) bring economic-social services to them.

A full-scale, multi-stranded dependency can include several values exchanged, such as client commitment of labor, political support, and physical security help for the patron, in return for use of a plow team, sharecropping acreage, and slack-season labor opportunities for the client. It is this kind of multi-sided relationship that, for anthropologists, qualifies as a full-scale patron-client one. In Tanzania since villagization, it might be asserted that villagization replaced dependencies on private patrons with a single dependency on the village party-government, which is now in a position to supply the basic needs impartially to all in need.

It may be that the incidence of full-scale clientelism was reduced somewhat by villagization, particularly where "capitalist farmers" owning large tracts had land redistributed. However, it is not necessary to the vulnerability of minimal significant choice and food access with which we are concerned that clientelism be multifaceted. Certainly many of the dependencies of the vulnerable will be such full-scale patron-client bonds, But many others will involve only a single-stranded economic exchange, such as one of timely plowing or weeding labor in return for late use of the cattle-owner's plow team. These are only referred to here as "clientelistic" due to having some relevant features of the patron-client relationship. Moreover, of course, there may be multiple dependencies for multiple needs, and the key suppliers may be local government officials as well as private individuals.

The supply of essential resources for basic needs in Tanzanian villages fell far short of demand after villagization, as it had before. The people in charge of any scarce resource from day to day, like the people in charge of the village water supply or the local health officials, may indeed have their perceived civil-political preferences anticipated by those on whom they depend, as the latter set significant limits on their civil-political behavior. Where there is a partial clientelistic dependency rather than a full-blown patron-client relationship, what may be most often expected of the dependent in civil-political fields for choice is not active participation in the faction to which the patron belongs in village politics, but more often, political quiescence on sensitive issues. Even if the resource lender actually has no political preferences regarding the dependent receiver's behavior, the latter will be apt to shy away from free expression and association in deference to assumptions about the anticipated reaction of the lender.

The poor villager will also have to remain on good terms with the top village administration, on whom, in the case of complete failure, the villager will depend for the distribution of food rations. This worst-case possibility may increase the poor household's choice constraint by adding other actual or presumed expectations to those of the ordinary kin or nonkin lender of occasionally needed resources in the normal year. That is, the village authorities do not represent a second significant alternative of economic endeavor or association; rather, they represent only a second dependency component of the single path of economic endeavor open to the poor household. To achieve the maximal degree of food access (inevitably still insufficient) in this one path, two sorts of better-off patrons must be pleased, as it were, both state and nonstate.

In practice, the expectations of the village authority and private-lender households are unlikely to diverge much. Available studies indicate that power in the local village political arena mainly reflects the relative strengths of the various well-off factions. As for ways out of the plight of the poorest 30 to 40 percent of the villagers, in Tanzania, the village authorities have little to offer other, than, within the constraints of prior claims, the use of distant land. Even that is unlikely to be forthcoming without demonstrated capacity by the poor household to farm additional land effectively, which shows that farming capacity in turn is often likely to depend on access to borrowed resources from a better-off kin or nonkin household, bringing us back to the original dependency. The overall imperatives leave only a single-alternative choice structure for economic endeavor. The strategy is to keep family labor (allowing migration to town labor only as is necessary) and try to increase access to land at workable distances from the homestead, and to secure small amounts of pesticides and fertilizers obtained through relationships with the village leadership as may be affordable and transportable to the fields.

Of course, some among the middle and upper strata of villages that did *not* have to move at the time of villagization can get workable access in older ways. Often retaining good, close land, they fared better initially as long as the fertility and soil structure of their more convenient plots held up. However, the scarcity of other land eventually ruled out shifting fields to fallow them, and required improved methods on the old convenient plots. Over time, the poorer among households not relocated by villagization are apt to sink into the same vulnerability as those who were.

Often presented as a new alternative opened by villagization was some sort of use of collective village land to provide the basis for greater economic security. Villagization did redistribute the land of some large "capitalist" farms and some larger peasant holdings. This land usually went for a communal village farm, for more land for successful (but "capitalist") farmers—sometimes as "block farm" allotments—and where necessary for small homestead plots for villagers who had been moved into already-existing villages. However, by the early and middle 1980s in most areas, village plots restricted to only collective activity had fallen into disuse. Alternatively, some were divided into block farms, which theoretically could present a significantly different route of economic endeavor by participating families under some degree of modernization-oriented regulation by the village. However, just as the better distant fields were allocated by the village leadership to the farmers most capable of making productive use of them, block farm land that was parceled out to qualified households would tend to go to those with the resources to potentially afford the often-expensive inputs and regulations imposed by the village for the use of such plots.

Another often-suggested economic alternative that proves to be largely illusory and insignificant for the poorer strata is the use of modern and intensified farming methods. Some experimentation with small amounts of pesticides and fertilizer has taken place by the poor where these are available through the village leadership (Rasmussen 1986, 55–57, 69–70), particularly on small plots close to the village homestead, out of desperation over declining fertility. However, food-grain plots of peasants so close to the survival margin are unlikely to be diverted from traditional-variety maize, with its superior nutritional value, greater reliability in case of rainfall variation, storage resilience, and early edibility (as "green maize") (Boesen, Havnevik, and Koponene 1988, 6). Adopting higher-yielding variety cultivation means that any irregularity in crop conditions will cause a sharp shortfall and put the household in even more stark dependency on the village authorities for food to make it through the year.

The new-variety alternative, however, is not insignificant for the better-off. Under the circumstances of concentrated settlement, members of the middle and upper strata who did well were those with the resources and labor availability to use improved methods of cultivation. One had to have a large enough complement of household labor to effectively cultivate distant plots (and herd cattle) as well as nearby ones. This required attracting at least some of the young male offspring to stay at home. This usually required an acceptable level of resources in the family, in turn heavily tied to being able to engage in productive agriculture. Effective means of plowing and transporting was necessary. Owning an ox team allows timely plowing of seven to ten acres (Kjaerby 1988, 64). This is best linked to the capacity to use the more productive hybrid varieties of maize, yielding sufficient maize stalks and bean straw to supply dry season fodder for the oxen. It also involves the common mixed farming approach of manuring the most intensely cultivated plots, in this case to preserve soil structure in perennially used plots as well as for fertilizing. In addition, the animals pull sledges for water and firewood (or, if the family is really well-off, wheeled carts), and biochemical inputs or manure to the more distant fields.

Those with such a favored situation could indeed afford the decision to send one or two family members to venture into urban education and employment, as an option promising the possibility of significantly heightened prosperity in the future. For the poorer strata, however, employment beyond household self-employment is, at most, an auxiliary component of the single rural strategy, not a significantly different alternative route to economic betterment. As in Botswana, the vast majority of urban migrants face far higher living costs and low earnings (Havnevik 1988, 261), and they fall far short of making up in remittances what is lost in absence of peak-period family labor (Schneider-Barthold et al. 1983). Only a small portion of poorer-stratum rural Tanzanians ventured into urban wage employment in the mid-1980s, most of which was then in patronage-dominated government and parastatal jobs. The government's policy response to budgetary austerity through the 1980s was to maintain overstaffed levels of urban government and parastatal employment while allowing erosion in real salary payouts by limiting or freezing the wages. The early 1980s economic crisis cut deeply into rates of utilization of industrial capacity and caused may layoffs and workweek cuts in this area.

High urban unemployment and especially underemployment continue; these now can be said to include many government and parastatal jobs, which are insufficient to feed the holders and their families. Many are partially vacated during working hours in favor of farming or other informal-sector activities to make ends meet. The IMF agreements may finally lead to large numbers of actual dismissals, and urban food insecurity may soon increase to the point of stimulating significant migration back to rural areas.

What was said about the general inadequacy of the Tanzanian diet largely applies to the poorer urban stratum there as well. Through economic crisis of the

1980s, a third or more of the urban population (concentrated in Dar es Salaam) benefited from the maize subsidy available to employees of government-linked institutions, including the military, parastatals, and hospitals, and, secondarily and unevenly, to lower-stratum ordinary residents going to the ration shops (Horton 1989, 157). The official parastatal marketing system, the National Milling Commission (NMC), the few large state farms, and most imported food aid thus mainly served the large cities, particularly Dar es Salaam. However, such subsidies for those able to get NMC grain were reduced in 1984, and IMF-influenced economic recovery programs since 1986 have bumped up food prices further for the favored recipients amidst a continuing 28 percent overall inflation rate and frozen official salaries since January 1987. Parallel market food prices have taken some big jumps and continue to be kept high in part by terrible road conditions, related truck shortages, and inadequate storage facilities, as well as general inflation. In the light of all this, for the poorest, flight to urban employment (though it might occur as a matter of desperate escape) is not a significant alternative for improving family food access.

CONCLUSION

In each of the three cases, then, achieving temporary food access in order to stave off malnutrition-related health risks for household members requires depending on one or more better-off households, each with some resource component of the survival package that amounts to the only significant alternative of economic endeavor for the household in clientelistic dependency. Each key component involves a scarce resource for which there is far more demand than can be supplied, and the clientelistic dependent cannot afford to alienate any of the patron-like suppliers. As population and resource stress increases, the key opportunities will look ever more like favors from the advantaged, and ever less like the impersonal consequences of the peasants' effective and determined effort, however much the latter is indeed required. Unable to do without any major component—e.g., access to credit or irrigation water in Bangladesh, or draft power in Botswana and Tanzania—the poor will tend to be inclined to please both benefactors and potential benefactors, where they can, in civil-political behavior. The ultimate question at which we arrive, however, is what can be done? It is to this that we now turn.

NOTES

1. See Jansen 1990, 34, note 2.
2. For good examples of active political entrepreneurship by wealthy patrons, see Jansen 1983, 134, 143–144, 149, and Jahangir 1979, 240–278.
3. Peasants understandably value a multifaceted patron-client relationship based on the idea that it increases the security of the relationship; see Jansen 1983, 171, 176 and Van Schendel 1981, 172, n. 72.
4. See chapter 1, note 1 above.

5. For proportions of draft team ownership in a typical village, and the resulting situation, see Van Schendel 1977, 166–167; for the generally poor condition and capacities of draft animals in Bangladesh, see Jansen 1983, 45. See also Van Schendel 1981, 86, 302, and Arens and van Beurden 1977, 87–88, 106.

6. For an analysis with extensive data on landowning and sharecropping in Bangladesh, see Jannuzi and Peach 1980.

7. In the areas studied by Hossain, animal hiring cost 15 percent of output, a devastating amount for sharecroppers (1977, 320–321). On the high cost in labor for bullock rental, see Hartmann and Boyce 1983, 163.

8. Sharecropping with hired labor, which can take over a quarter of the crop (half the sharecropper's share), on top of other tenant-paid expenses, seems to remove profit altogether in many cases (Hartmann and Boyce 1981, 19).

9. See Hossain 1977, 328, which cites the lower labor-intensity of aman paddy as a reason for its prevalence in sharecropped acreage.

10. According to Rahman 1983, 101, this has led to increased numbers of pure tenants, as the former owner (now a sharecropper) continues to farm plots beyond the mortgage interlude into the postsale period. However, overall the numbers of landless, "pure" tenant sharecroppers have not become significant, remaining around 6 to 7 percent (Jannuzi and Peach 1980, Tables D.4, E.5). Without a special income source (e.g., a commercial niche or government job) for a family member—not a common occurrence for cultivating families—it is highly unlikely for landless individuals to have the resources to provide required inputs on a cost-effective basis; it is much more common for families still owning a third of an acre, say, to sharecrop it *out* due to this problem.

11. For example, Van Schendel summed up the situation in five villages he examined in Bogra as one in which "an incessant scramble for employment among the poor resulted in a great number of often temporary pursuits yielding the smallest of pay or profit in return for very hard and long work. The middle groups who could subsist on agriculture did not need to join the fight for additional income. What they earned was sufficient for their needs, but they could not invest in other pursuits. . . ." (1981, 170).

12. In regard to low-return employment, in a village studied by Rahman, 31 percent of the income of .5–1.5-acre owners came from family-member wage labor (1983, 256). Compare Van Schendel's "category B" Goborgari household (1981, 90).

13. This reality is commonly referred to in sources that are in touch with village-level contexts. For examples, see Hossain 1981, 103; Jansen 1983, 143; Rahman 1983, 293–294, 297–298, 304; and Hartmann and Boyce 1983, 162–164, 198.

14. Concerning immediate sale at harvest, there is no possibility of the gains that can result from holding some grain off the market until prices go up, which is within reach of some owners of 1.5 acres or more. In another form of the same outcome, a moneylender may lend in advance of the harvest for repayment in rice at harvest time, but only at prices even lower than what the market rate will be at the harvest low point.

15. For concise surveys of land-mortgaging practices, see Jansen 1983, 128–132; Hartmann and Boyce 1983, 167–168 n. 1; and Arens and van Beurden 1977, 117.

16. For a detailed account of a patron-client relationship between two brothers, see Jansen 1983, 115–123. Where kin networks are unusually wide, wage labor alternatives may accordingly be greater, provided the general economic circumstances of the village permit. On the varying time frames involved in the land transfer process, compare Jansen's description of the Einuddin (1983, 117–122) with Khan 1977, 143.

17. For a vivid account of the death by illness of a starving landless laborer, see Hartmann and Boyce 1983, 169–176.

18. See page 91 above.

19. Rahman and Haque concede that despite a lowered overall *per capita* growth rate in the 1980s, the high growth rate in high-yielding-variety rice production "has enabled the bottom 40% of the rural population (consisting mostly of wage workers) to increase their relative share of the incremental income" (1988, 24).

20. Some economists call this phenomenon the "interlocking" of markets for labor, share tenancy, credit, and so forth.

21. Shamaj members included those of Adnan's shamaj P3, controlled by the JI party (Adnan 1987, 399).

22. An example of such a temporary cessation may be seen in Adnan 1989, 446.

23. This seems to include USAID (USAID 1983, 6).

24. For detailed examinations, see Jansen 1983; Hartmann and Boyce 1983, 202–205; Chisholm 1983; the numerous exemplary cases from various aid programs in Stroberg 1977; and, for more recent work, Adnan 1987, 234–241.

25. Recipient clients may have small land holdings but may be primarily involved in trading or money-lending operations that put them in the higher-income-earning strata of the villages.

26. Herdboys at cattle posts are traditionally given a few days off at planting time as well. These households also have the traditional cattle post dependent's benefit of access to milk from the herd.

27. See Vierich and Sheppard 1980. For *majako* from cattle post employees, see Hitchcock 1978, 358–359. Hitchcock found some cattle post household members whose migration to *majako* in large land areas brought them more crops than they could have had in their villages (1978, 359), but of course, this would depend on sufficiently good conditions.

Chapter 5

Conclusion: The Remedy

Without some stimulus to alter local social practices of the lack of operational human rights respect for the rural poor, the widespread lack of freedom and well-being in many third world rural areas can only worsen over time. I have argued that responsibility for the situation cannot be laid at the door of individual patrons as if the problem fit the individual perpetrator model pervasive in the conventional civil-political (freedom) sector of human rights doctrine. The patrons are simply participating in prevalent social practices with which their clients cooperate. These provide peasants with temporary, marginally improved food access compared to life without clientelistic dependency under the current circumstances, and they are part of an overall socioeconomic context extending beyond national borders. It would be fantasy to expect third world governments to make and implement laws prohibiting such practices within their jurisdictions. Formal government does not have the degree of authority, information, or other resources to enforce such laws—even if it had the intention to do so—without enacting change in the overarching socioeconomic context. Any attempts from the advantaged world or third world governments to impose some sort of top-down structural solution to the problem are unlikely to do more than change the form taken by clientelistic dependency. In any case, the rubric of human rights philosophy operates within the bounds of the requirement to respect national self-determination, which seems to rule out imposing unwilling compliance on a third world country in a matter so deeply ingrained in the local social practice of communities and governments.

Nonetheless, where national governments on the scene are structurally too weak to accomplish the task, humanity's duty to observe human rights and to promote their observance must, as a practical matter, lie with sufficiently advantaged peoples and governments that are in a position to stimulate real change in grass-roots social practices in third world rural areas. Current efforts by the advantaged world community to provide disaster food relief are required under human rights commitments, but they tend to be sporadic and focused only on the few cases of major war or famine that get news headlines. Ongoing programs for development aid tend substantially to miss the real ground level of poverty, as they are so commonly channeled, in one way or another, through intermediate and local patrons. This is particularly true for most credit programs, for which the aid is in the fluid form of money, which is easily diverted away from the target poor. Moreover, credit tends to have some implicit or explicit collateral requirement (like a landownership level above that of the vulnerable poor) or some collateral substitute, like quick repayment requirements, which rules out the wisely reluctant poor or requires petty trade niches that guarantee a quick return.

Data indicate that increasing homegrown food increases dietary adequacy, as to both quantity and quality (Holmboe-Ottesen 1992, 165). As I have suggested elsewhere (Smith 1986a, 1986b), the best prospect for change could be to complement the currently most effective international aid with the additional direct transfer of specific locally appropriate implements for agricultural production, to those members of the target group who are willing to undertake the hard and careful work they require. Such things would have to be fitted for particular local circumstances to actually enable some individuals in the vulnerable category to support themselves sufficiently independently of clientelistic dependency (a) to be able to make autonomous decisions in expression, association, movement, and economic endeavor, and (b) to establish this route as a believable alternative in the eyes of those who have not chosen it. The aid recipients may continue with some clientelistic relationships, but these would not be dependencies and instead would be freely chosen, in that they could be forgone. If a substantial proportion of the target group took up the new economic alternative, this would demonstrably present an option for those who did not take it up, thus rendering their own continuing clientelistic dependencies substantially more voluntary. The desired consequence could be a breakdown in the overall right-depriving complex of customary local social practices and their replacement with practices that assure human rights.

BANGLADESH

Data from Sri Lanka show that increased rice paddy production increased consumption of staples among the poorest, and among peasants brought more frequent consumption of foods of higher nutritional value (Holmboe-Ottesen 1992, 167–168). I would like to suggest that the Bangladesh situation points, first of all, to certain key things that must be added to the marginal cultivator's productive situation to render willing families in the target category capable of holding the line against land loss and malnutrition-related disease, even in a bad year. Most important initially are two things: local water access and draft animal power. Once minimal water and draft power are made accessible, we may proceed to the issue of the viable degree of land reform that must be undertaken, calibrated to provide opportunity for the landless and near-landless people who want more security of life than is provided by wage-labor opportunities in the country's newly altered agricultural environment. Also necessary is a supplementary food-for-work program, with projects chosen in consultation with the target group households and designed to address their infrastructural needs.

Recent experience in Bangladesh has shown that local water access can provide both (a) more stable and successful production conditions for broadcast and transplanted aman and aus (to compensate for variability of timing of onset and subsiding of monsoon rains and floods) and (b) an added crop of HYV *boro* rice in the dry winter season.[1] By itself, the available rechargeable underground water can provide those benefits over upward of 75 percent of the country (Friedkin, et al. 1983, 5), whereas now, between 12 and 20 percent is under some form of irrigation, which mainly benefits the better-off farmers.[2] Small handpump and other shallow tubewells can provide access to this water down to very small scales of plot cultivation. It has been demonstrated that intensity and efficiency of production increase in proportion to decreases in household-operated holding size, all the way down to agricultural holdings of between ½ and 1 acre.[3] This means that a ¾-acre holding can double or triple its productivity via HYV methods, depending on the availability and affordability of fertilizer and insecticide inputs, provided controlled water is available. Where well-situated plots are available, the owner of a ¾-acre holding can augment returns to a level not far from the that of the holder of 1½ acres of good, non-HYV land. As for smaller owners, it means significantly greater results from, say a third of an acre, meaning less family dependence on the labor market and, hence, fewer weeks of starvation or near-starvation in normal years and fewer months of this pain and vulnerability to disease in bad years. It may also mean slowing down or stemming the land loss involved in a further buildup of unpaid consumption loans.

"Irrigation" is much too abstract a term for our focus on the marginal cultivators and their conditions of choice and welfare. In fact, a big difference may be made by how a controlled supply of water is provided. For small owners, individual households, or groups in a cooperative, a much smaller-scale option is available which gives poor households control over their own production. Even in strictly economic terms, the small, cheap, movable handpump tubewells (HTW), which tap water within 20 to 40 feet of the surface for small plots, are by far the most appropriate and effective (Jansen 1979, 78–83; Friedkin, et al. 1983, 6–9; Howes 1985; Hannah 1976). In particular, they offer a timely application of water for planting and fertilizing small plots of winter *boro* (Howes 1985) in cases where other outlets for gainful labor are scarce. They can irrigate around half an acre, cost $60 to $80, and one man's labor is enough to irrigate a third of an acre (Biggs and Griffith 1987, 79–79). When purchased outright (typically by the owner of two acres or more who has the money), they can pay for themselves in a single *boro* season (Hartmann and Boyce 1983, 260–262; Friedkin, et al. 1983, 7). Since they break down less often than larger tubewells and are easily repaired, they do not risk the sacrifice of an expensive input.

In the 1980s the distribution of tubewell aid was mainly accomplished through the usual channels of influence to better-positioned households and their clients, or via market channels to those sufficiently well-off to have the surplus to purchase them. Even programs presumably aimed at the poor have not reached those in the lowest ownership rungs, who are not favorably connected and thus are currently shut out. However, the small, experimental expansion of HTWs has demonstrated their favorable economics for smallholders in cases where the agronomic circumstances, and particularly the water table, provide water close enough to the surface (Biggs and Griffith, 1987).

The central implication for the long-term development of minimal choice and welfare for the poor majority in Bangladesh lies, however, in the consequences of the small handpump tubewells for patron-client relations involving those owning less than one acre. Jansen's important survey (1979) of patron-client implications of tubewell size revealed a sharp contrast between households able to reach minimal economic independence via the availability of irrigation water under their own control and those who get water via the large and expensive deep tubewells; the latter find themselves sharecropping (with payment of a quarter of their earnings to the tubewell owner) the return on the new *boro* crop and often tightly bound in the patron-client relationship with the so-called owner or owners of large deep tubewells. The latter often refuse to supply water to anyone who will not become their social and political supporter, even at an exorbitant price; the command area of the tubewell thus becomes a checkerboard of green and brown in winter, reflecting who has obtained a *boro* crop (by being a client) and who has not (Jansen 1979, 74–75; see also Adnan 1987, 234–241). Where a poor peasant's main credit patron is not the tubewell owner, there will be the difficult choice of whether to take a chance on the new technology by trying to shift the land-mortgage or sale obligation to the tubewell owner in hopes of stemming land loss—and knowing that the frequent breakdowns and uneven input supplies (and their prices) could jeopardize the whole crop—and sticking to the current patron, even knowing that the plots have always been brown in the dry season and land loss always a risk. If considering a shift from a kin patron to a nonkin tubewell owner, the poor peasant must also consider the social and economic costs over the long term of alienating the *gusti* (patrilineage), wherein lies the only chance of help for the family in the peasant's old age.

Dependency on the owner of a deep tubewell for water (which costs between a quarter and a third of the crop on the irrigated land) provides relatively small incremental return on the new crop and tends to preserve or even exacerbate the absence of choice among significant alternatives for the poorer peasants. The small handpump tubewells, on the other hand, can lift owners of less than one acre over the great divide between clientelistic dependency, on one hand, and on the other, significant choice as to social, political, and economic association, and long-term endeavor.

To be sure, the delivery of handpump tubewell aid faces problems having to do with the agrarian circumstances in which the wells may be effective as well as with difficulties in conveying them to the target group. In particular where the water table has been drawn down by excessive tubewell exploitation, larger groups of less than one acre can make use of shallow tubewells, which can draw water up from 80 to 120 feet and irrigate an area of around 10 acres (Mandal 1988, 50). While this size is much smaller than the 250–300 feet and 35-acre area of the deep tubewells typically owned by larger landowners, it is still susceptible to being turned into a patronage machine under the influence of its strongest controller, since shallow tubewells are owned, on average, by owners of at least two acres. Nonetheless, it is notable that Proshika, a major poverty-oriented NGO in Bangladesh, has no less than 255 shallow tubewell irrigation schemes which, the NGO reports, are controlled by landless peasants (Task Forces on Bangladesh Development Strategies 1991, 35).

Handpump and shallow tubewells are important for additional reasons beyond the possibility of small (but important) additions to the scope and intensity of HYV rice cultivation. In periods of low rice irrigation activity, they are also recommended for homestead vegetable irrigation to improve diet, and to supply much healthier drinking water than with traditional sources (Friedkin, et al. 1983, 23). They can thus cut health risk in lean weeks and months, as well as supplying much safer drinking water the year around.

To take advantage of these values in ways adapted to the local circumstances, however, the implement must be mobile and under the control of the group of households that has received it. Aid involving HTWs that seeks to overly control the recipients' use of the items can miscarry from the point of view of sensitivity to an integrated system of human rights. For example, White (1991) relates the outcome of an NGO-provided handpump tubewell program that was aimed exclusively at the fixed-site field production of vegetables. Water table problems in the local area and the availability of water from nearby mechanized shallow and deep tubewells caused many to abandon their use for irrigating paddy, and move the metal-pipe HPTs closer to the homestead to supply convenient drinking water and homestead-plot vegetable cultivation (by the women); the program switched to the use of plastic pipes, which could not effectively be moved; the result was that the demand for the HPTs fell away (White 1991, 51–52). The strategic role of women, with their desperate need for labor-saving devices in contending with the health risks of food insecurity, has gone unrecognized here, along with the need for autonomous household control over any aid provided.

A second lesson from this case has to do with the role of other development aid programs. In White's village, apparently, an area development program provided deep tubewells which by 1989, had replaced the existing mechanized, shallow tubewells and, most important, had drawn down the water table to the point that the drinking water HTWs were running dry as early as February (White 1991, 52). Clearly, development avenues that cut off critical opportunities for the poor in this way must be reevaluated from a human rights point of view.

The costs of the handpump tubewell and its requirements are an important consideration and, currently, a barrier to access by poor peasants. Large numbers, however, can be very cost-effectively manufactured worldwide and delivered to areas such as rural Bangladesh. The real barriers—psychological, social, and political—lie in delivery to the target group (the landless and near landless). A major attitudinal problem now standing in the way is the view on the part of aid officials, both governmental and nongovernmental, that in order to try to convey things, we must do so in the form of credit for target individuals to use to try to buy the things.

THE CREDIT QUESTION

Most credit programs in Bangladesh have been unable to deliver for the poorest. In the end, they have been administered at the lowest level by, or with the approval of, the political machine and the habits of decades—in a phrase, the social practices at the grass-roots level.[4] Few people get credit for agricultural production without an acre or more of land as collateral, which is worth much more than the amount normally borrowed (for a typical example, see Friedkin, et al. 1983, 13–14). The basic purpose of many in lending to the poor has long been to acquire land, and prudent peasants know this. A relatively attractive number on a governmental or bank document that is supposed to represent an interest rate—even if way below the 50 percent per season the poor peasant may get from noninstitutional moneylenders—will mean little in the face of all the bribes and connections necessary to get the required signatures (see, e.g., Friedkin, et al. 1983, 15). The average marginal peasant already has too much debt, and would, in any case, have to become (or remain) incorporated into the clientele of the person who offered entry into the program. The peasant who can afford these costs, plus all the risks of HYV agriculture (including loss of the land), and avoid dependent incorporation is likely to own well above an acre and a half and thus, in any such relationship, to be a client by choice, anyway.

The well-off landowners (who have received the lion's share from most credit programs in the past) for their part have tended to use this additional resource, not for productive investment, but for such things as lending to others to acquire land and for speculation in rice (see Van Schendel 1981, 169, 173; Hossain 1981, 109–111). Even holders of two to five acres, whose tendency to invest resources in productive improvements is much higher, also are likely to use available credit, wherever feasible, to gain control of more land (Van Schendel 1981, 233). When wealthy people do invest productively, it often occurs only when the investment is subsidized substantially by the lending agency (as with deep tubewells), when they are likely to be able to escape repayment of most or all of the loan, and when the gains will serve their overall land acquisition strategy (e.g., by helping them acquire new clients through selling water).

Often taken to be a success in the credit area is the Grameen Bank program in Bangladesh, whose constraints in reaching the target group illustrate, I think, the limits of the credit approach. In an intelligent approach to limiting corruption and leakage, it makes short-term, small loans to qualified individuals owning under half an acre of land. In the few areas where the program has been implemented, it has had an identifiable impact. However, its requirement of the loan's repayment in full over six months in weekly installments more or less guarantees that it will not help the majority of the poorest strata, who are involved in food grain production (Ahmad and Hossain 1985, 87–88); rather, it supports either the activities of nonagricultural (trade or other employment) households that already have the resources to be able to make such prompt repayment, or activities that can produce rapid turnover into monetary return, like noncrop trading or shop-keeping niches (for which most male participants use the loans), or self-employment in small livestock husbandry, rice transport, or rice processing (favored by most female participants) (Ahmad and Hossain 1984, 86). It is unclear whether the Grameen Bank recipient households' higher standard of living than nonparticipants resulted from expanded income due to loan-supported activities or from a preexisting superior income position. Moreover, a large proportion of Grameen Bank support is given in repeat (often enlarged) loans to past loanees, more or less guaranteeing a high continuing record of prompt repayment. Finally, as an ILO-published evaluation concludes, the scope of Grameen Bank success may be limited by the limited size of the markets for its (often low-return) productive activities, to be demonstrated as the program expands (Ahmad and Hossain 1984, 91–93). Like subsistence-assuring town employment, there are niches securing long-term food adequacy for only a few. Grameen Bank is no doubt a good economic development program, but it should not be regarded as in any way sufficient to address rural poverty and clientelistic dependency.

The other realm of more effectively targeted credit effort is the NGO approach that combines consciousness-raising against poverty-engendering conditions with support for income-generating activities, as exemplified by Bangladesh Rural Advancement Committee (BRAC), Proshika, and others. Many of these efforts have their impact on the really poor. According to Hashemi's (1990) review of major NGOs, for almost all of them a majority of members are either functionally landless or own under one acre. Of poor peasants surveyed, 90 percent believe that relief distribution through the government is corrupt and 89 percent believed that NGOs are better; only 7 percent thought of the NGOs as corrupt (Hashemi 1990, 58). While a third of NGO members thought "that even NGO efforts led sometimes to corruption," Hashemi observed that at least NGOs take "severe steps" to stop corruption when it is discovered, which is not the case for governmental relief (1990, 58). However, even the most effective of these NGOs, in the areas in which they are strongest, reach no more than a third of the target group in those areas (Hashemi 1990, 26), and their beneficiaries generally experience no significant increase in incomes or assets (Hashemi 1990, 60–65). While traders and craftspeople in some cases are helped to continue working during lean periods (as with Grameen Bank recipients), Hashemi concludes that limited markets and low returns on the additional labor tend to rule out significant increases in the scale of cottage industry activity; any increases in income are used for hard-pressed consumption, production does not become self-sustaining, and dependency on the project funds continues (1990, 63). While the small improvements in income that often result certainly make a real difference in human terms for families struggling to increase the number of days or

weeks in which they eat a minimal diet, what is most striking is the absence of
effect on the underlying long-term conditions of clientelistic dependency emphasized here:

Economic coercion in rural Bangladesh occurs through the product market, the labour
market, the credit market and the interlocking of these markets. . . . This study examined
the prevailing markets in NGO areas and in non-NGO areas and discovered no changes in
NGO area markets having taken place because of NGO involvement. Agricultural product prices remained the same in all area markets. Labor wages too remained unaffected.
Interest rates on informal credit were invariant. NGO group members participated in
mortgages, dadan (credit against standing crops), and credit from moneylenders to the
same degree as non-NGO target people. However it is true that in some areas where
NGOs have provided extensive credit to their members, their need for informal credit has
decreased. But NGO mobilisations have not affected either the form of economic coercion or market rates for produce, labour and credit, in any area. (Hashemi 1990, 46–47)

Hashemi's look at BRAC credit for agricultural inputs in Sulla, Bangladesh, a
major area of BRAC activity, indicated that most was spent on pressing consumption needs (1990, 69). After pointing out data indicating that NGO groups
engaged in 23 percent more institutional (formal) borrowing than non-NGO
groups, and 6.5 percent less informal borrowing, Hashemi goes on, nonetheless,
to observe regarding the results of NGO credit programs that:

NGO groups have almost 90% of their debts outstanding and pay as much for middlemen
as do other groups. Additionally a much greater portion of borrowed funds (both formal
and informal) is spent on consumption. In regions of easy formal credit, as in NGO areas,
the observable trend has been of people receiving credit at low interest rates, spending it
on consumption, being unable to repay loans, having interest rates increased on defaulted
loans, and being back to square one with high indebtedness. This is of course assuming
no increases in productive capacities leading to increased incomes and repayments being
met internally. With traders and cottage industries under close NGO monitoring this scenario has worked, but in a large number of cases where credit was not tied to economic
activities, the first scenario holds. This was observed very clearly in the BRAC region of
Sulla. (1990, 70–71)[5]

Generally, Hashemi's review indicates that NGO efforts have not succeeded
broadly in building up improvements in self-generated income. Group savings
have been used to meet consumption needs; when applied to income-generating
enterprise, the activities have tended to be money lending, leasing land for
sharecropping, and hoarding or crop speculation, all of which tend to victimize
poorer nonmembers (Hashemi 1990, 63, 75). NGOs have generally not confronted local elites politically or taken up national political causes on behalf of
the poor—perhaps a condition of toleration of them locally and nationally.

The NGOs remain limited in scope and affect only small numbers of people in
part due to their reliance on heavy monitoring and an ideologically committed
and self-sacrificing leadership at the lowest organizational levels—a critical
element that is, unfortunately, in short supply for the task of supporting the

autonomous self-development of the rural poor of Bangladesh. Like the Grameen Bank program, these sorts of credit activities make a contribution to consumption relief for distressed peasants to the extent to which they are effective, and they provide some people with commercial financing in small trading or processing niches. Such niches are few, however, and the efforts fail to tackle head-on the fundamental problem of agricultural food-crop production and its implications for choice and well-being.

An interesting case of income-generating NGO intervention that proved successful at producing self-supporting agricultural income increases was Proshika's credit program at Dhamrai; it involved investment in irrigation equipment to produce a dry-season *boro* crop (Hashemi 1990, 63–65)—the kind of outcome our argument here supports in its emphasis on HTWs and cooperatively operated shallow tubewells. However, the scale of irrigation intervention was such that it provided enough for recipients to take up money lending, leasing land out for rent, and rice speculation, representing the "transfer of assets to a few members who immediately take on the function of the new agents of rent exaction" (Hashemi 1990, 65). These examples suggest the importance of transferring objects (or animals) rather than money, and of selecting those that are fitted to improving income to minimum subsistence levels (with the support of significant labor).

Unfortunately, the credit idea is dear to the hearts of aid officials, both governmental and NGO. The idea of an aid program giving outright, to average people, anything concrete makes the established givers feel somehow uncomfortable, despite the fact that so many less-targeted loans go at vastly subsidized interest, are never repaid, and in any case tend to go to people who do not really need them. This desire to cover over the gift aspect seems partly due to a paternalistic assumption that the recipient will feel better in the long run if he or she has returned a value equivalent to what is owed; this is commonly assumed without concern over whether the target group will ever be in a position to repay the full value of the loan and without certainty about what the peasants really do feel. A very competent, high-level NGO aid official once told me quite seriously that in his view giving something outright "corrupted" the recipient. Perhaps, however, in cases where corruption at the local level could not be any greater than it already is, and where credit programs have rarely reached the poor on any major scale, it is time to drop the paternalistic judgments and attend to the problem instead. This means getting needed things to the target people rather than floating money, pieces of paper, and procedures complex enough to require the "help" of those most skilled in taking advantage of them to divert the resources. What must be done is to give those in the distressed category something of long-run value without enmeshing them in the threatening, long-term ties of a new credit relationship.

A further misconception that stands in the way of delivering effectively targeted aid is the assumption that giving the poor peasant something implies no contribution of his or her own to the objective of human-rights-sensitive development. This misconception results from the usual sorts of international aid that do reach poor household heads (though not very many of them) in third world countries, such as emergency food relief. In these cases of necessary aid, little is put in by the recipient peasant. However, in the case of the small, handpump tubewell, there is a very significant resource the recipient peasant must add to get any value from the gift, large amounts of additional labor. An extra winter *boro* crop means hours of arduous pumping of water, plowing, and long, back-breaking days of weeding, harvesting, threshing, husking, and so forth, using family labor. Nothing comes for free to the poor peasant, whose well-being is inevitably substantially self-provided (on a household or small-group cooperative level). If one outcome is improved human rights conditions via minimal choice in economic, social, and political action, association, and endeavor, then the recipient peasant's labor will have made a truly significant contribution to the good the aid agency is pursuing. This amounts to a contribution that deserves to be considered a kind of repayment for the resource received at the outset.

FURTHER REQUIREMENTS

For Bangladesh, in addition to handpump tubewells, any choice-oriented package for the family (hypothetically, five members) owning less than an acre should consider draft power as well. As Jansen (1986, 43–44) and Dumont (1973b, 47–48) observe, in Bangladeshi villages there are already too many draft animals for the meager grazing land and available fodder, and a vast proportion of them are too frail and sickly to be effective anyway. However, this difficulty does not rule out the viability of a bullock team that is cooperatively owned and shared by three to four households with a total of three to five acres cultivated among them, for example.[6] Energy studies have shown that the actual product of wet rice agriculture in Bangladesh is sufficient to support healthy bullocks for plowing and threshing if the fodder components are not distributed so unequally (Briscoe 1979). By pooling the necessary paddy byproducts among the families cooperatively owning the bullock team, draft strength could be maintained as long as the viably cultivated land holdings of the households are sufficient. By moving the team rapidly and rationally from plot to plot at peak plowing times, with water supply stabilized, peasants can feel less at risk from the opportunity cost of wage-labor opportunities sacrificed by focusing on their own land.

The unit for such a cooperative practice might also serve for some degree of exchange of the water from the small, handpump tubewells. With a capacity of one-half to one acre only, a tubewell could be owned by one family. However, since the household holding is characteristically fragmented into smaller plots in different spots, it makes sense for neighbors sharing a bullock team to also engage in water exchange with owners of adjoining plots, so that each tubewell will have to be moved less often. This cooperative situation would also enable better peer observation of the usage of the tubewell and bullocks given by the aid agency. The bullock team and the tubewells could be given for the first year conditional on the peasant keeping them (rather than selling them) and maintaining them; if the items are sold, they could revert to the status of a loan that must be repaid. Only after a year's proper use (and no sale) would the given items be owned in a completely unencumbered way by the recipient household. The aid agency's local representative could double as the local tubewell repairer and bullock health advisor, allowing enough contact among the target group to yield information about how the use of the items is proceeding.

A practical problem in the last few years with reaching the great majority of poorer-stratum Bangladeshis with handpump tubewells is the lowering of the water table in many areas.[7] Apparently, in some areas the spread of deep tubewells and the attendant irrigation of more land for HYV agriculture in the 1980s have produced a self-fulfilling prophecy of the need for deeper tubewells as the water table recedes. It was reported of one area in the late 1980s that about half the hand tubewells in use earlier in the decade were no longer there because two private, shallow tubewells had made their entry (Mandal 1989, 56). A human rights orientation toward choice and needs in poverty-targeted development aid must also focus on restraining programs that extend and deepen clientelistic dependency among the food-insecure poor. Thus, dry-season water table preservation and, where necessary, restoration, should also be a top priority.

Beyond this, programs being talked about to bring the periodic water movements under centralized control by large-scale dam and embankment systems (Adnan 1991) may be the most dangerous threat of all to minimal choice and need satisfactions for the poor. The ordinary yearly flooding of plots, which restores fertility in this river delta region is a key component of potential for substantial independence for the poor, and central control of water would turn the vast majority of the population into clientelistic dependents.

As we move toward the land-reform requirements of this choice-oriented aid plan, it is important to notice the situation for labor opportunities, both within the family and in the wage labor market. Most obviously, much additional labor is needed to operate the handpumps on the tubewells. Households around the one-acre level tend to use family labor if available in sufficient quantity, and if they have the resources, to hire labor for the rest. Family labor seems especially appropriate in that tubewell pumping can be too tiring on the feet or back to be done for more than two to three hours at a stretch, and the work may have to be passed around in small parcels. This may be one function in the fields that Islamic tradition might allow women to undertake (as suggested in Friedkin, et al. 1983, 22), providing another outlet for available family labor resources. Where hand-pump tubewells come into general use, many more opportunities for hired wage labor in pumping open up, since the water control stabilizes monsoon aman and aus production as well as opening up a dry-season *boro* crop.

Furthermore, if the aid program has been extended to those poorer areas that tend to supply the migrating work gangs to the well-off owners in more affluent areas, the general lower availability of peak-season labor should help keep wages higher, making wage labor itself more rewarding to those depending on it. At present, HYV production tends to favor migrant labor in times of peak demand (see Van Schendel 1981, 97, 246; Jansen 1986, 191, 255–256; Arens and van Beurdon 1977, 97), lowering wages in these areas, but commonly providing the migrant with little more than his or her own survival. As development economics tells us, the generalized increase in well-being at the lower levels will support demand to a point that should encourage many sorts of small enterprises to spring up, offering more labor opportunities.

We are thus led to the question of the extent of land reform that would be needed to accompany this package. If a one-acre household holding with the proper aid package could produce to the level of a plot of one and a half to two acres under current conditions, many in our category would already have neared the goals of choice and well-being. A half-acre owner would need only another half acre, and so on. Furthermore, our cornerstone of choice would allow that those landless households that might wish to retain the wage-laboring alternative, given the greater surety of wage-labor opportunities with higher wages generally, be allowed to do so without the responsibility of an acre of their own ground to cultivate; certainly many in the labor or the trading sector would have no inclination in a generally improved rural economic environment to go back to family labor cultivation, despite the prestige it retains. Land-poor individuals are to be offered the option of choosing the second alternative, but they need not actually choose that alternative.

A significant advantage of this approach, however, is that it could be started on a demonstration basis in many parts of Bangladesh, providing experimental experience before extending the land reform component more widely. An initial project beginning with tubewells and bullock teams for holders of three-quarters to one acre could be launched right now, with some demand and employment effects that would prove generally somewhat beneficial. Small-scale land reform beginning with specific small parcels going to ½-acre owners could occur with little more than a degree of enforcement of current rules. With the results of this experience, perhaps knowledge and political momentum could spread to help expand the receptiveness to the program among the poor majority.

One might conclude from the kinds of grass-roots research cited here, for example, that (a) inexpensive, handpump shallow tubewells, together with (b) the comparatively modest transfer of enough land to bring volunteering households up to one-acre ownership per household (assuming protection of the safety of participants, however obtained), could effectively be conveyed directly to those households willing to invest the labor to achieve relatively autonomy as an individual household or small group cooperative. While undoubtedly only a portion of owners of less than an acre would choose the newly significant alternative, for others in the category, the alternative's availability as a possibility would indirectly yield, for them as well, an implicit option of choice, which might result in greater bargaining power with patrons and contribute to opening up at least minimal choice on a more widespread basis.

While landownership by the household of less than one acre seems to be the most useful indicator of the target group, it obviously cannot be regarded as the sole goal needing action, but rather as one component of a package. The extent of land reform in an aid package that is sensitive to the requirements of both nutritional and minimal choice structures would be much smaller than in most of the extant land reform proposals.[8] At least as important would be to get access, to the members of the target group who opt to take up a new labor-intensive alternative, to a healthy ox team and water under their own control. The focus could be on cooperative associations of four to five target households each, which have been brought up to the acre-per-household level in order to participate in the program. They could receive directly from an aid agency—provisionally, as a loan in kind—a healthy ox team and, say, two handpump (movable) shallow tubewells for irrigating a winter *boro* crop. After a year of proper use (as monitored, for example, by aid-agency repair technicians) these would become the property of the small cooperative or household.

Finally, for there to be the most minimal degree of assured food access so as to enable the new alternative to be feasible to take up, food-for-work programs must be available in the lean and dry periods when employment opportunities are scarce. These need not use the food grain with the highest local status (which may attract numbers outside the target group). As in current food-for-work programs in Bangladesh (under the World Food Programme aegis), wheat can be used rather than rice. In the past, food-for-work projects have mainly consisted of flood control embankments and road building, and the placement of projects (particularly those in the Ministry of Relief "local initiative" category) has been subject to the influence of the better-off networks among the local elite (see, e.g., Adnan 1987, 477), who are in a position to siphon off part of the funds, provided they are strong enough (Adnan 1987, 326). Now, apparently, projects are coordinated more by the various ministries in the context of their plans (Parkinson and Syeduzzaman 1993), which may aid their completion but leaves just as much in question about their poverty-targeting abilities and their relevance to the immediate food grain production needs of the landless and very land-poor. The range of projects should extend to more that are chosen by the peasants themselves and are of direct productive or consumption value to them, like drilling shallow tubewells for drinking water or vegetable production or building irrigation channels for several of the target group households. With the option of greater independence offered by shallow tubewell water, more peasants may, in turn, feel freer to assert themselves politically. This may serve more effectively to steer food-for-work projects in directions more beneficial to their stratum, thus creating a "virtuous circle" of bottom-up improvement.

Again, any right must take the form of an option, and many owners of less than an acre may choose not to take up the option offered, rejecting the additional hard work attending it in favor of wage labor. However, the presence of the option as an additional, significant alternative of endeavor in the poor peasants' field for choice may give, even to those not opting for it, additional bargaining power. This, in support of greater participant independence, may help turn grass-roots social practices in the direction of greater respect for minimalist degrees of well-being and choice possession, helping even the (still vulnerable) nonparticipants. Thus, a human-rights-based guidance, according to minimal needs and choice structure considerations for the particular context of Bangladesh, not only can clearly indicate a target group, but also can give a reasonable and affordable initial shape to abstract appeals for well-being and freedom.

BOTSWANA

In the case of rural Botswana we have a government that is comparatively well endowed, by third world standards, yet government rural policies have not addressed the production-related needs of the clientelistically dependent poor. The Arable Lands Development Program (ALDEP) was billed as a poverty-alleviating program; it was aimed at providing small farmers holding under 40 head of cattle and 10 hectares (24.7 acres) of agricultural land with grants for input factors and fencing. Under its revised version, the government provided grants for 60 percent of the costs for buying oxen and 85 percent for other inputs. However, the poorer households (characteristically employing multiple income-earning activities amid a shortage of male labor), have had a number of difficulties in availing themselves of the opportunities provided by this program. Its requirement of 40 percent of the cost of draft power up front from the recipients tended to rule out significant participation by the poor. In the 1985–1986 season, for example, only 15 percent of households owning no cattle and 30 percent of women participated in the program—and normally in minor ways, such as for fencing—in the 1985–1986 season, although this was an improvement on previous years. Particularly, the requirement of a down payment that many poor farmers cannot make, problems of increased weeding after the winter crop in the common absence of male labor for weeding, and generally high risks should drought hit have rendered the program unattractive to many poor households. In any case, the subsequent Accelerated Rainfed Arable Program (ARAP) begun in 1985, seems to have drawn many extension workers away from ALDEP and further weakened its effectiveness (Granberg and Parkinson 1988, 28).

The cornerstone of recent government policy from the last years of the drought of the 1980s up to the present has been ARAP, the program of full government subsidy for tractor rental. In theory, tractors can plow land much faster than oxen, and in theory peasants get full reimbursement from the government. However, the program rarely resulted in timely plowing of the small fields of the poor. Increasingly over the career of ARAP, a premium was required up front, beyond the government reimbursement level. Paid by acreage, tractor owners plowed day and night for the large field owners first, and equipment breakdowns tended to set in, rendering plowing help for the poor either unaffordable or late. Getting tractor hire under affordable and minimally effective conditions required special access, such as to a relative, on whom the poor household was, in effect, dependent for survival assurance even in a normal year. Even if the poor could get the tractor at the ARAP subsidy price, without up-front money, the lack of destumped land constrained the use that could be made of it for households that were short of labor and the cash to hire (the very scarce) destumping labor.[9] The cleared hectare or two of land that they might borrow from a neighbor would be ineligible for ARAP subsidy (Solway 1986, 18). Thus the poor were left only the traditional exchange of plowing or weeding labor for late access to an ox team.

What must be provided for rural Botswana directly, as gift—and not via a credit program—is draft animals, probably donkeys. Donkeys are much cheaper and lower in status than cattle, and while slower at plowing, they have more stamina for working a longer day and are easier to train (ATIP 1986, 124). The result is that donkeys can plow about 60 percent as much daily as cattle (Arntzen 1984, 14). Their use has been rising in some areas (Arntzen 1984, 21), as they not only can plow but can also transport items (including water), are more drought resistant than cattle, and require less grazing land. Where we see them owned by a lower-stratum household they are immediately available for the risk-lowering practice of plowing part of the field with each early rain shower (Arntzen 1984, 23). With donkey teams offered to cooperatives of between one and three households of the cattle poor or cattleless, under the control of the households themselves, small landowners would be able to plow with the crucial first rains in October–November rather than the late ones in December–January, as is often the case when people must borrow oxen. With the means for productive plowing available, males laboring in a town would be more encouraged to "shuttle" back, as described by Hesselberg (1985), to provide this high-return, peak-season labor for the household. As low-status animals, donkeys are less likely to arouse the ire of local cattle owners if given by an outside program, and they are less likely to attract demand for retargeting to higher-stratum households. It is notable that the ALDEP program chose donkeys as the form of draft power form to be offered to the poorest (though as requiring them to put up 40 percent of the cost was, of course, typically beyond the reach of those in the really vulnerable category).

Again, food-for-work programs can have a supplementary role. Drought monitoring and food distribution to identified drought-stricken areas have been comparatively efficient in Botswana relative to other developing areas under such risks, due to past donor concern and present government wealth from diamond revenues. However, additional relief to smaller pockets of needy people can be provided via awarding grain for work on water control or other projects of local benefit to the poor, while providing that increment of food security necessary for independent choice among a range of alternatives that include new and potentially risky choices.

The overall result of introduction of this alternative economic path might be not only many people taking it up in order to gain more economic and civil-political independence, but the added effect that even those who do not take up the independent plowing alternative would have the ready option of doing so, thus letting them hold bargaining power over their patrons. There might follow a change in local social practices generally, with real improvements in respect for civil-political choice. Then, existing aid programs fed through local patron-client networks could continue without contributing to strengthening the clientelistic dependencies of the rural poor; current programs would be rendered more human-rights-neutral and less problematic.

TANZANIA

In Tanzania, as elsewhere, we are unlikely to be able to use top-down political methods successfully to alter the situation fundamentally, either in trying to ensure a blind attitude by influential villagers to the civil-political behavior of the poor or in trying to reallocate much land. The government's investments in food grain production have mainly emphasized the state farms, which have produced rice and wheat as a controllable supply for the larger cities to encourage a taste for these (mainly imported) grains. Local research and extension work concerning agricultural production, as in most of the third world, ignore the subsistence sector and focus instead on increasing overall marketed output (often for export), which tends to mean the better-off farm stratum, those with the resources to take advantage of fertilizers, insecticides, row-planted weeding regimens, etc. Extension advice tends to be directed to the better-off cultivators and the male heads of households, who are still considered the household representative by the village authority structures that were set up under villagization (McCall 1987, 200–201), the program of the 1970s to bring scattered homesteads together into villages where they could be reached by government services. Little extension work is directed to the wives, who do most of the work to ensure food security and consequently bear the greatest risks and burdens. Even giving simple advice to the poor on, for example, planning how much to store and protecting stores against pest damage is ruled out in many areas by the current general decline of agricultural extension and local health work. In Tanzania, as elsewhere, channeling benefits through the better-off and middle-level strata (which together often make up only a minority of village inhabitants) tends to foster clientelistic dependency as the affluent permit the trickle down of scarce slack-season employment opportunities, discretionary loans, and so forth to favored kin and neighbors.

In a few places, sophisticated strategies have been tried, such as providing no-interest, single-season credit for a package of inputs of improved seeds, fertilizer, and anti-pest chemicals, which can multiply output for the recipients. Even this approach, however, may not be well geared to households with poor resource endowments in labor, draft animal access, land in close proximity to the homestead, or labor-saving tools such as a cart and plow. An example is the fertilizer credit program run by the Norwegian Agency for Development Cooperation (NORAD) in Kighoma region. The program operated in one of the most favored areas in Tanzania in terms of reliability of rainfall and basic fertility of the soil. The average (and median) farmer of the 1,000 farmers in the program got 12 to 13 bags of maize per acre—double or triple the average of 4 to 5 bags per acre in the areas without the package—and 83 percent of the farmers were able to repay the loan at the end of the season (NORAD 1993, A2–4). There is no question that a well-run fertilizer-subsidy program can have a positive general impact on village economies. Not unusually, however, reporting on the program failed to focus on how performance may have varied according to different household resource endowments; it only mentioned that "the two villages with the lowest average maize yields (Bugaga and Mkundiutsi) had a very low recovery rate of only ⅓" (NORAD 1993, A2–4). That is to say, when all factors were taken into account (including the opportunity cost of applying labor in other ways), poorer households and villages could not repay the loans.

This kind of outcome is often used to rationalize directing aid only to better-off farmers, but this ignores both the resource endowment factor and human rights criteria. The fault is not with the program, which, by its lateral-impact application and intelligent donor-country control, is probably the best that top-down development can do. The failure lies in not complementing such programs with a bottom-up component of simple-technology aid to the poorer strata, so that they, too, can enjoy increased food security and achieve greater independence in their clientelistic linkages, rendering them voluntary clientelistic relationships rather than imposed dependencies.

Every calorie that is burned in work must be provided in food, and the labor time and effort required of women is deplorable, with drastic effects on the children as well. Particularly among the poor, women must collect and transport—by headloading—all water, firewood, seeds, and harvested grains, as well as do the farming and processing tasks, complete the household chores, and brew beer to get cash for necessities like salt, sugar, kerosene, clothes, and utensils, as well as school costs. The weakened condition of many women may rule out their taking timely advantage of health care services, which may be located 10 or 20 kilometers away.

A realistically human-rights-sensitive budget for Tanzanian circumstances might start, for example, with 80 percent devoted to conveying, directly into the hands of poor women, the cheap, small, locale-appropriate labor-saving devices they need to increase production on both nearby and distant plots and thus save their scarce time and energy. Again, draft power should be a practical focus. A draft team for timely plowing adds significantly to cultivable acreage (Rasmussen 1987, 28). If land at greater distance becomes workable with the draft power to provide transport to get there, labor will become productive enough to become an incentive to keep male labor at the village. In addition, the transport capacity would be available to ease the burden of women for the movement of water, firewood, and other requirements.

As important, or more so, improvements become possible in the often ignored realm of weeding. Kjaerby (1983) argued that the plow can be used for weeding (apparently, by turning it in a certain way) under row cultivation, thus helping address the weeding labor bottleneck. Timely earlier weeding (e.g., at 5 to 10 centimeters of plant height) can substantially improve productivity, in some cases nearly doubling the crop (Loewen-Rudgers et al. 1988). By making two adjustable passes between rows of maize (or beans), there is no need for the precisely maintained distances between rows that are required by more expensive mechanical cultivators and are, in practice, impossible for the poorer farmers.[10] Also interesting is the new, small animal-drawn "over-the-row" weeder being developed by the Canadians to enable row cultivation without requiring precise distances between rows (Loewen-Rudgers et al. 1988); nonetheless, it would be more expensive than simply using the plow, with which the peasants are already familiar. In any case, such approaches promise to lessen further the women's burden of weeding as well as provide timely access to animal draft power. The possibility thus emerges of producing a surplus for tiding the household over a bad crop year.

Finally, there seems to be a strong possibility of food-security-oriented improvements in plant breeding, particularly in small-grain, drought-resistant varieties. Friis-Hansen (1988), in the context of communal-area Zimbabwe, focuses on work that has been done on breeding sorghum and millet for sustainability and ease of milling (as opposed to hybrid maize), particularly in the context of an appropriate-technology milling machine being developed.

As elsewhere, of course, the introduction of draft power (and, if necessary, appropriate light plows, weeders, and new seeds) may have to avoid use of intermediary credit, for which the really poor could not qualify, or which they might find too risky. In any case, credit arrangements tend to be captured, or at least influenced, by the well-off members of the local party government and private elite, who redirect them to their clients or to the better-off farmers. To reach the target group, animals, tools, and seeds would have to turn into outright gifts following an appropriate period of serving as a probationary loan-in-kind.

Several traditional problems, however, get in the way. Giving one healthy ox team to every household might be too expensive, as the great majority of Tanzanians are too cattle-poor, and postvillagization grazing is too scarce to universalize the cattle-centered "mixed-farming" approach considered the most appropriate traditional technology by many agriculturists. As in Botswana, then, we may need a special focus, not only on the whole range of features and benefits of mixed farming (i.e., including the production of milk for the children) to be had with the luxury of owning adequate cattle herds, but also on what will get done the most necessary jobs of plowing, transport, and weeding help. Again, I think, the logical choice may be donkeys and either weeders or plows usefully fitted to double as weeders, which may be given cooperatively to two or three target-group households to share. The more distant land that is available in rural Tanzania could then become workably productive, and a significant independent alternative could thus emerge alongside the status quo. Again, food-for-work programs can augment food security (particularly reforestation projects).

Of course, this will in no way determine what portion of the vulnerable-category members will, in fact, choose to take up the new alternative considering the attendant hard work (even with the labor-saving resources included). It is essential in human rights analysis and action that the recipients choose between significant alternatives and that the outcomes of the choice are known in advance. However, even those who elect to stay in their current dependent associations and arrangements would gain the option at any time to choose an alternative to their status quo. The presence of that alternative promises to expand their civil-political choice structure almost as much as that of people taking up the new economic path and the attendant greater economic independence.

CONCLUSION

Conventional aid programs for rural development and increasing agricultural productivity have suffered discouraging degrees of corruption via the influence of indigenous patron-client networks. What aid does make it to the village level mainly reaches the rural well-off and middle class. In particular, programs involving handling money and credit tend to be influenced by the local rural elite, and ultimately reinforce the kinds of economic dependencies that bring to the poor fragile and subminimal economic levels and vulnerability to coercion. A credit program for nearly assetless poor people will be considered too risky or as a grab for their remaining assets.

I have suggested that what must be conveyed to the rural poor for assuring the option of minimal significant choice and minimal well being are, instead, production-related items that poor peasants can take in their hands immediately to use for the next harvest. In Bangladesh, I recommend draft animals, plows, simple-technology water-control devices such as handpump tubewells, and land (if necessary) to bring unencumbered ownership up to an acre. In Botswana and Tanzania, I have recommended donkey teams and plows for cultivating and transportation. After a provisional period of a couple of years of loan-in-kind status (to make sure the animals are used and not sold during the period), the production aids must turn formally into gifts. Local repair and advisory workers with the aid program might be able to monitor the probationary period, and security for the program and its recipients against possible violence would, of course, have to be assured. The successful experience of the Heifer Project in giving dairy animals in Tanzania (Kinsey 1994) demonstrates that the gift approach can work.

Many economists observing the rural developing world, from conservatives to Marxists, have assumed that "peasantries" and their problems are a passing phenomenon, in the face of inevitable urbanization (accompanying modernization) and its impersonal labor market. To be sure, the early stages of urban expansion made migration to the city and some of its access to services attractive. It is increasingly apparent, however, that employment for the migrating males in their shantytowns for which remuneration is sufficient to feed their households is growing more scarce rather than less so. The poor rural population falls into ever-greater misery as the survival-crucial male labor power is drained off in futile urban migration. Urban wage rates for the split households are unable to effectively subsidize the peasant women, children, and elderly on their marginal rural food base. Under these circumstances, food-effective job opportunities in urban as well as rural areas will increasingly be granted as personal favors, to be highly prized by the recipients as scarce resources critical for household survival, thus adding to the vulnerability to potential choice constraint, on one hand, and food insecurity, on the other. For the poor and poorly educated, there is little evidence that access to labor opportunities that are adequately food-effective for their households will be impersonally dispensed on a wide scale in the near future.

The strategy of providing productivity-enhancing animals and implements directly to the rural target group has the advantage of not fostering choice-constraining dependency on the local middle and upper strata. It leaves use of the aid up to the recipients, who, we can expect, will be the most reliable trustees of their own well-being. With an independent rural food viability as a foundation, both economic and civil-political risk taking will tend to be fostered. Households will be in a position to branch out from the rural base both economically and politically. At least for those households taking up the offered aid package and gaining minimal independent food viability, there will be a home base as a fall-back alternative in case of failure or unacceptable conditions encountered in other ventures, such as an urban job opportunity taken by a family member.

If enough target-group peasants take up the offer, customary local social practices—currently authorizing the undue influence of the rural haves over the civil-political choice and the minimal food security of the have-nots—could erode overall because those choosing not to take up the newly offered alternative (to instead remain in their current circumstances), would nonetheless retain the option of taking up the independent path in the future; they could, hence, acquire a strengthened bargaining position with their patrons, to the point in sharing, to some degree, in significant choice as well.

Under these more favorable circumstances, the status of other sorts of development aid programs targeted at the poor might be transformed. From the point of view of human rights analysis, the target poor would face other development aid possibilities as optional alternatives rather than new channels of clientelistic dependency. The giving of this sort of concrete aid, as obligatory under the human rights rubric, is not aimed to replace other strategies of appropriate-technology development aid for the poor, such as projects supplying sanitary water, small-scale local grain milling, health posts, and so forth. Other immediate human rights obligations such as food relief to the distressed must remain in effect, whether or not the sort of aid I recommend here is forthcoming. Indeed, if production for self-provision is fostered as well, the scope of the problem of immediate food distress will be reduced to more manageable proportions, and it may then be more widely recognized as immediate obligation as well. The argument here aims to provide a secure platform of minimally adequate food and the accompanying natural resistance to health threats, under the peasant household's own control, for a more effective use of the opportunities that can come from the whole range of intelligent development aid strategies targeted at the poor.

Under the human rights rubric, there is an immediate obligation to promote the observance of respect for human rights in the freedom sector as well as the economic-social sector. To meet this obligation, there should be mounted an affordable program of direct, production-oriented aid from the world's advantaged North to the target populations of the less-advantaged South. Thus, there could be major improvements with only a relatively limited cost in redistributed resources if current conventional political, social, and financial channels of intermediate patron-client structure can be sidestepped with a simple, direct transfer of the things into the hands of the target group. This aid could have widespread effects fostering new social practices of human rights respect, weakening arguments that the costs of meeting human rights obligations are beyond what the (mostly) northern advantaged nations can manage.

NOTES

1. See the discussion of the work of Bose, by R. Dumont, K. Griffin, B. Horvat, N. Islam, S. D. Chowdhury, and others, in Robinson and Griffin 1974, 160–162. See also Van Schendel 1981, 150; USAID 1983, 18.

2. This phenomenon involves, of course, the association of tubewell water with HYV production. See USAID 1983, 6; Van Schendel 1981, 97–98, 150, 183; and De Vylder 1982, 106–117. For an excellent short bibliography on this sort of effect of the "Green Revolution" generally, see Van Schendel 1981, 251.

3. Bose, quoted in Robinson and Griffin 1974, 147. The slightly superior productivity of 2–4 acre farms is accounted for by their favored position regarding material inputs (see De Vylder 1982, 114–117) and the timing of marketing, which means that they can keep some paddy off the market until later on, when better, postharvest prices can be had.

4. For an overall survey of the credit situation, see De Vylder 1982, 111–114.

5. By the end of the 1980s BRAC was trying to reorganize at Sulla in order to improve repayment without the sale of assets (Hashemi 1990, 71).

6. The consensus seems to be that while a pair of bullocks in good condition can plow 5 to acres, Bangladeshi teams in their most common condition today can only do 2 to 3 acres well (Jansen 1983, 45; Dumont 1973b, 47–48).

7. The UNDP Agricultural Sector Review volume on "Land, Water and Irrigation" states that a minimum water table of 12 meters or less and "good aquifer conditions" (plus "high unemployment") are required for the use of handpump tubewells to be feasible (UNDP 1989, 55).

8. For examples, see the discussion of land reform proposals in Robinson and Griffin 1974.

9. Personal communication from Philip Escali, April 7, 1989.

10. Personal communication, Finn Kjaerby, February 2, 1989.

Selected Bibliography

Abecassis, David. 1990. *Identity, Islam and Human Development in Rural Bangladesh*. Dhaka: University Press Ltd.

Abrahams, R. G., ed. 1985. *Villagers, Villages and the State in Modern Tanzania*. Cambridge African Monograph 4. Cambridge: African Studies Centre.

Adnan, Shapnan. 1987. "The Roots of Power: A Re-Study of Daripalla in Rural Bangladesh." Unpublished ms.

——. 1989. *Annotation of Village Studies in Bangladesh and West Bengal: A Review of Socio-Economic Trends over 1942–88*. Dhaka: Bangladesh Academy for Rural Development.

——. 1990. *Birds in a Cage: Institutional Factors and Changes in Women's Position in Bangladesh*. Dhaka: Winrock International; Bangladesh Agricultural Research Council.

——. 1991. *Floods, People and the Environment*. Dhaka: Bangladesh Research and Advisory Services.

Agricultural Technology Improvement Project (ATIP). 1986. *Farming System Activities at Malapye, 1982–1985*. ATIP Research Report No. 1. Dar es Salaam: ATIP.

Ahmad, Q. K., and Mahabub Hossain. 1983. *Rural Poverty Alleviation in Bangladesh—Experiences and Policies*. Rome: Food and Agricultural Organization of the United Nations.

——. 1985. "An Evaluation of Selected Policies and Programmes for the Alleviation of Rural Poverty in Bangladesh." In Rizwanul Islam, ed., *Strategies for Alleviating Poverty in Rural Asia*. Dhaka: Bangladesh Institute of Development Studies; Bangkok: International Labor Organization, Asian Employment Program.

Ahmed, Muzaffar, Philip English, Shelley Feldman, Mosharaff Hossain, Eirik G. Jansen, Florence E. McCarthy, Koen de Wilde, and Roger Young. 1990. *Rural Poverty in Bangladesh: A Report to the Like-Minded Group*. Dhaka: University Press Ltd.

Alam, Mustafa. 1986. "Special Employment Programmes in Bangladesh—An Evaluation of Major Schemes." In M. Muqtada, ed., *The Elusive Target: An Evaluation of Target-Group Approaches to Employment Creation in Rural Asia*. New Delhi, India: ILO

Asian Regional Team for Employment Promotion and World Employment Programme.

Ames, Glenn W., and Paul A. Wojtkowski. 1988. "Feast or Famine: Projections of Food Supply, Demand, and Human Nutrition for Five African Countries." *Journal of African Studies* 14, no. 4 (Winter 1987–1988): 207–212.

Andreasson, Bard-Anders, Tor Skalnes, Alan G. Smith, and Hugo Stokke. 1988. "Assessing Human Rights Performance in Developing Countries: the Case for a Minimal Threshold Approach." In Bard-Anders Andreasson and Asbjorn Eide, eds., *Human Rights in Developing Countries, 1987–88.* Copenhagen: Akademisk Forlag.

Andreasson, Bard-Anders, Alan G. Smith, and Hugo Stokke. 1992. "Compliance with Economic and Social Human Rights: Realistic Evaluation and Monitoring in the light of Immediate Obligation." In Asbjorn Eide and Bernt Hagtvet, eds., *Human Rights in Perspective: A Global Assessment.* London: Blackwell.

Arens, Jenneke, and Jos van Beurden. 1977. *Jhagrapur: Poor Peasants and Women in a Village in Bangladesh.* Amsterdam: Third World Publications.

Arntzen, Jaap. 1984. *Rural Agricultural Activities and Resource Utilization in Mmathubudkwane during a Period of Drought.* Gaborone: University of Botswana, National Institute of Development Research and Documentation.

Bantje, Han. 1980. "Floods and Famines, a Study of Food Shortages in Rufiji District." Bureau of Resource Assessment and Land Use Planning, Research Paper No. 63. Dar Es Salaam: University of Dar Es Salaam.

———. 1986. *Household Differentiation and Productivity: A Study of Smallholder Agriculture in Mbozi District.* Dar Es Salaam: University of Dar Es Salaam, Institute of Resource Assessment.

Beitz, Charles R. 1979. *Political Theory and International Relations.* Princeton: Princeton University Press.

Beneria, Lourdes, and Shelley Feldman, eds. 1992. *Unequal Burden: Economic Crises, Persistent Poverty, and Women's Work.* Boulder, Colo.: Westview Press.

Bertell, Taina. 1985. *Effects of Finnish Development Cooperation on Tanzanian Women: Tanzanian Rural Women and Their Crucial Role in Development.* Institute of Development Studies Report 5/1985. Helsinki: University of Helsinki.

Biggs, Stephen, and Jon Griffith. 1987. "Irrigation in Bangladesh." In Frances Stewart, ed., *Macro-Policies for Appropriate Technology in Developing Countries.* Boulder, Colo.: Westview Press.

Blair, Harry W. 1982. "The Elusiveness of Equity: Institutional Approaches to Rural Development in Bangladesh." In D. Uphoff, ed., *Rural Development and Local Organization in Asia*, Vol. 1, Introduction and South Asia. Delhi: Macmillan.

Boesen, Jannik. 1988. *Peasant Responses to Increasing Social and Ecological Vulnerability.* Center for Development Research Project Papers, D.88.4. Copenhagen: Center for Development Research.

Boesen, Jannik, Kjell J. Havnevik, and Juhani Koponene, eds. 1986. *Tanzania: Crisis and Struggle for Survival.* Uppsala, Sweden: Scandinavian Institute of African Studies.

Boesen, Jannik, and Helle Munk Ravnborg. 1992. *Peasant Production in Iringa District, Tanzania.* Copenhagen: Center for Development Research.

Booth, David, Flora Lugangira, Patrick Masanja, Abu Mvungi, Rosemarie Mwaipopo, Joaquim Mwami, Alison Redmayne. 1993. *Social, Cultural and Economic Change in Contemporary Tanzania: A People-Oriented Focus.* Stockholm: Development Studies Unit, Department of Social Anthropology, Stockholm University.

Briscoe, John. 1979. "Energy Use and Social Structure in a Bangladesh Village." *Population and Development* 5, no. 4: 613–641.

Bryceson, Deborah Fahy. 1988. "Peasant Cash Cropping versus Self-Sufficiency in Tanzania: A Historical Perspective." *IDS Bulletin* 19, no. 2: 37–46.

Chen, L. C., A. K. M. A. Chowdhury, and S. L. Huffman. 1980. "Anthropometric Assessment of Energy-Protein Malnutrition and Subsequent Risk of Malnutrition among Preschool Aged Children." *American Journal of Clinical Nutrition* 33: 1836–1845.

Chisholm, N. 1984. *Whose Rural Development? Socio-Economic Change in DTW (Deep Tubewell) Pumpgroups in Bogra District, Northwest Bangladesh*. Dhaka: Swedish International Development Authority.

Chowdhury, Omar Haider. 1992. "Nutritional Dimensions of Poverty." In H. Z. Rahman and Mahabub Hossain, eds., *Re-Thinking Rural Poverty*. Dhaka: Bangladesh Institute for Development Studies.

Colclough, Christopher, and Peter Fallon. 1983. "Rural Poverty in Botswana: Dimensions, Causes, and Constraints." In Dharam Ghai and Samir Rhadwan, eds., *Agrarian Policies and Rural Poverty in Africa*. Geneva: International Labor Organization.

Collier, Paul, Samir Radwan, Samuel Wangwe, and Albert Wagner. 1986. *Labour and Poverty in Rural Tanzania: Ujamaa and Rural Development in the United Republic of Tanzania*. Oxford: Clarendon.

Cranston, Maurice. 1962. *What Are Human Rights?* New York: Basic Books.

Dahl, Robert A. 1976. *Modern Political Analysis*. 3rd ed. Englewood Cliffs, N.J.: Prentice-Hall.

De Vylder, S. 1982. *Agriculture in Chains—Bangladesh*. London: Zed Press.

Dewey, John. 1963. *Liberalism and Social Action*. New York: Capricorn.

Donnelly, Jack. 1989. *Universal Human Rights in Theory and Practice*. Ithaca, N.Y.: Cornell University Press.

Due, Jean M. 1988. "Intra-Household Gender Issues in Farming Systems in Tanzania, Zambia, and Malawi." In Susan V. Poats, Marianne Schmink, and Anita Spring, eds., *Gender Issues in Farming Systems: Research and Extension*. Boulder, Colo.: Westview Press.

Due, Jean M., P. Anandajayasckcram, N. S. Mdoe, and Marcia White. 1984. "Beans in the Farming Systems in Langali and Kibaoni Villages, Mgeta Area, Morogor Region, Tanzania." Economic Research Bureau Paper No. 84.2. Dar Es Salaam: University of Dar Es Salaam.

Duggan, W. R. 1983. "Botswana's Rural Economy." In M. A. Oomen, F. K. Inganji, and L. D. Ngcongco, eds., *Botswana's Economy Since Independence*. New Delhi: Tata McGraw-Hill.

Dumont, Rene. 1973a. *Problems and Prospects for Rural Development in Bangladesh*. Dhaka: Ford Foundation.

——. 1973b. *A Self-Reliant Rural Development Policy for the Poor Peasantry of Sonar Bangladesh*. Dhaka: Ford Foundation.

Economist Intelligence Unit (EIU). *Country Reports*. London: The Economist.

Egner, E. B., and A. L. Klausen. 1980. *Poverty in Botswana*. Prepared for the U. S. Agency for International Development (USAID). Gaborone: Republic of Botswana.

Faaland, Just, and J. R. Parkinson. 1976. *Bangladesh: The Test Case for Development*. London: C. Hurst and Co.

Farrington, T., and K. D. V. Marsh. 1987. *An Assessment of the ARAP and Drought Relief Farmer Assistance Policies*. Gaborone: Republic of Botswana.

Feinberg, Joel. 1973. *Social Philosophy*. Englewood Cliffs, N.J.: Prentice-Hall.

Feldman, Shelley, and Florence E. McCarthy. 1984. *Rural Women and Development in Bangladesh*. Oslo: Norwegian Agency for Development Cooperation.

Ferreira, M. L. 1993. *Tanzania: A Poverty Profile*. Washington, D.C.: The World Bank.

Fortmann, Louise. 1980. *Peasants, Officials and Participation in Rural Tanzania: Experience with Villagization and Decentralization.* Ithaca, N.Y.: Cornell University, Center for International Studies, Rural Development Committee.

——. 1983. *The Role of Local Institutions in Communal Area Development: A Summary Report.* Gaborone: Botswana Ministry of Local Government and Lands, Applied Research Unit.

Fortmann, Louise, and Emery Roe. 1982. "Settlement on Tap: The Role of Water in Permanent Settlement at the Lands." In R. Renee Hitchcock and Mary R. Smith, eds., *Settlement in Botswana.* Marshalltown, South Africa: Heinemann.

Friedkin, Tom, Robert Lester, Herbert Blank, Nizam U. Ahmed. 1983. "Bangladesh Small-Scale Irrigation." AID Project Impact Evaluation Report No. 42. Dhaka, Bangladesh: USAID (U. S. Agency for International Development).

Friis-Hansen, Esbern. 1987a. *Changes in Land Tenure and Land Use Since Villagization and their Impact on Peasant Agricultural Production in Tanzania: The Case of the Southern Highlands.* CDR Research Report no. 11, Institute for Resource Assessment (IRA) Research Paper No. 16. Copenhagen: Center for Development Research (CDR).

——. 1987b. "Environmental Problems in Tanzania–A Case Study." Seminar paper presented at the General Conference of Environment and Development International (EADI), Amsterdam.

——. 1988. "The Role of the Seed: Prospects of Food Security and Sustainable Farming in Communal Areas of Zimbabwe." Research proposal presented to the Research Council of Zimbabwe.

Gewirth, Alan. 1981. "The Basis and Content of Human Rights." In J. Roland Pennock and John W. Chapman, eds., *Human Rights.* New York: New York University Press.

Ghafur, Abdul. 1990. "Food Policy of Bangladesh and Some Constraints." In Ole David Koht Norbye, ed., *Bangladesh Faces the Future.* Dhaka: University Press Ltd.

Granberg, Per, and J. R. Parkinson, eds. 1988. *Botswana Country Study and Norwegian Aid Review.* Bergen, Norway: Chr. Michelsen Institute.

Gulbrandsen, Ornulf. 1980. *Agro-Pastoral Production and Communal Land Use: A Socio-economic Study of the Bangwaketse.* Gaborone: Government of Botswana.

——. 1984. *Access to Agricultural Land and Communal Land Management in Eastern Botswana.* Gaborone: Botswana Ministry of Local Government and Lands, Applied Research Unit, and University of Wisconsin–Madison, Land Tenure Center.

——. 1990. *Enduring Poverty: A South African Labor Reservoir.* Bergen Studies in Social Anthropology No. 45. Bergen, Norway: University of Bergen.

Hamid, Shamim. 1992. "Gender Dimensions of Poverty." In H. Z. Rahman and Mahabub Hossain, eds., *Re-Thinking Rural Poverty.* Dhaka: Bangladesh Institute of Development Studies.

Hannah, L. M. 1976. "Hand Pump Irrigation in Bangladesh." *Bangladesh Development Studies* 4, no. 4 (October): 441–454.

Harrison, G. A., and J. C. Waterlow, eds. 1990. *Diet and Disease in Traditional and Developing Societies: 30th Symposium Volume of the Society for the Study of Human Biology.* Cambridge: Cambridge University Press.

Hartmann, Betsy, and James K. Boyce. 1983. *A Quiet Violence: View from a Bangladesh Village.* London: Zed Press.

Harvey, Charles, and Stephen R. Lewis, Jr. 1990. *Policy Choice and Development Performance in Botswana.* London: Macmillan.

Hashemi, Syed M. 1990. NGOs in Bangladesh: *Development Alternative or Alternative Rhetoric.* Manchester: University of Manchester, U.K.: Institute for Development Policy and Management.

Havnevik, Kjell J. 1983. *Analysis of Rural Production and Incomes, Rufiji District, Tanzania*. Development Research and Action Programme Puglications No. 152. Bergen, Norway: Chr. Michelsen Institute.

——. 1988. "State Intervention and Peasant Response in Tanzania" Ph.D. dissertation, University of Bradford. Bradford, U.K.: University of Bradford.

Havnevik, Kjell J., Finn Kjaerby, Ruth Meena, Rune Skarstein, and Ulla Vuorela. 1988. *Tanzania: Country Study and Norwegian Aid Review*. Bergen; Norway: University of Bergen, Center for Development Studies.

Havnevik, Kjell J., and Rune Skarstein. 1985. "Agricultural Decline and Foreign Aid in Tanzania." Development Research and Action Program (DERAP) Working Paper A 341. Bergen, Norway: Chr. Michelsen Institute.

Hayek, Frederick. 1960. *The Constitution of Liberty*. Chicago: University of Chicago Press.

Helle-Valle, Jo. 1992. "Consumption Patterns and Food in Letlhakeng Village, Botswana." In Alhassan Manu, ed., *Health and Environment in Developing Countries*. Oslo: University of Oslo, Center for Development and the Environment.

Henkin, Louis. 1978. *The Rights of Man Today*. Boulder, Colo.: Westview Press.

Hertel, Thomas W. 1977. *The System of Mafisa and the Highly Dependent Agricultural Sector*. Gaborone: Botswana Ministry of Agriculture, Division of Planning and Statistics.

Hesselberg, Jan. 1981. *New Trends in the Settlement Pattern of Botswana*. Oslo: University of Oslo, Department of Geography.

——. 1985. *The Third World in Transition: The Case of the Peasantry in Botswana*. Uppsala, Sweden: Scandinavian Institute of African Studies.

Hitchcock, R. Renee, and Mary R. Smith, eds. 1982. *Settlement in Botswana–The Historical Development of a Human Landscape*. Marshalltown, South Africa: Heinemann.

Hitchcock, Robert K. 1978. *Kalahari Cattle Posts: A Regional Study of Hunter-Gatherers, Pastoralists, and Agriculturalists in the Western Sandveld Region, Central District, Botswana*. Gaborone: Botswana Ministry of Local Government and Lands.

——. 1982. "Tradition, Social Justice and Land Reform in Central Botswana." In Richard P. Werbner, ed., *Land Reform in the Making*. London: Rex Collings.

——. 1987. "Socioeconomic Change among the Basarwa in Botswana: An Ethnohistorical Analysis." *Ethnohistory* 34, no. 3 (Summer): 219–254.

Hitchcock, Robert K., and Sam Totten. 1988. "Socioeconomic Rights and Development among Southern African San." Paper presented in a symposium entitled "International Human Rights and Indigenous Peoples: A Professional Responsibility" at the 87th Annual Meeting of the American Anthropological Association, Phoenix, Arizona, November 16–20.

Hoffman, Stanley. 1981. *Duties beyond Borders: On the Limits and Possibilities of an Ethical International Politics*. Syracuse, N.Y.: Syracuse University Press.

Holm, John D. 1982. "Liberal Democracy and Rural Development in Botswana." *African Studies Review* 25, no. 1: 83–102.

——. 1985. "The State, Social Class and Rural Development in Botswana." In Louis A. Picard, ed., *The Evolution of Modern Botswana*. Lincoln: University of Nebraska Press; London: Rex Collings.

Holm, John D., and Patrick Molutsi, eds. 1989. *Democracy in Botswana. Proceedings of a symposium Held in Gaborone, August 1–5, 1988*. Gaborone: Macmillan Botswana Publishing Company Ltd.

Holmboe-Ottesen, Gerd. 1992. "Food Security and Economic Strategies in Relation to Consumption: The Cases of Tanzania and Botswana." In Alhassan Manu, ed., *Health and Environment in Developing Countries*. Oslo: University of Oslo, Center for Development and the Environment.

Holmboe-Ottensen, Gerd, and Margareta Wandel. 1988. "Child Nutrition, Women, and Agriculture in a Seasonal Perspective: Determinants of Child Malnutrition in Msanzi and Pito." Interim report from an ongoing field study in Sumbawanga District, Rukwa Region. Oslo: University of Oslo, Institute for Nutrition Research.

———. 1991. "Men's Contribution to the Food and Nutritional Situation in the Tanzanian Household" *Ecology of Food and Nutrition* 26: 83–96.

Holmquist, Frank. 1983. "Tanzania's Retreat from Statism in the Countryside." Working Paper no. 399, Institute for Development Studies. Nairobi: University of Nairobi.

Horton, Susan. 1989. "Food Subsidies and the Poor: A Case Study of Tanzania" in Richard M. Bird and Susan Horton, eds., *Government Policy and the Poor in Developing Countries*. Toronto; Buffalo, N.Y.; London: University of Toronto Press.

Hossain, Mahabub. 1977. "Farm Size, Tenancy and Land Productivity: An Analysis of Farm Level Data in Bangladesh Agriculture." *Bangladesh Development Studies* 5, no. 3: 285–348.

———. 1981. "Agrarian Structure: Some Considerations of Equity, Productivity and Growth." In W. Mahmud, ed., *Development Issues in an Agrarian Economy–Bangladesh*. Dhaka: Center for Administrative Studies.

———. 1989. "Food Security, Agriculture and the Economy: The Next 25 Years." In Government of Bangladesh, Planning Commission, ed., *Food Strategies in Bangladesh: Medium and Long Term Perspectives*. Dhaka: University Press Ltd..

———. 1992a. "Nutritional Dimensions of Poverty." In H. Z. Rahman and Mahabub Hossain, eds., *Re-Thinking Rural Poverty*. Dhaka: Bangladesh Institute of Development Studies.

———. 1992b. "Socio-Economic Characteristics of the Poor." In H. Z. Rahman and Mahabub Hossain, eds., *Re-Thinking Rural Poverty*. Dhaka: Bangladesh Institute of Development Studies.

———. 1992c. "Structure and Distribution of Household Income and Income Dimensions of Poverty." In H. Z. Rahman and Mahabub Hossain, eds., *Re-Thinking Rural Poverty*. Dhaka: Bangladesh Institute of Development Studies.

Hossain, Mahabub, and Binayak Sen. 1992. "The Political Economy of Poverty Alleviation." In H. Z. Rahman and Mahabub Hossain, ed., *Re-Thinking Rural Poverty*. Dhaka: Bangladesh Institute of Development Studies.

Hossain, Mosharaff. 1987. *The Assault That Failed: A Profile of Absolute Poverty in Six Villages of Bangladesh*. Geneva: United Nations Institute for Social Research.

Howes, M. 1985. *Whose Water? An Investigation of the Consequences of Alternative Approaches to Small Scale Irrigation in Bangladesh*. Dhaka: Bangladesh Institute of Development Studies.

Hyden, Goran. 1980. Beyond Ujamaa in Tanzania: *Underdevelopment and an Uncaptured Peasantry*. Berkeley: University of California Press.

Inger, D. 1986. "Constraints to Popular Participation in Rural Development." In B. D. Tsiane and F. Youngman, eds., *The Theory and Practice of People's Participation in Rural Development*. Proceedings of the Rural Extension Co-ordination Committee (RECC) Workshop Held in Kanye, Botswana, November 18–22, 1985. Gaborone, Botswana: Government of Botswana, Ministry of Finance and Development Planning.

Institute of Nutrition and Food Science (INFS), University of Dhaka. 1983. *Nutrition Survey of Rural Bangladesh, 1981–82*. Dhaka: University of Dhaka.

International Commission of Jurists. 1977. *International Bill of Human Rights, Final Authorized Text*. New York: American Association for the International Commission of Jurists.

Jahan, Rounaq. 1989. *Women and Development in Bangladesh: Challenges and Opportunities*. Dhaka: Ford Foundation/Bangladesh.

Jahangir, B. K. 1979. *Differentiation, Polarisation, and Confrontation in Rural Bangladesh*. Dhaka: Centre for Social Studies, University of Dhaka.

Jannuzi, F. T., and J. T. Peach. 1980. *Agrarian Structure of Bangladesh: An Impediment to Development*. Boulder, Colo.: Westview Press.

Jansen, Eirik G. 1979. "Choice of Irrigation Technology in Bangladesh: Implications for Dependency Relationships between Rich and Poor Farmers." *Journal of Social Studies*, no. 5: 61–84.

——. 1986. *Rural Bangladesh–Competition for Scarce Resources*. Oslo, Norway: Norwegian University Press.

——. 1990. "Processes of Polarization and the Breaking Up of Patron-Client Relationships in Rural Bangladesh." In Ole David Koht Norbye, ed., *Bangladesh Faces the Future*. Dhaka: University Press Ltd.

Jerve, Alf Morten. 1982. *Cattle and Inequality: A Study in Rural Economic Differentiation from Southern Kgalagadi in Botswana*. Bergen, Norway: Chr. Michelsen Institute, DERAP Publications.

Jones, David. 1982. "The Implications of Agricultural Development Planning for Rural Settlement." In R. Renee Hitchcock and Mary R. Smith, eds., *Settlement in Botswana*. Marshalltown, South Africa: Heinemann.

Jorgensen, Steffen, Mikael Jorgensen, and Torben Birch-Thomsen. 1988. *Agricultural Intensification–the Role and Risks in the Introduction of Ox-Mechanization*. Copenhagen: University of Copenhagen, Institute of Geography.

Kamenka, Eugene. 1978. *Human Rights*. London: Edward Arnold.

Kauzeni, A. S. 1984. *Increasing Agricultural Production and Productivity in Rukwa Region. Institute of Resource Assessment*, Research Report no. 61 (New Series). Dar es Salaam: University of Dar es Salaam.

——. 1985. *Accelerating and Sustaining Village Development. Institute of Resource Assessment*, Research Report no. 61 (New Series). Dar es Salaam: University of Dar es Salaam.

Kavishe, Festo P. 1993. *Nutrition-Relevant Actions in Tanzania*. Tanzania Food and Nutrition Center, 20th Anniversary, 1973–1993, Monograph Series no. 1. Dar es Salaam: Tanzania Food and Nutrition Center.

Kerven, Carol. 1979. *Urban and Rural Female-Headed Households' Dependence on Agriculture.*, National Migration Study Paper. Gaborone: Botswana Ministry of Agriculture, Rural Sociology Unit.

Khan, Azizur Rahman. 1977. "Poverty and Inequality in Rural Bangladesh." In International Labor Office, ed, *Poverty and Landlessness in Rural Asia*. Geneva: International Labor Organization.

Khan, Azizur Rahman, and Mahabub Hossain. 1989. *The Strategy of Development in Bangladesh*. London: Macmillan.

Kinsey, Erwin. 1994. *Some Aspects of Credit: the HPI Tanzania Experience*. Dar es Salaam: Heifer Project International (HPI).

Kjaerby, Finn. 1983. *Problems and Contradictions in the Development of Ox-Cultivation in Tanzania*. Research Report no 66. Uppsala, Sweden: Scandinavian Institute of African Studies.

——. 1986. "The Development of Agricultural Mechanization." In Jannik Boesen, Kjell J. Havnevik, and Juhani Koponene, eds., *Tanzania*. Uppsala, Sweden: Scandinavian Institute of African Studies.

——. 1988. "Villagization and the Crisis: Agricultural Production in Hanang District, Northern Tanzania." Draft Project Paper. Copenhagen: Center for Development Research.

Koojman, Kunnie. 1978. *Social and Economic Change in a Tswana Village*. Leiden, Holland: African Studies Center.

Kossoudji, Sherrie, and Eva Mueller. 1983. "The Economic and Demographic Status of Female-headed Households in Rural Botswana." *Economic Development and Cultural Change* 31, no. 4 (July): 831–859.

Kramsjo, Bosse, and Geoffrey D. Wood. 1992. *Breaking the Chains: Collective Action for Social Justice among the Rural Poor of Bangladesh*. London: IT Publications.

Kuper, Adam. 1970. *Kalahari Village Politics: An African Democracy*. London: Cambridge University Press.

Lein, Haakon. 1988. *Water to the Fields: Technological Change in Bangladesh Agriculture*. Bergen, Norway: University of Bergen, Department of Geography.

——. 1989. *Persistence and Polarization: the Case of the "Green Revolution" in Bangladesh*. Bergen, Norway: University of Bergen, Institute for Geography.

Lindstrom, Jan. 1986. "Grain for Livestock and Livestock for Grain." In Jannik Boesen, Kjell J. Havnevik, and Juhani Koponene, eds., *Tanzania*. Uppsala, Sweden: Scandinavian Institute of African Studies.

Loewen-Rudgers, L., E. Rempel, J. Harder, and K. Klassen Harder. 1988. Appendix C: "Constraints to the Adoption of Animal Traction Weeding Technology in Mbeya Region of Tanzania." Mbeya Oxenization Project Papers. Dar Es Salaam: Canadian International Development Agency.

Lyons, David. 1970. "The Correlativity of Rights and Duties." *Nous* 4 (1970): 45–55.

McCall, Michael. 1987. "Carrying Heavier Burdens but Carrying Less Weight: Some Implications of Villagization for Women in Tanzania." In Janet Henshall Momsen and Janet G. Townsend, eds., *Geography of Gender in the Third World*. London: Hutchinson.

McCall, Michael, and Margaret Skutsch. 1983. "Strategies and Contradictions in Tanzania's Rural Development: Which Path for the Peasants?" In David A. Shea and D. D. Chandri, eds., *Rural Development and the State: Contradictions and Dilemmas in Developing Countries*. London: Methuen.

McCloskey, H. J. 1976. "Rights: Some Conceptual Issues." *Australasian Journal of Philosophy* 54: 99–115.

McGregor, J. Allister. 1989. "Boro Gafur and Choto Gafur: Development Interventions and Indigenous Institutions." *Journal of Social Studies* 43 (January): 39–51.

Madsen, Birgit. 1984. *Women's Mobilization and Integration in Development: A Village Case Study from Tanzania*. Center for Development Research (CDR) Report no. 3. Copenhagen: Center for Development Research.

Mahmud, Simeen. 1987. *Gender Aspects of Nutrition and Mortality among Children in Rural Bangladesh*. Bangladesh Institute of Development Studies Research Report No. 63. Dhaka: Bangladesh Institute of Development Studies.

Mandal, M. A. S. 1989. "Market for and Returns from Groundwater Irrigation in Bangladesh." In United Nations Development Program (UNDP), ed., *Bangladesh Agriculture Sector Review: Compendium Volume III, Land Water and Irrigation*. Dhaka: UNDP.

Manu, Alhassan, ed. 1992. *Health and Environment in Developing Countries: Proceedings from an International Workshop*. Oslo: University of Oslo, Centre for Development and the Environment.

Martin, Rex. 1980. "Human Rights and Civil Rights." *Philosophical Studies* 37: 391–403.

Mbilinyi, Marjorie. 1989. "Women as Peasant and Casual Labor and the Development Crisis in Tanzania." In Jane L. Parpart, ed., *Women and Development in Africa: Comparative Perspectives*. New York: University Press of America.

Mbughuni, Patricia. 1988. "Women of Tanzania: Struggle for Progress." In *The Arusha Declaration 20 Years After. Proceedings of the International Conference of the 20 Years of the Arusha Declaration*. Dar es Salaam: University of Dar es Salaam.

Merafe, Y., D. Baker, and D. Norman. 1986. "Socio-Economic Constraints to Farm Equipment Innovations in Botswana." In International Labor Office (ILO), ed., *Initiatives for Farm Equipment Programmes in Botswana: Improving Co-ordination*. Papers and proceedings of a national workshop on farm tools and equipment technology, basic needs and employment, Gaborone, Botswana, December 3–5, 1985. Geneva: ILO.

Mhina, A. K. 1987. "The Viability of the Village as Institution to Serve the Interest of Peasants in Tanzania." *Taamuli* 17 nos. 1, 2: 25–41.

Miranda, Armindo. 1989. *Focussed Balance: A Prescription for Dutch Assistance to the Population Sector in Bangladesh*. Amsterdam: Royal Tropical Institute.

Mlay, Wilfred. 1985. "Pitfalls in Rural Development: The Case in Tanzania." In Fassil G. Kiros, ed., *Challenging Rural Poverty*. Trenton, N.J.: Africa World Press.

——. 1986. "Environmental Implications of Land-Use Patterns in the New Villages in Tanzania." In J. W. Arntzen, L. D. Ngcongco, and S. D. Turner, eds., *Land Policy and Agriculture in Eastern and Southern Africa*. New York: United Nations University.

Muqtada, M. 1989. *The Elusive Target: An Evaluation of Target-group Approaches to Employment Creation in Rural Asia*. New Delhi: International Labor Organization, Asian Regional Team for Employment Promotion, of the World Employment Programme.

Muqtada, M., and Rizwanul Islam, eds. 1986. Bangladesh: Selected Issues in Employment and Development. New Delhi: International Labor Organization, Asian Employment Programme.

Nelson, William N. 1974. "Special Rights, General Rights, and Social Justice." *Philosophy and Public Affairs* 3: 410–430.

Nickel, James W. 1980. "Is There a Human Right to Employment?" *Philosophical Forum* 11: 149–170.

Noppen, Dolf. 1982. *Consultation and Non-Commitment: Planning with the People in Botswana*. African Studies Center Research Report no. 13. Leiden, Holland: African Studies Center.

Norbye, Ole David Koht, ed. 1986. *Bangladesh: Country Study and Norwegian Aid Review: 1986*. Bergen, Norway: Chr. Michelsen Institute.

——, ed. 1990. *Bangladesh Faces the Future*. Report on the BIDS/CMI Bangladesh Seminar, Bergen, 15–17 February 1989. Dhaka: University Press Ltd.

Norwegian Agency for Development Cooperation (NORAD). 1993. "Two Case Studies of Economic and Financial Aspects, Agriculture Projects–KIDEP and RUDEP" (Kigoma Integrated Rural Development Program and Rukwa Integrated Rural Development Program). Appendix 2 in NORAD, *An Economic and Financial Evaluation of RUDEP and KIDEP" Draft report*. Dar es Salaam: NORAD.

Odell, Marcia. 1980. *A Land Shortage in Botswana: Truth or Fiction?* Gaborone: Institute of Development Management.

Odgaard, Rie. 1986. "Tea–Does It Do the Peasant Women in Rungwe Any Good?" In Jannik Boesen, Kjell J. Havnevik, and Juhani Koponene, eds., *Tanzania: Crisis and Struggle for Survival*. Uppsala, Sweden: Scandinavian Institute of African Studies.

Omari, C. K. 1986. "Politcs and Policies of Food Self-sufficiency in Tanzania." *Social Science and Medicine* 22, no. 7: 769–774.

Opschoor, Johannes B. 1986. "Crops, Class and Climate: Environmental and Economic Constraints and Potentials of Production in Botswana." In M. A. Oomen, F. K. Inganji, and L. D. Ngcongco, eds., *Botswana's Economy Since Independence*. New Delhi: Tata McGraw-Hill.

Oygard, Gunnar, Jaap Arntzen, and Onalenna Selowane. 1983. *Botswana's Arable Sector and the Role of Government with Special Reference to the Accelerated Rainfed Arable Program*. Report to the Royal Norwegian Ministry of Development Cooperation. Gaborone: Government of Botswana.

Parkinson, J. R., and M. Syeduzzaman. 1993. "Joint WFP Evaluation, Draft Rapid Assessment Report: Bangladesh." Bergen, Norway: World Food Program.

Parthasarathy, G. 1989. "Growth and Equity Issues: Rural Poor." In United Nations Development Program (UNDP), ed., *Bangladesh Agriculture Sector Review, Bangladesh Agriculture, Performance and Policies: Compendium Volume I, The Agricultural Sector in Context*. Dhaka: UNDP.

Pennock, J. Roland, and John W. Chapman, eds. 1981. *Human Rights: Nomos XXIII*. New York: New York University Press.

Perry, Thomas D. 1977. "A Paradigm of Philosophy: Hohfeld on Legal Rights." *American Philosophical Quarterly* 14: 41–50.

Quddus, M. Abdul. 1984. "Food Habits in Bangladesh: Changing Pattern in Adversities." Comilla, Bangladesh: Bangladesh Academy for Rural Development (BARD).

Rahman, Atiq. 1986. "Poverty Alleviation and the Most Disadvantaged Groups in Bangladesh Agriculture." *Bangladesh Development Studies* 14, no. 1 (March): 29–55.

Rahman, Atiq, and Trina Haque. 1988. *Poverty and Inequality in Bangladesh in the Eighties: An Analysis of Some Recent Evidence*. Research Report No. 91. Dhaka: Bangladesh Institute of Development Studies.

Rahman, Atiq, Simeen Mahmud, and Trina Haque. 1988. *A Critical Review of the Poverty Situation in Bangladesh in the Eighties*. Vol. 1. Research Report No. 66. Dhaka: Bangladesh Institute of Development Studies.

Rahman, Atiur. 1983. "Differentiation of the Peasantry in Bangladesh: An Empirical Study with Micro Level Data". Ph.D. thesis, University of London.

Rahman, H. Z. 1992a. "Crisis and Insecurity: The Other Face of Poverty." In H. Z. Rahman and Mahabub Hossain, eds., *Re-Thinking Rural Poverty*. Dhaka: Bangladesh Institute of Development Studies.

——. 1992b. "Ecological Reserves and Expenditure-Saving Scopes for the Poor." In H. Z. Rahman and Mahabub Hossain, eds., *Re-Thinking Rural Poverty*. Dhaka: Bangladesh Institute of Development Studies.

——. 1992c. "Mora Kartik: Seasonal Deficits and the Vulnerability of the Rural Poor." In H. Z. Rahman and Mahabub Hossain eds., *Re-Thinking Rural Poverty*. Dhaka: Bangladesh Institute of Development Studies.

——. 1992d. "The Political Economy of Poverty Alleviation." In H. Z. Rahman and Mahabub Hossain, eds., *Re-Thinking Rural Poverty*. Dhaka: Bangladesh Institute of Development Studies.

——. 1992e. "Re-Thinking the Poverty Debate." In H. Z. Rahman and Mahabub Hossain, eds., *Re-Thinking Rural Poverty*. Dhaka: Bangladesh Institute of Development Studies.

Rahman, H. Z., and Mahabub Hossain, eds. 1992. *Re-Thinking Rural Poverty*: A Case for Bangladesh. Dhaka: Bangladesh Institute of Development Studies.

Raikes, Philip. 1986. "He Who Eats the Carrot Wields the Stick: The Agricultural Sector in Tanzania." In Jannik Boesen, Kjell J. Havnevik, and Juhani Koponene, eds., *Tanzania*. Uppsala, Sweden: Scandinavian Institute of African Studies.

Raphael, D. D. 1967. *Political Theory and the Rights of Man*. London: Macmillan.

Rasmussen, Torben. 1986. "Green Revolution in the Southern Highlands." In Jannik Boesen, Kjell J. Havnevik, and Juhani Koponene, eds., *Tanzania*. Uppsala, Sweden: Scandinavian Institute of African Studies.

Rawls, John. 1971. *A Theory of Justice*. Cambridge: Harvard University Press.

Robinson, E. A. G., and Keith Griffin. 1974. *Economic Development of Bangladesh*. New York: Wiley.

Safilios-Rothschild, Constantina, and Simeen Mahmud. 1989. "Women's Roles in Agriculture: Present Trends and Potential for Growth." In United Nations Development Program (UNDP), ed., *Bangladesh Agriculture Sector Review*. Dhaka: UNDP and UNIFEM.

Schneider-Barthold, Wolfgang, Nina Boschmann, Stefan Gruchmann, Wolfgang Hehn, Wolfgang Leidig, Michael Plesch. 1983. *Farmers' Reactions to the Present Economic Situation in Tanzania with Respect to Production and Marketing: A Case Study of Five Villages in the Kilimanjaro Region*. Berlin: German Development Institute.

Sen, Binayak. 1992a. "Income-Earning Environment of the Poor." In H. Z. Rahman and Mahabub Hossain, eds., *Re-Thinking Rural Poverty*. Dhaka: Bangladesh Institute of Development Studies.

——. 1992b. "The Poor and the Poorest." In H. Z. Rahman and Mahabub Hossain, eds., *Re-Thinking Rural Poverty*. Dhaka: Bangladesh Institute of Development Studies.

——. 1992c. "Rural Poverty Trends, 1963/64 to 1989/90." In H. Z. Rahman and Mahabub Hossain, eds., *Re-Thinking Rural Poverty*. Dhaka: Bangladesh Institute of Development Studies.

——. 1992d. "Selected Living Standard Indicators." In H. Z. Rahman and Mahabub Hossain, eds., *Re-Thinking Rural Poverty*. Dhaka: Bangladesh Institute of Development Studies.

Seshamani, Lalitha. 1981. *Food Consumption and Nutritional Adequacy in Iringa—A Case Study of Four Villages*. Economic Research Bureau Paper 81.5. Dar Es Salaam: University of Dar Es Salaam.

Shahabuddin, Quazi. 1989. "Pattern of Food Consumption in Bangladesh: An Analysis of Household Expenditure Survey Data." *Bangladesh Development Studies* 17, no. 3: 101–117.

Shao, I. F. 1987. "People's Power and People's Participation in the Rural Sector: The Case of Tanzania" *Taamuli* 17, nos. 1, 2: 42–57.

Shao, John. 1986. "The Villagization Program and the Disruption of the Ecological Balance in Tanzania." *Canadian Journal of African Studies* 20, no. 2: 219–239.

Shue, Henry. 1979. "Rights in the Light of Duties." In Peter G. Brown and Douglas MacLean, eds. *Human Rights and U.S. Foreign Policy*. Lexington, Mass.: Lexington Books.

——. 1980. *Basic Rights: Subsistence, Affluence, and U.S. Foreign Policy*. Princeton: Princeton University Press.

Silberbauer, G. B., and A. J. Kuper. 1966. "Kgalagari Masters and Bushman Serfs: Some Observations." *African Studies* 25, no. 4: 171–179.

Silitshena, R. M. K. 1983. *Intra-Rural Migration and Settlement Changes in Botswana*. Research Reports 20. Leiden, Holland: African Studies Centre.

Smith, Alan G. 1986a. "Human Rights and Choice in Poverty." *Journal of Social Studies* 32 (April): 44–78.

——. 1986b. *Poverty, Choice, and Human Rights in Rural Bangladesh.* Development Research and Action Program (DERAP) Publications no. 212. Bergen, Norway: Chr. Michelsen Institute.

——. 1989. "Botswana." In Manfred Novak and Theresa Swinehart, eds., *Human Rights in Developing Countries,* 1989 Yearbook. Kehl; Strasbourg, Germany; Arlington, Va.: N. P. Engel.

——. 1991a. "Bangladesh." in Bard-Anders Andreassen and Theresa Swinehart, eds., *Human Rights in Developing Countries,* 1990 Yearbook. Kehl; Strasbourg, Germany; Arlington, Va.: N. P. Engel.

——. 1991b. "Tanzania." in Bard-Anders Andreassen and Theresa Swinehart, eds., *Human Rights in Developing Countries, 1990 Yearbook.* Kehl; Strasbourg, Germany, Arlington, Va.: N. P. Engel.

——. 1994. "Tanzania." In Peter Baehr, Hilde Hey, Jacqueline Smith, Theresa Swinehart, eds., *Human Rights in Developing Countries, Yearbook 1994.* Deventer, Holland: Kluwer Law and Taxation Publishers.

Solway, Jacqueline S. 1980. *People, Cattle, and Drought in Western Kweneng: Report on Dutlwe Village.* Gaborone: Botswana Ministry of Agriculture, Division of Planning and Statistics.

——. 1986. *Commercialization, Drought and Social Change, Fieldwork in Western Kewneng, 1977–9 and 1986–Field Report.* Toronto: University of Toronto, Department of Anthropology.

Sosovele, Hussein. 1986. *Agricultural Production and the Use of Animal-Traction in Iringa Rural District.* Research Report No. 69, Institute of Resource Assessment. Dar es Salaam: University of Dar es Salaam.

Spurr, G. B. 1990. "The Impact of Chronic Undernutrition on Physical Work Capacity and Daily Energy Expenditure." In G. A. Harrison and J. C. Waterlow, eds., *Diet and Disease in Traditional and Developing Societies.* Cambridge, U.K.: Cambridge University Press.

Stroberg, Per-Arne. 1977. "Water and Development: Organizational Aspects on a Tubewell Irrigation Project in Bangladesh." Unpublished ms.

Swantz, Marja-Liisa. 1985. *Women in Development: A Creative Role Denied? The Case of Tanzania.* London: C. Hurst; New York: St. Martin's.

——. 1992. "The History of Informal Organizational Structures in Tanzania." In Pekka Seppala, ed., *Civil Society in the Making: People's Organizations and Politics in the Third World.* Helsinki, Finland: University of Helsinki, Institute of Development Studies.

Tanzania Food and Nutrition Center (TFNC), and World Health Organization. 1992. *The Food and Nutrition Situation in Tanzania.* TFNC Report no. 1445. Dar es Salaam: Tanzania Food and Nutrition Center.

Task Forces on Bangladesh Development Strategies for the 1990s. 1991. *Report of the Task Forces on Bangladesh Development Strategies for the 1990's: Policies for Development.* Vol. 1. Dhaka: University Press Ltd.

Therkildsen, Ole. 1986. "State, Donors and Villages in Rural Water Development." In Jannik Boesen, Kjell J. Kavnevik, and Juhani Koponene, eds., *Tanzania.* Uppsala, Sweden: Scandinavian Institute of African Studies.

Thiele, Graham. 1985. "Villages as Economic Agents: The Accident of Social Reproduction." In R. G. Abrahams, ed., *Villagers, Villages and the State in Modern Tanzania.* Cambridge, U.K.: African Studies Centre.

——. 1986a. "The State and Rural Development in Tanzania: The Village Administration as a Political Field." *Journal of Development Studies* 22, no. 3 (April): 540–557.

——. 1986b. "The Tanzanian Villagisation Programme: Its Impact on Household Production in Dodoma." *Canadian Journal of African Studies* 20, no. 2: 243–258.

Thompson, Graham. 1985. "The Bewitchment and Fall of a Village Politician." In R. G. Abrahams, ed., *Villagers, Villages and the State in Modern Tanzania*. Cambridge, U.K.: African Studies Centre.

Tobisson, Eva. 1980. *Women, Work, Food and Nutrition in Nyamwigura Village*, Mara Region, Tanzania. TFNC Report No. 548. Dar Es Salaam: Tanzanian Food and Nutrition Center (TFNC).

Tripp, Aili Mari. 1992. "The Impact of Crisis and Economic Reform on Women in Urban Tanzania." In Lourdes Beneria and Shelley Feldman, eds. *Unequal Burden*. Boulder, Colo: Westview Press.

Ulijaszek, S. J. 1990. "Nutritional Status and Susceptibility to Infectious disease." In G. A. Harrison and J. C. Waterlow, eds., *Diet and Disease in Traditional and Developing Societes*. Cambridge: Cambridge University Press.

United Nations Children's Fund (UNICEF). 1990. *State of the World's Children 1990*. New York: UNICEF.

United Nations Development Program (UNDP). 1989. *Bangladesh Agricultural Sector Review (BASR); Main Report, Bangladesh Agriculture: Performance and Policies*. Dhaka: UNDP.

——. 1990. "Human Development Indicators." In *Human Development Report*. New York: UNDP.

U.S. Agency for International Development (USAID). 1983. "Bangladesh Small-Scale Irrigation." AID Project Impact Evaluation Report No. 42. Dhaka, Bangladesh: USAID.

Van Hekken, P. M., and H. U. E. Thoden Van Velsen. 1972. *Land Scarcity and Rural Inequality in Tanzania*: Some Case Studies from Rungwe District. The Hague: Mouton.

Van Schendel, Willem. 1981. *Peasant Mobility—The Odds of Life in Rural Bangladesh*. Assen, Holland: Van Gorcum.

Vierich, Helga, and Christopher Sheppard. 1980. *Drought in Rural Botswana, Socio-economic Impact and Government Policy*. Botswana Ministry of Agriculture, Rural Sociology Unit.

Wagao, Jumanne H. 1993. "The Nutrition Situation in Tanzania." Paper presented at the conference of the 20th Anniversary of the Tanzania Food and Nutrition Center. Dar es Salaam: Tanzania Food and Nutrition Center (TFNC).

Wandel, Margareta, and Gerd Holmboe-Ottesen. 1992. "Food Availability and Nutrition in a Seasonal Perspective: A Study from the Rukwa Region in Tanzania." *Human Ecology* 20, no. 1: 89–107.

Wasserstrom, Richard. 1964. "Rights, Human Rights, and Racial Discrimination." *Journal of Philosophy* 61: 628–641.

Wellman, Carl. 1967. "A New Conception of Human Rights." In Eugene Kamenka and Alice Erh-Soon Tay, eds., *Human Rights*. London: Macmillan.

Werbner, Richard P., ed. 1982. *Land Reform in the Making: Tradition, Public Policy and Ideology in Botswana*. London: Rex Collings.

White, Sarah. 1991. "Arguing with the Crocodile: Class and Gender in Rural Bangladesh." Ph.D. dissertation, University of Bath, England.

Wikan, Gerd. 1981. *Absenteeism, Crop Cultivation and Level of Living in Rural Botswana*. Oslo: University of Oslo, Department of Geography.

Wilmsen, Edwin N. 1982. *Remote Area Dwellers in Botswana: An Assessment of Their Current Status*. Working Paper No. 65. Boston: Boston University, African Studies Center.

Wynne, Susan G. 1981. *Local Institutions and Development in Botswana*. Gaborone: Botswana, Ministry of Agriculture, Division of Planning and Statistics.

Index

About the Author

ALAN G. SMITH is Associate Professor of Political Science at Central Connecticut State University. His publications relating to human rights and development have appeared in the *Journal of Social Studies*, in the yearbook *Human Rights in Developing Countries,* and in reports and papers of human rights institutes.

ISBN 0-275-95826-4

90000>

EAN

9 780275 958268

HARDCOVER BAR CODE